# Caring for Troubled Children

*Residential Treatment in a Community Context*

James K. Whittaker

*with chapters by*
*Richard W. Small and Robin B. Clarke*
*and Jerome Beker*

ALDINE DE GRUYTER

New York

First published © 1979 by James K. Whittaker
Jossey-Bass Inc. Publishers
San Francisco, California

First paperback edition
Published 1997 by Walter de Gruyter, Inc., New York

ALDINE DE GRUYTER
A Division of Walter de Gruyter, Inc.
200 Saw Mill River Road
Hawthorne, New York 10532

This publication is printed on acid free paper

**Library of Congress Cataloging-in-Publication Data**
Whittaker, James K.
    Caring for troubled children : residential treatment in a
community context / James K. Whittaker ; with chapters by Richard W.
Small and Robin B. Clarke and by Jerome Beker. — 1st pbk. ed.
        p.  cm.
    Originally published: San Francisco : Jossey-Bass, 1979, in
series: The Jossey-Bass social and behavioral science series.
    Includes bibliographical references (p.      ) and indexes.
    ISBN 0-202-36104-7 (paper : acid-free paper)
    1. Problem children—Institutional care.  2. Problem children—
Family relationships.  I. Title.
HV713.W48  1997
362.7'4—dc20                                                    96-30185
                                                                    CIP

Manufactured in the United States of America
10  9  8  7  6  5  4  3  2  1

# Contents

# Preface

Since children in trouble do not come neatly packaged, neither should our approaches to helping them. Much current wisdom holds that the need for specialized out-of-home care—residential treatment, for example—is minimal at best and that our major energies should be directed to reaching troubled children earlier and in the context of their own families. In part, this attitude reflects two things:

- Recent and shocking examples of both personal and institutional abuse of children in some substitute care arrangements.
- A long-standing and deep-seated distrust of group care settings as childrearing (or child helping) environments.

Many children who have found their way to group care settings undoubtedly can and should be helped in their own homes. The moves in this direction are unmistakable and include the closing of large institutions that do little more than warehouse children and the recent development of a number of creative and promising home-based services for troubled children and their families. The central assumption of this book, however, is that any intervention strategy—home-based or residential—will succeed according to its ability to affect the total ecology of the child's world: family, peer group, school, neighborhood, and community. While much current debate has quite properly focused on the shortcomings of the isolated child caring institution in meeting the needs of troubled children for either effective treatment or humane care, recent past history has also shown that simply changing the *locus* of treatment

vii

from institution to community or family is not enough. We must also attend to the *focus* and the *purpose* of treatment—whether it occurs in a residential center, group home, community agency, or the child's own home.

I believe that group care—in particular, residential treatment—has both a proper place and a purpose in the continuum of child and family services. This potential will be realized only after several basic questions are addressed: (1) Where does residential treatment fit in the total continuum of child and family services? (2) What are the critical elements in a specialized helping environment for troubled children, and what are their various strengths and limitations? (3) How is the temporary group living environment linked with and supportive to the other important systems in the child's life—particularly the family and the public school? My motivation for writing *Caring for Troubled Children* stemmed from a desire to provide at least partial answers to these basic questions. Although it is not intended as a practice manual, the book hopefully will provide some practical suggestions for all whose mission is the care and treatment of children with special needs.

In the chapters that follow, I attempt to do two things: first, provide a perspective on residential treatment that includes some analysis of where we have been, where we are presently, and where we ought to be headed; second, to suggest some positive approaches and directions to counter what I consider indiscriminate condemnation and an unjustly negative view of group care existing in some quarters today. In essence, I try to deal honestly with some of the problems confronting residential treatment—for which no easy solutions exist—as well as to indicate some of the promise of this area of service, one that we have barely begun to explore. Inevitably, the results of such an ambitious undertaking are, at times, uneven—partly because of my own limitations and partly because of the limitations of our present knowledge and technology in a still very new field. Yet I feel that the book's coverage reflects accurately my own experience as well as my view of others in the field—child care workers, clinicians, and executives—whose concerns during a single day may range from weighty questions of organizational survival to strategies for getting the kids to bed at night. Throughout the book I offer these professionals concrete suggestions that are readily transferable to the real-life problems of children in need of help.

Chapter One examines four critical issues on which the future of residential treatment rests and suggests guidelines for the development of new programs. Chapter Two develops a paradigm for a therapeutic milieu based on the special needs of troubled children. Chapter Three describes several different approaches to residential treatment and analyzes their relative strengths and weaknesses. Chapter Four details the major elements in the residential environment—the culture of group living. Chapter Five looks at residential treatment in its broadest community context and, in particular, examines the linkages between the group living environment and the other major systems in which the child participates. Chapters Six and Seven provide in-depth perspectives of two such systems—the family and the school—and suggest the relationship of each to the group life environment. Chapter Eight examines the multiple functions of program evaluation in residential treatment, and Chapter Nine analyzes the emerging child care profession.

From the outset, I felt that someone other than myself could provide a more substantive perspective on two important areas— the school program and the emerging profession of child care. The thoughtful and rich contributions of Richard W. Small and Robin B. Clarke (Chapter Seven) and Jerome Beker (Chapter Nine) confirm my initial judgment. I deeply appreciate their efforts, as well as their helpful criticism on other sections of the book. I also wish to acknowledge numerous conversations with E. C. Teather and James R. Mann, which greatly enriched my thinking. I continue to learn from old colleagues and friends like Albert E. Trieschman. More recently I have also benefited from the work of Montrose M. Wolf of the University of Kansas and Elery L. Phillips and his staff at Boys Town in Nebraska. In a larger sense, I acknowledge the hundreds of child care professionals—executives, child care workers, social workers, and other clinicians, as well as teachers and parents—who have participated in my workshops and consultations over the past ten years. I also acknowledge the contribution of my students at the University of Washington's school of social work. Many of them are former child care workers and their questions led me to areas I might not otherwise have explored. I am, more than ever before, convinced of the tremendous amount of knowledge and skill that exists at the grass-roots level in the child care field. As always, I am grateful to Dean Scott Briar for providing support and envouragement in numerous ways. Mitsi Vondrachek typed the entire manuscript and deserves special recognition for continuing good cheer in the face of countless revisions. Finally, I owe a special debt to those in my own immediate "environment"—my wife, Kathleen, and children, Matthew, Patrick, and Abby—for providing support, more than occasional insight, and much joy.

*London*                                                        James K. Whittaker
*November 1978*

# The Authors

James K. Whittaker is a professor in the school of social work at the University of Washington. He received his A.B. degree in sociology from Boston College, his M.S.W. degree from the University of Michigan, and his Ph.D. degree from the University of Minnesota, where he also served on the faculty. A former child care worker, therapist, and administrator in residential child care, Whittaker has been a consultant to governmental and voluntary children's agencies throughout North America. During the academic year 1978-79, he studied the delivery of children's services in Britain and was a visiting scholar at the National Institute for Social Work in London. His books on child care and social work practice have been translated into four languages and include *The Other 23 Hours: Child Care Work in a Therapeutic Milieu* (1969, with Albert E. Trieschman and Larry K. Brendtro), *Children Away from Home: A Sourcebook in Residential Treatment* (1972, with Albert E. Trieschman), and *Social Treatment: An Approach to Interpersonal Helping* (1974).

Richard W. Small has worked in residential settings for emotionally disturbed children since 1967. His direct experience includes child care work, classroom teaching, and administration—most recently as coordinator of clinical services at the Walker School in Needham, Massachusetts. He holds a M.A. degree in education from Harvard University and is currently a doctoral candidate in social welfare at the University of Washington's school of social work.

Robin B. Clarke is an educator with extensive experience in both public and private schools. She has taught in the North Haven, Connecticut, public schools and at the James Jackson Putnam Clinic in Roxbury, Massachusetts. At the time this chapter was written, she was director of special education at the Walker School in Needham, Massachusetts. Clarke holds a M.A. degree in special education from Boston University and a certificate of advanced graduate study from Harvard University's graduate school of education. She currently resides with her family in Washington, D.C.

Jerome Beker is director of the Center for Youth Development and Research at the University of Minnesota. He also serves as editor of *Child Care Quarterly* and *Child and Youth Services* and as United States correspondent for the *International Child Welfare Review*. He earned his B.A. degree in psychology at Swarthmore College and holds the Ed.D. degree from Teachers College, Columbia University, in youth guidance and student personnel administration. Beker is the author or coauthor of three books, including *Critical Incidents in Child Care: A Case Book* (1972), and numerous articles in the field. His wide experience in the field of child and youth care covers practice, policy, research, and teaching.

## THE AUTHORS TODAY (1997)

James K. Whittaker, Ph.D. is Professor, School of Social Work, The University of Washington, Seattle, Washington.

Richard W. Small, Ph.D. is Executive Director, The Walker Home & School, Needham, Massachusetts.

Robin B. Clarke, M.A. is an educational consultant in private practice in North Carolina.

Jerome Beker, Ed.D. is Professor, Youth Studies Program, School of Social Work, The University of Minnesota, St. Paul, Minnesota.

# 1

# The Changing Character of Residential Child Care

This is a book about building helping environments for troubled children. The notion of the importance of environment to residential care or "the ecology of child treatment" is not new. We "knew," for example, even before Taylor and Alpert (1973) that what happens to the child on his or her return to the community is probably more important than anything that happened while the child was in care. Though it is presently small, the literature on ecological approaches to child treatment is growing. Broadly speaking, ecological theory looks at the interaction between organisms and their environments. The arena for research and intervention is the natural environment in which the individual resides. Instead of focusing

*Note:* An earlier version of a portion of this chapter appeared in "The Changing Character of Residential Child Care: An Ecological Perspective," *Social Service Review,* 1978, 22 (1), 21-36.

only on the question of individual deficit, ecological theorists are more interested in examining ecosystems or the interaction system comprised of living things and the nonliving habitat. (Central to the ecological model is the seminal work of Barker, 1968; see also Apter, in press; Kelly, 1969; Rhodes and Tracy, 1972; Garbarino, 1976, 1977a, 1977b; Whittaker, 1975; Collins and Pancoast, 1976; Wahler, House, and Stambaugh, 1976; Bronfenbrenner, 1977; and Rogers-Warren and Warren, 1977.) In the area of child treatment, recognition must be given to the special contributions of Hobbs (1964, 1966, 1967), who expanded our notion of helping environment to include the total community.

The ecological perspective encourages us to view residential treatment as a complex interplay of many different elements both within and outside the formal treatment program. It also encourages us to place as much emphasis on environmental assessment as on individual assessment, particularly on identifying natural helping networks in the community to which the child will return. In short, it provides us with an expanded view of the residential treatment center (see Figure 1). This book will provide an expanded definition of the key variables in the residential environment and explain their relationship to several important systems in the external environment—in particular, the family and the school.

Exactly where the ecological perspective will take us is not yet clear. I have not attempted to provide, nor does there yet exist, a fully developed "ecological model" of residential treatment. In fact, an ecological perspective, by definition, suggests that no single model of therapeutic group care will suffice but rather that residential programs need to be tailored to the special needs of the children and families they serve and the larger environments of which they are a part. In stressing the importance of ecological variables on individual children and the programs that serve them, we may be merely stating the obvious—but I do not think so. Rather, I believe that the confluence of ecological theory and child treatment theory will eventually result in a redefinition of mission for residential treatment, a new conceptualization of problems, and a new way

Figure 1. Group Living in Context: The Ecology of Child Treatment

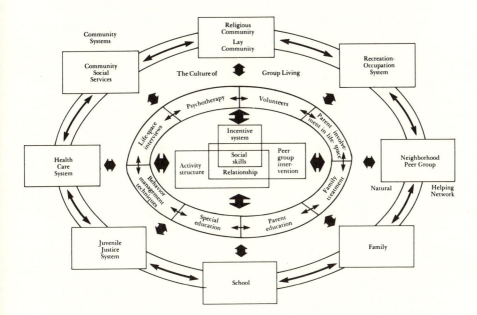

of thinking about interventive strategies. In short, it could lead us to a more precise understanding of what a therapeutic milieu —or helping environment—actually means. By focusing attention on the specialized environment of the residential center and on the broader environment of the community, this book will, I hope, constitute a first step in defining the components of an effective treatment strategy.

## Current Issues in Residential Treatment

*Continuity of Care.* Providing continuity of care has plagued the development of American social, health, and welfare services generally and has made the development of services for troubled children and their families particularly difficult. For example, we have tended to see most services as temporary remedies for children and families in a state of crisis, and our typical view of services takes on an "either/or" quality: children

are either full time in residential care, or they are considered
out of the service system; a family's case is "closed" or "open."
Agencies are not reimbursed for services provided to siblings of
the "referred" child, and some agencies are pressured by funding bodies to "close out" those cases where there is little or no
current activity. Consider for a moment the difference between
this view of a service system and that which is characteristic of a
health cooperative (or a prepaid health insurance plan). In the
latter case, although people frequently use the service system at
times of physical crises, their relationships with the system are
not severed during periods when they are in relatively good
health. In fact, they undoubtedly take great comfort in knowing that the system is there when and if they need it. Neither
the patient nor the provider nor, for that matter, society in general regards a continued dependent relationship with the health
care system as intrinsically wrong.

To my knowledge, in the field of children's services there
are very few analogues. We do not sanction continued dependence on the child welfare system, and we have not developed
an integrated continuum of services for troubled children and
their families. We have, instead, an aggregate of isolated, sometimes overlapping programs with no apparent connections between them. Particularly critical is the gap in aftercare services
for children returning to their home communities from residential treatment programs. Also lacking are adequate community-
based preventive services to reach children and families before
out-of-home placement is indicated. As a result, we have come
to regard the various elements of the service continuum as sufficient in themselves to meet the needs of children in trouble.
Nowhere is this type of argument more evident than in the current debate over deinstitutionalization, a controversy that leads
me to my first guideline in planning for services:

*Our goal should be to develop an integrated continuum
of care that provides a full range of home-based and residential
options and contains an easily activated set of linkages between
the various service programs and the other major systems in
which the child participates: family, peer group, school, church,
and community.*

The current controversy over deinstitutionalization in child mental health and juvenile corrections rests in part on a false and misleading dichotomy between residential and community-based programs. (For an introduction to the controversy over deinstitutionalization, see Bakal, 1973; Coughlin, 1977; Reid, 1974; Whittaker, 1975; Ohlin, Coates, and Miller, 1974; Miller and Ohlin, 1976; Lerman, 1975; Koshel, 1973; Morrison, 1977; Levine, 1977.) While the rationale for community-based treatment—to bring the remedial effort closer to the child's natural environment—is both sound and defensible, some advocates of community care have overstated the case: all institutions are bad, all community programs are good—or, at least, less detrimental. I would argue that this is an unfair characterization of child caring institutions, which, in fact, differ significantly in size, staff competence, degree of community relatedness, family involvement, and a host of other factors. Generalizations about child caring institutions as intrinsically bad suffer the same flaws as generalizations about "the family" as inherently good. Certainly no one would argue the desirability of large, impersonal, isolated institutions that do little more than warehouse children. There does exist a clear and pressing need for more humane, family-centered, neighborhood-based services that reach troubled children sooner and in more effective ways. But if the "locus" of treatment is important, so is the "focus"; buying a home in the community and staffing it with a set of untrained houseparents, opening a drop-in center, or offering "cookbook-style" parent education to multiproblem families does not make for a sophisticated, effective, or more humane treatment program. Further, just as some children can remain at home while they and their families receive help, others will continue to require total or partial care away from home. In any event, some "community-based" residential programs house upward of twenty to twenty-five children, so that the differences between these "community-based" services and their "institutional" counterparts tend to evaporate; we are dealing in both cases with the total or partial away-from-home care of significant numbers of children.

The real issue is not the relative merits of residential

versus community treatment; rather, it is the question of how best to translate the most useful knowledge from clinical research and practice wisdom to a total continuum of services, ranging from programs that provide help while the child remains in his own home, through smaller, open, community-based residential and day programs to larger, more secure residential facilities for those few children who need them. The goal in any program should be to build what Wolins (1974) has called a "powerful environment," whether or not that environment includes an out-of-home placement for the child. What we need is a continuum of care that softens rather than hardens the line between residential and nonresidential options. Most certainly such a continuum would include foster care, respite care, shelter care, day treatment, and family-centered intervention along with a variety of residential and home-based options. The key element in developing a service plan for any particular child would not center on whether he or she remained at home or was placed out; it would focus instead on how the elements in the total ecosystem could be so mobilized as to constitute a powerful environment for positive change. Such a focus would require the presence of an easily activated set of linkages between the treatment program and the other major systems in which the child participates: family, school, church, peer group, juvenile justice system, recreation-occupation system, health care system, social service system, as well as any informal helping networks (see Figure 1). A truly ecological view of child treatment requires intervention in a number of different supporting systems to ensure continuity of care. The goal of planning should be the development of an integrated service net, rather than the creation of isolated programs.

*Definition of Purpose.* Granted the need for an integrated continuum of child and family services, what is the place of residential and day treatment in such a spectrum? For example, should residential care be seen as a temporary support for a family under stress or as a substitute for a family that has failed? While the majority of residential programs would probably choose the former as their primary purpose, much current practice indicates the latter. In many programs, parents are still not regarded as full and equal partners in the treatment process, and the general integration of residential services in their host communities remains incomplete, as witnessed by the reluctance of many neighborhoods to accept therapeutic group homes in their midst: "Community care is fine—but not in my neighborhood." Now, however, largely because of the rising costs of care and the gradual change of mental health services to a more consumer-focused, educational orientation, the field of residential care is entering a period of change that goes to the very core of its existence and necessitates a reassessment of basic purpose. Recognition of that impending change leads to my second guideline in planning for services:

*Residential and day programs for troubled children should function as a family support system rather than treating the child in isolation from his family and home community.*

This guideline is based on the assumption that the nuclear family, natural or foster, will continue to be seen as the optimal environment for child rearing in American society. Partly because of physical isolation from their clients' communities and partly because of the presumed involvement of parents as causative agents in the child's problems, many residential treatment centers developed practices that isolated parents from the treatment of their child. However, the literature that exists on the permanence of therapeutic change in children suggests the importance of involving parents in the child's treatment. In those programs where parents have been full and equal partners in the helping process, the results have been impressive (see Schopler and Reichler, 1976; Johnson and Katz, 1973; Patterson and others, 1975). In my view, therefore, child treatment programs should not be regarded as substitutes for family living but, rather, as instruments for helping natural or foster parents or other guardians develop successful methods of caring for children with special life adjustment problems.

On another level, I would argue that the creation of a broad-based citizens' lobby—including parents of children in need of residential and day programs—is critical to the continued viability of those programs. The counterargument to fuller parental involvement holds that many of the parents of the children we serve are themselves overburdened, troubled, or apathetic, so that they are incapable of participating as full and equal partners in the treatment for their own child, much less assuming active responsibility for advocating on behalf of others. While such assertions may be true for any particular family, I prefer to look at the problem from another perspective: What barriers have we erected in our service programs, treatment philosophies, and professional education that tend to exclude parents from full and equal participation? Have we relied too heavily on the "family etiology hypothesis" to explain disturbed behavior (Whittaker, 1976a)? Have we selectively defined a role for parents—individual treatment with a therapist—that effectively isolates them from the child care worker, the staff member who has the most complete and detailed view of their child's day-to-day behavior? Have we actively sought to engage parents in political efforts on behalf of all the children in care through board participation, legislative efforts, and the like, or have we tended to see them in unidimensional terms as "clients" or "patients." My hesitancy in believing that parents cannot or will not be actively involved at all levels of the program stems partly from the fact that, until a very few years ago, similar arguments about nonparticipation could be extended to parents of other handicapped children, such as the mentally retarded and the autistic. Today each of these groups presents a strong, visible, national political voice, a new "image," and a new relationship to the professional community—all of which must certainly lead to better services. Therefore, the fact that (to my knowledge) no comparable organizations presently exist for, say, parents of delinquent children or for natural parents of foster children should be taken as a challenge for action and not as a confirmation of the diagnosis of incapability.

Along with a refocus on residential treatment as a support rather than a substitute for family care, we need to redefine what the "treatment" in residential treatment actually means. More specifically, I would offer a third guideline in planning for services:

*Residential and day treatment programs should focus on growth and development in the child's total life sphere rather*

*than on the remediation of psychiatrically defined syndromes
or the extinction of certain problematical behaviors.*

The basic purpose of all child helping should be the
teaching of skills for living. Our goal should be the development
of a model of child rearing which emphasizes the competence
and mastery that all children need to develop in basic life skills
and then demonstrates how these skills may be taught to children with special needs. The illness model of residential treatment that pervades our case records has not served us well; in
fact, a majority of the children we serve do not suffer from
underlying disease processes, psychoneuroses, or character disorders. We should therefore make use of assessment procedures
that are behaviorally specific and contextually grounded; that
is, directly applicable to the real-life environments the children
encounter in their home communities. We should also proceed
on the assumption that no single format for teaching skills is
sufficient; neither psychotherapy nor behavior modification of
itself provides education for living. We need instead to think
about a variety of teaching formats, including group intervention, behavioral modification, games and activities, special education, and family work. Such an orientation to total child
growth and development requires us to take three additional
steps:

1. *Demystification of the helping process.* Parents and
child care workers are most often the best experts on the children in their care. Both should be involved as central actors in
the helping process; specifically, they should have access to all
information possessed by the clinicians. Too often parents and
parenting persons are kept in the dark regarding clinical assessments, which themselves are often couched in jargon that con-
fuses more than clarifies. Assessment should include a look at
the child's total range of functioning and begin not with clinical
presuppositions but with those areas that are causing parents
and child the most pain and strain. Finally, taking the mystery
out of child treatment means saying honestly, "I don't know,"
when the situation warrants.

2. *Relabeling of program elements.* Hobbs (1975a,
1975b) and his associates have written of the dangers of labeling

individual children. Similarly, program labels help the child define himself. The basic elements of the child treatment program require a relabeling to reflect a living/learning rather than an illness/treatment orientation. For example:

"Campus" *not* "Grounds"
"Student" *not* "Patient"
"Dormitory" *not* "Cottage"
"Graduation" *not* "Discharge"
"Residential" *not* "Treatment"
"School" *not* "Center"

The reason for this semantic change (for which I am indebted to my colleague Albert E. Trieschman, whose own program—the Walker School—uses this terminology) is partly political—"education" is more positively valenced in the society than "treatment." In addition, however, the new terms provide a much better set of descriptors for what the program is all about: teaching the child something about the reasonable limits of his own behavior and, at the same time, providing him with the opportunity to acquire competence in a whole range of life skills. The illness/treatment terminology suggests the presence of some identifiable psychic disease processes in children—a view that is not supported by the available evidence.

3. *Designing learning experiences with an eye toward maximum "portability."* Adjustment within the program should be seen as the means and not the end of the helping process. Developing "marketable peer skills" should mean just that: how to make a friend, join a game, or negotiate with someone who is bigger and tougher than oneself. The ultimate proving ground should be the child's own home, school, and community. As we know from clinical experience and from the available research, adjustment *within* the program is not necessarily a good predictor of how the child will fare on his return to the community.

Finally, the residential or day program should have relevance for all of the community's children, not just those in care. For example, residential treatment centers should begin to offer an increasingly diversified array of services, including milieu therapy, special education, day treatment, community-centered programs, consultation, and parent education. Knowledge gained from the day-to-day management of children with special life adjustment problems is also of importance to parents, teachers, and other caring persons. The need for such child rearing and child management information, particularly as it relates to group care settings, will increase as the society moves toward day care for older "normal" children who suddenly begin to exhibit many of the same problem behaviors as their "special" counterparts. Residential treatment can provide a valuable laboratory for exploring home-based methods of working with the most difficult children; and these methods, in turn, will have great applicability to child management in general. The whole move toward the "normalization" of services requires that we bring the community into the treatment agency, as well as the agency into the community.

*Theory in the Service of Program.* We need an adequate theory for changing children's behavior—and we needed it yesterday! As the children entering residential treatment programs have changed in recent years (see Maluccio and Marlow, 1972; Weintrob, 1974; Mayer, Richman, and Balcerzak, 1977), so has our knowledge of how best to help them. The origin of many childhood disorders is now seen in a different light. Strictly functional or psychogenic explanations of problem behavior have given way to explanations stressing the complex interplay of neurobiological, emotional, familial, and sociocultural factors. In residential treatment, psychoanalytically oriented therapy as the treatment of choice is slowly giving way to therapeutic intervention in the life space. Perhaps the greatest change in the clinical process of residential treatment in the last decade has been the infusion of behavior modification into the therapeutic milieu. Several studies have demonstrated the efficacy of behavior management techniques in residential settings for behavior-disordered and psychotic children, while others have developed techniques for the behavioral treatment of antisocial children in their own homes (Phillips and others, 1973a; Browning and Stover, 1971; Patterson and others, 1975). As the research from one prominent behavioral program suggests, however, behavioral interventions will not be effective unless they take into account the host of subtle but powerful interactions that occur between staff and children (Phillips and others, 1973a). In short, "relationship" continues to play a key role in constructing a therapeutic milieu, but we have to develop a common understanding of what exactly a "relationship" is. Moreover, although treatment will continue to become more oriented to specific measurable and limited goals for each individual child, a successful program must also effectively harness the power of the peer group to work toward positive goals. Individual treatment alone, as Polsky (1962) and others have pointed out, simply does not have the power to overcome a negative peer culture. Finally, just as our knowledge of "what to do" has changed, so has our understanding of "who" should do it. A new orientation to the total ecology of the child's world will mean realignment of staff both within and outside of the core treatment program. Where, then, will we find an adequate theory to describe just what a therapeutic milieu is and how it should work? In response to this question, I would offer a fourth guideline for practice:

*No single theory or set of practice prescriptions will answer the needs of a program that is geared to the total range of children's development and oriented to the total ecology of their world.*

We lack a unified theory for residential treatment and will probably continue to do so for the immediate future. This should not be viewed as particularly problematic, since we are still a field that is developing. It suggests a continued period of experimentation with many different models and an essentially inductive rather than a deductive approach to the development of a theory of intervention. Our theory should be used in the service of our stated program purpose—to provide education for living. Instead, residential treatment programs too often have tried to bend their purposes or objectives to meet preconceived theoretical biases. Thus, some residential programs have suddenly switched from a totally psychodynamic to a totally behaviorist orientation—simply through a change in executive directors. On occasion, even whole service systems, particularly in juvenile corrections, have shifted from one total approach to another—for example, from "casework" to positive peer culture and then back again, as if "truth" lay only on one or the other side of the argument. This either/or approach to the development of a practice theory has been counterproductive in that it has constantly kept alive the spark of hope that somewhere, somehow, we will discover the "answer" in a single approach, theory, or treatment model.

But there is no simple solution to the complex problems that confront us in the child care field. Rather than continuing a search for an encompassing theory of milieu treatment, we should accept the fact that theory development will proceed slowly through a series of experiments and program demonstrations in which the wisdom of clinical practice and the knowledge from clinical research and theory are tested against the real-life problems of children and families in need of care. We must therefore guard against overreliance on a single body of theory, even though there is a need for coherence and a value in commonly held precepts. Perhaps our primary unity should come not so much from commonly accepted and defended theory as from a common commitment to basic purposes: to teach skills for living and to build a powerful environment. Such an open, flexible, and eclectic orientation to a theory of residential treatment demands a program that is data based and capable of being evaluated.

*Social Cost and Public Accountability.* The development of effective, humane, and ecologically sound services requires a built-in capability to measure the effectiveness of what we do. Therefore, my fifth guideline for the development of services is as follows:

*Children's residential and day treatment programs should be able to demonstrate what they do in simple, clear, and jargon-free terms that can be understood by the general public.*

Simply stated, sound evaluative procedures should be built into all child helping programs. Evaluation need not be esoteric or highly complex; we are a problem-focused group, so our research should be action research. The impetus for evaluation is not simply political. We need to learn more about what works and what does not in children's programs and to build knowledge in an area of practice sorely in need of hard data. The choice, then, is not whether to evaluate but who will do the evaluation and what will be the outcome criteria? In many studies "success" has been narrowly defined and often in ways not warranted by the treatment effort. The goal for evaluation should be as broad a set of measures as possible rather than a single criterion such as "recidivism," "grades in school," or "absence of police contact." In order not to be stampeded in the rush for cost effectiveness and accountability, child care practitioners must themselves get involved in the process of goal setting, development of outcome criteria, and instrument development. We need to be sure not only that our methodology is correct but also that we are asking the right questions. We also need to determine a wide range of outcome criteria and to tailor evaluation to individual programs.

Fortunately, research methodology has advanced to the point where we can overcome some of the practical and ethical problems involved in implementing the traditional group design. A review of the literature on the effectiveness of residential treatment, however, yields a mixed picture (Shyne, 1973; Kadushin, 1974) vis-à-vis outcome. Many studies are conducted without benefit of controls. Therefore, although a change in the dependent variable sometimes occurred, the precise nature of independent variables responsible for the change can rarely be specified. Service units are often poorly conceptualized and extremely difficult to quantify. For example, virtually all group care services now classify themselves as "treatment" centers, though individual programs vary considerably. In actual practice, agencies need both program evaluation, which yields a cumulative measure of total agency performance, and clinical evaluation, which measures progress in an individual case.

Basically, each program needs to build an information system that permits both formative evaluation and summative evaluation. A formative evaluation of the program will yield helpful information to staff about treatment effectiveness with individual children while the children are still in care. Such a system, which should include measures of individual progress and program effectiveness, allows us to alter individual treatment plans and agency programs on the basis of a continuous flow of information. Formative evaluation is crucial in a field such as residential treatment, where our knowledge of what constitutes effective programs for an individual child or group of children is still at a primitive phase. Summative evaluation answers the following question: "Over time, did our treatment have an effect on the behavior of the children after they returned to neighborhood, school, family, and peer group?"

A final issue concerns the cost of care in child treatment and, particularly, the cost of residential care. The cost of care per child in residential treatment ranges anywhere from $6,000 to $25,000 a year, with some centers exceeding $30,000. Though heavily subsidized through public funding, many private centers operate at a deficit level. Therapeutic group home services are less expensive in capital investment and annual operating costs, though cost comparisons often do not reflect services provided "free" outside of the group home and in the community—services such as special education, casework services, and aftercare.

State legislatures and private funding sources, under increasing demand for shrinking resources, are raising questions like: "Why so much money for so few children?" and "Couldn't we achieve the same results at a lower cost through community-based services?" In a sense, these questions assume a false dichotomy between residential and community-based services, since there will continue to be children in need of care away from their own homes, whether that care is provided in a treatment institution or a community-based program. It is also becoming apparent that the provision of quality community-based treatment is not as inexpensive a service as it first appeared, particularly when expenses like staff training and auxiliary support services are factored into the budget. For example, Lerman's (1975) secondary analysis of the California Youth Authority's decade of experimentation with community treatment calls into serious question not only the agency's claim of treatment effectiveness but also its cost effectiveness when compared with institutional services.

Another problem has to do with the cost reimbursement

policies in some localities. For example, many residential programs receive funds only for children in full-time residence,
which creates the tendency to keep bed spaces filled even when
partial care or day treatment might be indicated. Part of the
problem stems from the fact that we lack precise instruments
for measuring the social costs of not serving children in need of
help. Clearly, such measurement would include the added costs
to the school system, juvenile justice system, and social service
system for services provided in the absence of specialized care.
But how one goes about measuring the ultimate costs, monetary
and psychic, of not serving children is a problem that has not
yielded an easy solution. Occasionally, the specter of a troubled
child turned assassin, or the realization that our adult prison or
mental hospital populations might have responded to earlier
intervention, touches a responsive chord. But we have usually
responded to such revelations—if we have responded at all—by
developing a crash program, say, for runaways, instead of looking critically at the total system of care. We need to face the
cost-of-care issue squarely from two perspectives: Are there
more cost-effective ways to deliver our services, and are there
predictable and measurable social and economic costs that will
follow from lack of action?

## Conclusions

I have attempted to identify four broad areas of concern
to residential and day treatment programs:

*Continuity of Care.* The controversy over deinstitutionalization is based on a false and misleading dichotomy between
residential and community-based programs. Our goal should be
to develop an integrated continuum of care, which provides a
full range of home-based and residential options and contains an
easily activated set of linkages between the various service programs and the other major systems in which the child participates: family, peer group, school, and community.

*Definition of Purpose.* Residential and day programs for
troubled children should function as a family support system
rather than treating the child in isolation from his family and

home community. Child treatment programs should focus on growth and development in the child's total life sphere, rather than on the remediation of psychiatrically defined syndromes or the extinction of certain problematical behaviors.

*Theory in the Service of Program.* No single theory or set of practice prescriptions will answer the needs of a program that is geared to the total range of children's development and oriented to the total ecology of their world.

*Social Cost and Public Accountability.* Children's residential and day treatment programs should be able to demonstrate what they do in simple, clear, and jargon-free terms that can be understood by the general public.

What all this suggests is that the field of remedial group child care is entering a period of change that goes to its very core. This change will, among other things, require existing programs to reexamine their basic goals and objectives. The increasing emphasis on accountability and cost effectiveness will bring about internal structural changes as well as changes in treatment philosophy. Shorter-term treatment focused on specific, limited, and measurable goals will become more commonplace, with parents playing a much more active role as developmental therapists for their own children as well as being advocates for the total program. Indeed, if community-based treatment is to work effectively, a new set of linkages between agency and community will be needed. Continuity of care requires a spectrum of services that vary from secure institutions for those few children who need them, through a variety of open, low-visibility, community-based residential and day treatment programs, to a set of services that can be offered to children while they remain at home or in a foster home. We must discard once and for all the notion that institutional care and community care are mutually exclusive options, when they are, in fact, different points on a needed continuum of services.

Let us proceed now to a look at the children in need of help—who they are, what are their special needs, and what type of helping program they require.

# 2

## Assessing Child Problems and Creating a Helping Environment

Jean Itard's (1962) classic account of Victor, *The Wild Boy of Aveyron*, portrays the painful and moving efforts of a clinician-scientist to reach out and help a profoundly troubled child—the origin of whose illness he did not understand. Was Victor in fact a "feral" child suckled by wolves and devoid of human emotion? Or was he, perhaps, a severely retarded deaf-mute abandoned by parents incapable of caring for him—or, as some have more recently hypothesized, an autistic child whose bizarre behavior and absence of social skills predated his exposure to the wild? For Itard and later for his student Sequin, Victor represented a challenge to the notion of irreversible trauma and, perhaps, as has been suggested by others, something deeper besides. "To Itard he represented questions without answers; to Sequin he provided answers to questions; but to us his life signifies one of the eternal questions: Who was he and what are we ourselves" (Balthazar and Stevens, 1975, frontispiece)?

18

The world of the troubled child today is a world no less filled with questions. As clinicians and educators, we are faced with the task of teaching and treating in problem areas whose origins are little understood. While logic decrees that a theory of etiology should precede a theory of clinical intervention, in reality the reverse is more often true: like Itard, we come to truly *understand* a troubled child's behavior only after attempting to change it. What follows should be taken equally as evidence for what we do not know as well as what we do. Precisely because we are so often pressed for a theory of changing children's behavior, it is well to begin again with the question raised by every novice child care worker who has for the first time experienced the sound and fury of a full fledged temper tantrum or tried, unsuccessfully, to reestablish contact with a sullen and aloof runaway adolescent: *Who are these children and how did they get this way?*

The number of troubled children in the United States—as reported by the 1970 White House Conference on Children—indicates a target population and a social problem of considerable magnitude: Approximately 10 percent of the 50 million school-age children had moderate to severe emotional problems. One out of three poor children had serious emotional problems requiring attention. Ninety-two percent of all public elementary schools reported some children with severe reading problems. Nearly two million children were enrolled in special education programs. While 682,000 children and their families received mental health care in an average year, they represented only a fraction of those families in need of such services. (*Profiles of Children,* 1972, Charts 43, 45, 121, 130.)

Excluding the physically handicapped, there were approximately 220,000 children under the age of 18 in institutional care in 1970 (Kadushin, 1974). They were housed in some 2,400 child caring institutions (Pappenfort, Kilpatrick, and Roberts, 1973). In addition, over one million cases are handled in our juvenile courts yearly, and these figures may not accurately reflect the need for services or the number of children who were improperly placed. In fact, the collection of accurate data in any segment of the children's field presents significant problems, since no single agency has overall responsibility for tracking children in the child welfare system. One government expert recently testified that we have a more accurate count of the number of camp stoves and picnic tables in national parks than the number of children in need of care.

Clinically, the children coming into residential and day treatment programs seem more disturbed than just a few years ago (Maluccio and Marlow, 1972; Weintrob, 1974). Most present a multiplicity of problems: interpersonal, emotional, learning, familial, physiological. This population encompasses a wide range of presenting problems and diagnostic labels: infantile autism, childhood schizophrenia, character disorder, minimal brain dysfunction, depressed, hyperkinetic, socially maladjusted, delinquent, and developmentally disordered. Hobbs' (1975a, 1975b) study of the effects of labeling on troubled children and their families recalls the earlier work of Goffman (1962), who spoke of the "paper shadow" of case records, labels, and the like, that follows the career of the child in special education like the dossier of the mental patient. In what is an understandable desire for specificity and closure, parents, professionals, and helping agencies use the label to explain the child's problem—almost as if the acquisition of a diagnostic label signifies that a treatment plan is now self-evident. Unfortunately, we are not yet at the stage where diagnostic labels lead ineluctably to clear and determinative plans for treatment or education. This fact, coupled with the frequently cited harmful effects of labeling, should lead us to reexamine the typical behavior of children coming into residential or day treatment programs; we might thereby learn whether there are any common categories of presenting problems.

### Children at Risk: A Naturalistic Assessment

The question of whether children who are referred to group care facilities present common patterns of behavioral deficits is an empirical one. The categories presented here are only in part based on clinical research and to a large extent are impressionistic. My intention is neither to identify discrete syndromes nor to suggest that conclusions are based on a rigorous epidemiological study of the population at risk—though both types of research activity are clearly needed as a base for planning services. Rather, my intention is to provide a conceptual framework for describing what appear to me to be the behaviors of many troubled children in need of care—a framework that takes into account the full range of developmental difficulties and that yields practical suggestions for intervention by child care workers, teachers, therapists, and parents.

When one attempts to identify certain common problem categories, he runs the risk of obscuring real etiological and behavioral differences between various subpopulations of troubled children. Clearly, the program for the profoundly disturbed autistic child and the aggressive, acting-out preadolescent will differ significantly. In fact, the bulk of the behavioral description will best fit the middle range of the child population at risk—having less validity for the child who is frankly psychotic or for the adolescent culturally trained delinquent. What all these children share, however, is the fact of their development: the need to acquire competence in a wide range of emotional and interpersonal areas. From a competency-based perspective, such a child may be diagnosed as having failed to develop emotional, social, and physical competence. "Acting out" (as with the delinquent or hyperactive child) or repetitive activity (as with the psychotic or special-learning-disabled child) may indicate crude attempts to master an environment that is seen as threatening and unpredictable (a notion introduced by Robinson and Robinson, 1976, with respect to mentally retarded children. Their speculation was based on the earlier work of White, 1960, on "competence"). The problem categories shown in Figure 2 are more or less representative of the population at risk.

*Poorly Developed Impulse Control.* Numerous clinicians have noted the low frustration tolerance and limited ability to postpone gratification characteristic of many of the children who come into residential or day treatment (Browning and Stover, 1971; Redl, 1966; Redl and Wineman, 1957; Trieschman, Whittaker, and Brendtro, 1969). Disruptive outbursts at home and in school are often part of the initial reason for refer-

Figure 2. Some Commonly Observed Problem Categories

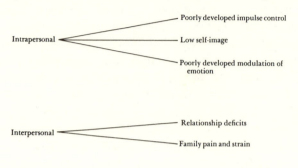

ral. Many children exhibit faulty connections between thought, feeling, and action in the course of a temper tantrum (Trieschman, Whittaker, and Brendtro, 1969, pp. 170-198). Lashing out at other persons, at objects, or at self becomes the characteristic way of dealing with frustration, strain, or anxiety. In purely behavioral terms, the "aggressive child" of Redl and Wineman (1957) possesses only a limited repertoire of responses for dealing with frustration or provocation. A related characteristic is the apparent inability of many of those children to screen out peripheral stimuli; they are easily "contaged" by the misbehavior of other children and are especially prone to group excitement. Etiological explanations for the inability to control impulses have varied predictably according to theoretical biases. Psychoanalytic theoreticians at first viewed acting-out behavior as a function of faulty superego development. These conscience deficits—or "superego lacunae"—were thought to be the result of faulty early developmental experiences and were to be remedied primarily through therapeutic attempts at filling in the lacunae with a more socially acceptable set of values (Johnson, 1950). A somewhat later and more widely held explanation laid the blame for impulsivity on faulty ego development—specifically, on the inability to channel instinctual impulses into socially acceptable forms of expression. In this view, the disturbed child acts out his id drives using activity rather than language to cope with his impulses (Grossbard, 1962)—not unlike the infant, who dissipates tensions through kicking and crying; the drive structure of the disturbed child spills over into all areas of bodily function and is reflected in hyperactivity and restlessness. Along with this characteristic impulsivity, the child manifests other disruptions of normal ego function—specifically, (1) a distortion in the sense of *time*, reflected in a limited ability to postpone gratification and an almost total focus on the present; and (2) *perceptual* deficits, whereby the child demonstrates an apparent inability to learn from experience despite negative consequences. The ego selects from reality those factors that fit in with the child's world view and excludes those that do not. Characteristic behaviors include avoidance, denial, and negation. In sum, the ego of the impulsive child is thought to be lacking in the basic ability to control impulses and to discharge them through appropriate forms of language, sublimation, and fantasy (Grossbard, 1962).

From a neurobiological point of view, an almost identical symptom picture has led to a different diagnosis: minimal brain dysfunction (MBD). The basic characteristics of MBD are as follows: (1) short attention span; (2) distractibility; (3) hyperactivity; (4) impulsiveness; (5) emotional lability; (6) poor motor integration; (7) deficits in the perception of space, form, movement, and time; and (8) disorders of language or symbol development (Peters and others, 1973, pp. 6-8).

While evidence on the incidence of this disorder is incomplete, the direction of the research findings appears to support the general conclusion that organic factors play a critical role in explaining the etiology of much impulse-ridden and learning-disordered behavior.

Finally, behaviorists have long pointed to the effects of attention and other forms of social reinforcement on the maintenance of impulsive, acting-out behaviors. While it is doubtful that such social learning explanations can completely account for all the impulsive behavior observed in the population at risk —given the growing body of neurobiological evidence to the contrary—social learning explanations do help to explain why

such behaviors are maintained at home and in the treatment setting, where such symptoms may be actually nurtured as a conscious part of the treatment process as "regression in the service
of the ego" is allowed to occur.

   *Low Self-Image.* To the extent that the child's self-
concept may be understood in terms of "I am what I learn"
(Langer, 1969), many of these children (because of their special
learning difficulties) have an extremely low or negative self-
image. The troubled child is likely to see himself as "bad,"
"evil," "stupid," "troublemaker." A fatalistic view of the potential for change ("It's always been this way") may be supported by a string of unsuccessful experiences in school, at
home, and with friends. In the Eriksonian sense, we see the
antithesis of "I am what I will be" in the hollowness of the delinquent adolescent on whose forearm is etched "Born to Lose"
(see Erikson, 1963, 1964). Such a low self-concept may be reflected in the child's dress, gait, posture, and demeanor, though
it may sometimes be masked with a thin veneer of bravado or
indifference. Often children's drawings or written narratives
(Long, Morse, and Newman, 1971, p. 60) reflect the sense of
emptiness within.

   *Poorly Developed Modulation of Emotion.* Many disturbed children also lack skills in dealing appropriately and
effectively with the normal range of human emotions: anger,
fear, elation, and sadness. In addition to the problem of expressing emotion congruently, these children have difficulty in sorting out mixed emotions—particularly anger and sadness—or are
emotionally labile. A common example is the child who reacts
with full-blown rage when told by a teacher or child care
worker that he must "wait his turn" in a lesson or favorite
activity. The sheer force of anger which these children are capable of expressing has been noted by Redl and Wineman (1957);
Trieschman, Whittaker, and Brendtro (1969); and others. A
puzzling aspect of these emotional storms is the rapidity with
which they often pass and the haziness with which they are remembered by some children: "The aftermath of a tantrum
varies considerably. Some children talk and look as though
'nothing ever happened'—except for a little fatigue or a slight

redness of the eyes or face. . . . To all appearances, these children have 'shot their wad,' blown up, ventilated in the extreme, and now seem in their usual condition. Their dissociated anger outburst seems to have cleared the register for new transactions" (Trieschman, Whittaker, and Brendtro, 1969, p. 190). Other youngsters more typically lapse into a mildly depressed state—shunning human contact and retreating in solitude to the farthest corner of the ward or cottage. As mentioned, many of these children appear to have difficulty in recognizing the comingling of anger and sadness that occurs within them. For example, children who, for one reason or another, cannot return to their natural family are often quick to acknowledge the sadness they feel but slower to recognize the considerable anger they feel toward their parents for letting them down. Often this side of the emotion is expressed through displacement to child care workers, teachers, and foster parents.

While the mastery of emotional states is a learned skill, the literature on teaching emotional competence to children is sparse. Trieschman and Levine (1972) have devised methods of helping children learn to deal with grief and unhappiness. Fagen, Long, and Stevens (1975) have developed a model for teaching children to master emotions in a classroom environment, and a recent literature has emerged on helping children deal with the separation and trauma involved in death, divorce, and physical illness (Furman, 1974; Gardner, 1971). Hobbs (1967, p. 353) has stressed the importance of helping children attain cognitive control of their emotions and of allowing children to "know joy." The behavioral literature contains some examples of the use of operant and respondent procedures to help the child overcome excessive fears and the avoidance behaviors that often accompany them (Patterson, 1965). At least one preliminary study has indicated that biofeedback and relaxation techniques show real promise for helping children control muscular activity and its accompanying tension and emotionality (Braud, Lupin, and Braud, 1975; Finch and others, 1975). For the child who flies off into uncontrollable rages at the slightest provocation, or whose mood swings from euphoric highs to depressive lows, or who desperately needs to know how to cope with the feelings attendant to the loss of relationship, learning emotional competence—and the mastery of inner environment that accompanies it—is every bit as important as mastering an academic or a physical skill.

*Relationship Deficits.* Many of the children coming into residential or day treatment programs exhibit clear and significant deficits in their ability to form close and meaningful relationships with peers and helping adults. Interpersonally, one sees the range of relationship deficits from the isolating autistic child who avoids even eye contact, to the clinging, overpowering child who seems ready to submerge or be submerged in another. Some children are fearful of closeness and leery of adult relationships, while others react stereotypically to male or female authority figures. For example, they may view all female child care staff members as "bitches" or all male staff members as physically threatening. Often, these are children who have few friends, perhaps because of their unpredictability, or their proclivity to "con" and manipulate, or their tendency to "overload" an individual relationship with too many demands. Such children may have difficulty in joining and leaving peer groups and in handling partialized as opposed to diffuse relationships (a relationship with a teacher as opposed to a parent, for example). Finally, some children simply lack the social skills (such as small talk) that one uses to facilitate new relationships; thus, they resort to disruptive, silly, or bizarre behavior as a way of handling their discomfort. Several common styles of interacting are frequently observed among these children:

The *manipulative child* has the finely honed ability to play one individual off against another. Teacher, child care worker, and parent are left feeling that much of the child's "problem" lies with the insensitivity of the other adults in the child's life. Children habituated to this style of relating are often into their "con" almost reflexively, even when the situation is a nonstressful one. Such a child may also "set up" other children in the cottage or group home by selectively feeding provocative information to each and then stepping back to watch the sparks fly. Many adolescents become skilled at conning the therapist by providing the "right" answers in therapy.

Basic to their style of relationship is an extremely low level of trust in peers and helping adults and significant gaps in conscience development.

The *intimidating child*, because of physical size or sheer force of presence, assumes a position of dominance over the rest of the group. The cottage "duke" moves rapidly to establish authority over turf—possessions, physical space, privileges—and is often abetted in his activity by the tacit sanction of the staff, who allow him free rein in exchange for order. Polsky (1962) discovered such a phenomenon in a large residential institution for delinquents. This child is frequently called upon to reassert his dominance over the group—particularly as new members are added.

The *bizarre child* displays some physical or mental abnormality which is both repulsive and frightening to the rest of the group. Often children who show certain psychotic symptoms—hand flapping, grimacing, stereotypical movements—will have this effect on a group of more nearly normal behavior-disordered children. Epilepsy and physical handicaps, such as a prosthesis, can elicit a similar effect. These youngsters often learn to use their abnormality as a way of keeping peers at arm's length. Generally these children will be left alone by the group, which is never really sure what to expect of them.

The *overdependent child* makes excessive demands on the time and emotional resources of the helping adults, from whom he or she never strays very far. This child checks every decision with an adult, to see whether it is "OK"; engages in activities with other children only when adults are present; lives in constant fear of what the other children will do to him or her out of the sight of the teacher or houseparent; and provides a steady stream of information to the staff about the underlife of the group. Adult approval and nurturance are constantly sought on a demand schedule.

The *isolated child* exists in a space-time dimension apart from the rest of the group. Peer relations are sparse, and a good deal of time is spent in private activity—daydreaming, reading. Adult relationships are pleasant but perfunctory. The isolated child generally knows how to stay out of the limelight and out of trouble; he or she has developed a preventive avoidance reaction for dealing with potentially difficult situations.

The *scapegoat* has salient characteristics that are easy to identify (Allport, 1966). In an extended analysis of scapegoating phenomena in children's groups, Garland and Kolodny (1972) report that the most commonly observed characteristic of scapegoats is their inability to deal with aggression. The authors (p. 225) suggest that the persecutee's role is often a purposeful one, since (1) the scapegoated child tends to put himself in situations that are clearly injurious to him; (2) he frequently denies that he is seeking persecution; and (3) he insists that the situation is beyond his control and hopeless. This purposefulness on the part of the scapegoat is complemented by the group's simultaneously cherishing and reviling the scorned member—thus keeping the undesirable trait, habit, or behavior quite literally on someone else's back. Garland and Kolodny also identify four different problem clusters that seem to elicit non-purposeful scapegoating on the part of the victim: confused sexual identity; the overriding need for inclusion, which may contain the willingness to undergo "secondary pain" as the price of acceptance—as with the obese child; the easily provoked child, who resorts to physical retaliation at the drop of a hat; and the child who possesses any of a number of cultural or physical unorthodoxies—skin color, religion, physical deformity, and the like.

Two final points regarding relationship deficits:

1. Many children exhibit gaps in interpersonal skills that do not fit precisely into any of the previously mentioned categories. Such things as the inability to "make small talk," invite a friend out to play, join a game already in progress, ask a teacher for help, or say "I like you" are part and parcel of the presenting problems of many of these youngsters. What we take for granted as "innate" responses in normal adult interaction are, in fact, acquired social skills that can be actively taught to promote social competence and the feeling of confidence that accompanies it.

2. Interpersonal assessment must be undertaken only with respect to a specific context. Scapegoating, bullying, and

isolative behaviors may be as much a function of the group living context as anything the child brings with him. Thus, we
must be wary of pinning the label of "pathological" on what is,
in fact, system-caused "illness." At the same time, interpersonal
deficits will tend to show the general manner and direction in
which a child is likely to react and thus are useful as diagnostic
indicators for other life situations: family, school, peer groups.

*Family Pain and Strain.* Two fundamental assumptions
can be made of the great majority of troubled children and their
families: (1) Most troubled children do not come "unpack-
aged"; they live with, or will return to, natural or foster families, who represent their primary source of nurturance, support,
and socialization. (2) "Success" in "treatment"—however we
wish to define both of these terms—will vary according to the
ability of the helping person to involve these parents or parenting persons as full and equal partners in the helping process.

Although many troubled children do come from troubled
families, the overwhelming predisposition toward seeing parents
as the witting or unwitting cause of their child's problems has
led to the development of what I would call the "family etiology hypothesis," best stated in the following form: *Troubled
children nearly always come from families that exhibit a certain
amount of pain and strain; since the family—in particular, the
parents—represents the major source of influence on the child's
early development, the child's problem is either directly caused
by or unconsciously influenced by the pathology or shortcomings of the parent.* Evidence for the existence of this hypothesis may be found in almost any standard psychiatry text used in
clinical education from roughly the late 1940s to the mid
1960s. The following is illustrative: "It is probably safe to say
that the majority of emotional problems in children are created
by emotional problems of their parents. . . . One of the most
common pathological family conditions is that of the dominat-
ing, authoritative, ruling mother figure, with the father the
more passive and, at least emotionally, less contributing member" (English and Finch, 1954, pp. 136-137).

For the individual practitioner, this hypothesis appeared
to be validated in the countless families where parental pathol-

ogy of one sort or another did have a profoundly damaging effect on the development and adjustment of the child. It is not the total rejection of the family etiology hypothesis that is sought here—clearly, troubled parents can bring about troubled children. What needs to be questioned is its blanket application to all families of children with problems.

Recent research is shedding new light on the origins of some childhood disorders. This evidence—while incomplete and tentative—suggests a probable neurobiological base for at least two children's disorders: infantile autism and learning disorders. Epidemiological studies indicate that a fairly high proportion of children with behavioral problems in school may have specific learning difficulties as well. Allowing for the fact that troubled parents can and do bring about problems in their children (as the literature on child abuse, family disorganization, and adult psychosis will readily confirm), as a profession we continue to be overwhelmingly predisposed to functional or psychogenic explanations of childhood disturbances. On the basis of the available evidence, such a predisposition—at least with respect to autism and learning disorders—appears to have no justification. Further, at least some of the "pathology" exhibited by parents of troubled children may well be *responsive to* rather than *causative of* the child's disturbance.

Perhaps the most damaging consequence of this predisposition to "blame the parents" is that it causes us to underutilize our most valuable "natural resource" in child treatment: the parents themselves. Parents are often the best "expert" on their troubled child. No battery of diagnostic tests can match the knowledge gained by the parent, who loves, disciplines, teaches, feeds, clothes, and plays with the handicapped child twenty-four hours a day, seven days a week. Parents can provide infinite detail on the nuances of behavior, habits, patterns, and preferences; and such information is invaluable to the professional in diagnosis and treatment planning. Specific strategies for involving parents as full working partners in residential and day treatment programs will be discussed in Chapter Six.

*Limited Play Skills.* A child's world is, in many respects, a world of play and activities. Through play, children learn mastery of their own bodies and the physical space that surrounds them, as well as the complex array of social behaviors that support the play situation. The importance of play in social development has long been recognized among child development specialists. In addition, some recent research by Singer (1973) and his associates at Yale indicates the importance of imaginative and solitary play in cognitive development. Both lines of research suggest for the child care professional that solitary and group play is a critical medium for competency acquisition with the troubled child and will provide—through games, dramatics, and crafts—both the means and the context for acquiring mastery over the internal and external environment.

Simply stated, many of these youngsters do not know how to play very well. Their range of skills may be quite narrow, with the child running one or two favorite activities into the ground by overloading on them in much the same way that relationships become overloaded. Such a fixation is often followed by boredom and mild depression: "There's nothing to do around here"; "It probably wouldn't work for me anyway." A good indicator of the relative skill level of a particular child is mirrored in his or her bedroom (at home or in the cottage or group home) and possessions. Contrast the systematically collected "clutter" of the competent preadolescent—endless collections of "things," favorite toys, mementos, pictures of folk heroes, completed projects—with the relatively empty and unadorned space of the troubled child.

Deficits may occur in group play skills—as reflected in the child's inability to follow a set of rules, or to enter a game already in progress, or to make constructive use of private time. Child care workers, parents, and teachers sometimes try to help the child get involved with the group at the expense of learning specific skills to use when alone. Such a one-sided approach to teaching activity skills is particularly unfortunate for the hyperactive, easily distracted, emotionally labile child, who needs to develop skills for "tuning out" the group as well as for joining it.

Often the child with limited play skills, his peers, and the helping adults around him get caught in a vicious cycle: failure in play is followed by avoidance of novel play situations. For example, the child fails to manage a specific play situation successfully: he can't wait his turn in a softball game and begins drawing jeers from the other children; he then throws a bat at someone and storms off the playfield. Unless an incident like this is fully worked through, three outcomes are likely: the child will tend to avoid similar group play situations with "those kids"; the other children will not view the child as a favored teammate or participant; and the caring adult will be wary of suggesting a similar activity, because the child may not be "ready for it." Thus, the ineptitude of the child in a group play situation becomes a kind of self-fulfilling prophecy for all concerned. (The therapeutic-educational uses of play with both individual children and groups will be covered in Chapter Four.)

*Special Learning Disabilities.* Hobbs (1975a, pp. 79-81) points out that *learning disability* is a catch-all phrase used to imply a handicapping condition associated with the inability of a child to perform school tasks at a level expected of him; children with learning disabilities often display hyperactivity, emotional lability, impulsivity, distractibility, perseveration, and perceptual difficulties. Some forty different terms have been used to describe this condition, which affects about 700,000 children nationally. Terms like *minimal brain damage, maturational lag, perceptual disability, dyslexia, anomia, aphasia,* and *language disorder* have grown out of the effort to define and extend our understanding of why children do not learn. They enable us to label learning disorders (and children), but they do not explain why there are so many children today who do not learn (Sapir and Nitzburg, 1973, p. xiii).

In the past, because of the difficulty in diagnosing these disorders and their unclear origins, great emphasis was placed on psychogenic explanations of school-related problem behavior. Early psychoanalytic studies of learning disorders in children suggested that certain types of learning disabilities were a manifestation of an inhibition in ego functioning related to exploration and curiosity. Later studies attempted to find the cause of the learning disorder in a disturbed communication between mother and child (Skillman, 1964, p. 140). Somewhat similarly, English and Pearson (1957, p. 132) attributed hyperkinesis in children to parental rejection, which overstimulated the child's autoeroticism. By attempting to dam up his autoerotic behavior in order to secure himself with his parents, he would over-innervate the general muscular system and become hyper-kinetic. "Acting-out" behavior was explained as follows: "The parents may find vicarious gratification of their own poorly integrated forbidden impulses in the acting out of the child, through their unconscious permissiveness or inconsistency toward the child in these spheres of behavior" (Johnson and Szurek, 1965, p. 120).

Classical treatment often involved psychotherapy or play therapy with the child to uncover the emotional blocks to learn-ing; the parents were seen separately if at all. Critical to this formulation was the assumption that the learning disorder or the behavioral difficulty flowed from the emotional problem and, again, that the parents may have been at least unwitting causal agents of the child's difficulty. Apart from the fact that the field no longer views "emotional" and "learning" problems as totally separate and discrete entities, what else can be said about the origin of these disorders?

The first finding of interest is an epidemiological one. Learning disorders appear a far more widespread problem among children than was suspected even a few years ago. In addition to the figures from the White House Conference cited earlier, Wright (1974) found that a high percentage of children (51 percent) referred for conduct problems in an elementary school had specific, identifiable learning disorders. Thus, the "acting out" of many children referred to residential and day treatment programs may be the symptom and not the cause of a specific learning disorder. In the area of etiology, there is still little known about the origin of these disorders, though recent studies have tended to suggest neurobiological involvement (Sapir and Nitzburg, 1973, pp. 187-287). Some studies of hyperactive children seem to point toward an organic-genetic base for at least some hyperkinesis. Morrison and Stewart (1973), in a study of hyperactive adoptive children, found a high prevalence of hysteria, sociopathy, and alcoholism in the biological parents of these children. No such prevalence was found among the adopted parents. Such studies suggest an in-

volvement of parental disturbance in the child's disorder, but
the relationship appears to be genetic rather than functional
(Gross and Wilson, 1974, p. 138). Other studies report a statistically higher incidence of complications in the mother's preg-
nancy and in the birth and early development of hyperkinetic
children—suggesting at least some organic involvement (Prechtl
and Stemmer, 1962; Huessy, 1967; Werry, Weiss, and Douglas,
1964; Walzer and Wolff, 1973; Quay and Werry, 1972; Lievens,
1974). The research of Rourke (1975) and his associates strongly suggests that cerebral dysfunction plays a part in most disorders of learning. While one gets a mixed and inconclusive picture of the etiology of learning disorders generally, there does
seem to be a trend in the direction of organic-perceptual factors as
at least the partial cause of some disorders. There does not at this
time appear to be any conclusive evidence for the psychogenic
explanation of these disorders.

Since Chapter Seven is devoted entirely to the role of special education in residential and day treatment, I will make only
three additional points about school-related problems:

1. The public school represents the largest single system the
   child has to negotiate in the community. As such, it is the
   source of a great many potential rewards and sanctions.
2. Many children entering residential or day treatment programs have some form of specific learning difficulties.
3. School programs—both public and on campus—continue to
   represent an underdeveloped area in far too many residential
   and day treatment programs. This is perhaps a residual effect
   of the view once prevalent in the child mental health field
   that the etiology of learning-related problems was more
   psychogenic than neurobiological. Consequently, greater emphasis was given to the "treating" rather than the teaching
   components of the program.

### The Therapeutic Milieu

Given this wide range of presenting problems, it is clear
that any effective treatment program must be broadly based
and geared to the total development of the troubled child. Let

us therefore proceed to an analysis of the essential elements in the immediate environment of the therapeutic milieu.

How does one go about building a therapeutic milieu? What are its critical features, and how does it act as a positive force for growth and change? (Because this is a book about children in need of temporary out-of-home care, I will not deal with the question of building a "powerful environment" for those children who can be successfully helped in their own homes, though many of the strategies for family involvement are clearly applicable.) In fact, the residential center may constitute the ideal organizational foundation for home-based care (see, for example, Small and Whittaker, in press).

First of all, the residential treatment center should have low visibility. Large institutions are undesirable for a number of reasons. They tend to separate children from the communities to which they are to return; they create, with their size, a need for regimen and routine which far exceeds that necessary in a family living environment; they tend to develop deviant subcultures, and they stigmatize both staff and children. Precisely because they are large and easily identifiable, they perpetuate the myth that the children they serve are inherently different from the rest of us. Just as we would not build a skyscraper in a residential neighborhood, we should not build residential facilities that are grossly out of harmony with their surrounding communities.

In addition to low visibility, child care programs need as much as possible to be involved with the communities that support them. Specifically, professional staff should make use of public schools and of volunteer workers whenever possible; seek the support of local merchants; participate in recreation and other community programs; and form an advisory or governing board that reflects the various segments of the host community. We also need to develop agency information systems that actively solicit feedback from all consumer groups: the children, their families, teachers, and referring agencies. Consumer validation should rank equally high with other "hard" criteria as a measure of program effectiveness.

Another characteristic of a therapeutic milieu is flexibility. All too often, residential treatment programs are unable to quickly shift gears in response to changing service demands. For example, programs may be committed to long-term, residential treatment when what is needed is a variety of shorter-term residential and day treatment options. One relatively recent change that caught many programs off guard was the influx of a more aggressive, assaultive child, who presents a challenge to any program, especially an open, community-based facility.

Finally, our programs should be capable of being understood by the lay public. That is, we need to weed out unnecessary jargon and talk about program goals in plain, simple language. We also should develop audiovisual materials that describe what the program is all about. Every staff member, from the executive director to the maintenance staff, as well as parents and children, should be able to provide a clear and succinct account of what the program is, whom it serves, and how it relates to the larger community.

Let us turn now to an operational definition of the therapeutic milieu: *A therapeutic milieu is a specially designed environment in which the events of daily living are used as formats for teaching competence in basic life skills. The living environment becomes both a means and a context for growth and change, informed by a culture that stresses learning through living.*

Teaching occurs in a wide range of formats, including rules, routines, games and activities, and quiet conversations with staff. Moreover, it covers a full curriculum of basic life skills: emotional, academic, interpersonal, and environmental. The essential process of change is educational. Instead of simply being treated for an underlying psychic illness, the child is helped to learn alternate behaviors. Attention is paid to the full range of the child's developmental difficulties—cognitive, social, emotional—not just to the most obvious or troublesome "symptoms."

The acquisition of competence occurs on three different levels. (For the seminal work on competence, see White, 1959, 1960, 1963.) *Intrapersonally,* the child learns to deal appropriately and effectively with impulses and emotions: anger, fear, sadness, boredom, and joy. Children are helped to identify feelings and link them with thoughts and behaviors. For example, "I think about home—I feel sad—I get in an argument with the housemother." Through such varied teaching formats as incentive systems, individual life-space interviews, and biofeedback, the child is helped to gain control over his or her inner environment. *Interpersonally,* the child is helped to learn more adaptive and rewarding ways of interacting with the important people in his life space:

- How do you say "I like you" to a favorite friend?
- How can you make it so the other kids will want to play with you?
- How do you handle someone who bullies you?
- What steps can you take to get unfrozen from the role of scapegoat or flunky?

On the *environmental* level, the child is helped to learn various ways of dealing effectively with the multiple systems that he or she inhabits. Thus, the child is taught to develop physical competence (motor coordination, physical dexterity, and athletic skills—all of which have high "market value" in the peer group), academic competence (living and study skills leading to increased reinforcement in school and in the community), and competence in new social situations (interviewing for a job, joining a church youth group, taking a bus crosstown, asking a friend for a date, opening a bank account).

In this approach to the milieu, all areas of competence development are viewed as equal in importance. For a given youngster, learning how to deal constructively with solitude, kick a soccer ball, or make an omelette may be just as important as learning how to join a group of peers, master an angry impulse, or achieve in a classroom environment. Moreover, the development of competence in one area often has positive "spillover" to other areas of life functioning; for example, the child who learns something about managing his behavior in the classroom increases the likelihood that he will remain in the learning environment long enough to acquire some skills in reading. Competency acquisition—whether in sports, crafts, interpersonal skills, or emotional skills—enhances the child's self-image and provides incentive for the mastery of new and more difficult challenges, such as moving to a new foster home or changing schools. Competence is closely related to "confidence"—the feeling that accompanies mastery experiences: "I am what I can do." Finally, the development of a broad range of competencies means that any single area of functioning—home, school, peer group—assumes less importance in the child's overall sphere of activity.

*The Teaching Context.* It is assumed that children learn in not one but in many different ways—for example, through insight, reward and punishment, and imitation. The power of the milieu is enhanced to the extent that particular teaching formats activate all these processes of learning. Overreliance on a single process—for example, insight learning—means that certain competencies can be taught less well and that certain children will be less likely to learn effectively. In short, a therapeutic milieu seeks to activate every possible medium for learning—realizing that for some children the most effective "teachers" may be the cook or caretaker and the most fruitful lessons may be learned in a crafts shop or kitchen rather than a therapy room or classroom. While the following list of teaching formats is by no means inclusive, it does represent the major "ingredients" in a therapeutic milieu:

1. *Rules:* The formal and informal "do's" and "don'ts" of the helping culture which tend to define what is important and what is not.
2. *Routines:* Waking up; mealtimes; going to bed—all the basic activities that all children participate in.
3. *Program Activities:* Arts, crafts, games, sports, and the whole array of informal individual and group activities.
4. *Group Sessions:* Cottage group meetings; group therapy; special-interest groups.
5. *Individual Psychotherapy:* Conceived of here not as the cornerstone of milieu treatment but as an important adjunctive therapy for those children who can develop and act on the basis of insight.

6. *Life-Space Interviews:* A set of interviewing strategies—developed by Redl and Wineman (1957) and elaborated by Long, Morse, and Newman (1971)—designed specifically for use in the life space by child care workers. The life-space interview may help the child manage a particular upset ("emotional first aid"), or it may deal with a chronic pattern of behavior ("clinical exploitation of life events").
7. *Incentive System:* The contingent use of generalized reinforcers (tokens) throughout a total system—cottage, ward, or classroom—for the purpose of teaching alternative, prosocial behavior.
8. *Special Education:* The formalized on-campus or community school program.
9. *Conjoint Family Treatment:* Therapeutic intervention with the family as a total system.
10. *Parent Education Groups:* Didactic group sessions on effective parenting.
11. *Parent Involvement in Life Space:* Use of parents as participants in life-space intervention.
12. *Individual Behavior Modification Program:* The individualized use of any of a number of behavioral protocols with a given child.

Figure 3 shows the overall relationship of the various teaching formats within a therapeutic milieu and some typical problem areas encountered in children entering residential treatment. Although each format is applicable to any problem area, the effect of each typically differs by problem area. Similarly, each of the formats is capable of utilizing any of the learning processes, though in practice certain styles of learning tend to receive greater emphasis than others. For example, "program activities" typically involve reward and punishment, imitation and are most effective in dealing with poor impulse control, low self-image, poorly developed modulation of emotion, relationship deficits, and limited play skills. Similarly, the use of "routines" involves several processes of learning and is particularly effective in dealing with problems of impulse control and is only marginally effective in alleviating poorly developed modu-

**Figure 3. Paradigm of a Therapeutic Milieu**

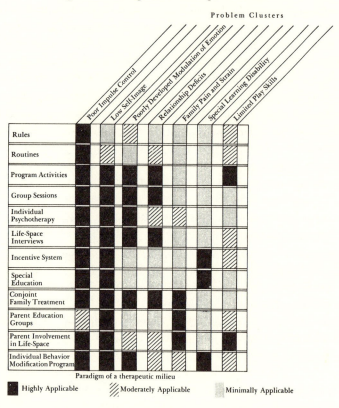

Paradigm of a therapeutic milieu

■ Highly Applicable    ▨ Moderately Applicable    ▨ Minimally Applicable

lation of emotion, family pain and strain, or special learning disabilities. If taken as a guide for discussion, Figure 3 can serve as a framework for assessing the major presenting problems of a given child or group of children and the most likely teaching formats for addressing those problems. It can also be used as a grid for measuring the teaching formats in a total program—for the purpose of identifying areas of strength and weakness.

The milieu, then, must be conceived of as a "multidimensional" context for teaching competence if it is to impact the multiple life problems which children bring with them. No single teaching format—however powerful—can do the job alone.

*Staffing and Consultation.* Child care workers should play an increasingly important role in child treatment, parent education, and school consultation. The more traditional clinical roles

—for example, that of the child therapist—should be transformed and expanded to include educational and administrative functions. The child care role, along with that of the classroom teacher, should be seen as pivotal, with all other clinical professionals acting as support staff. The social work role should be redefined to include less treatment of individual children and more consultation to child care staff, in-service education, family therapy, and community liaison work. Increasingly, the separation between family work and child care is difficult to justify. A total team approach should become the norm—particularly as education and certification for child care workers become more readily available. Such a role shift will require accompanying changes in the educational preparation of social workers for residential treatment; they will need to receive training in supervision, management, in-service education, and program evaluation as well as in clinical treatment.

Another role that needs reformulation is that of the clinical consultant. In many centers, the weekly visit from the psychiatrist is the only source of consultation, and the trend in many residential centers toward hospital-type accreditation increases the likelihood that this form of consultation will become the dominant mode. Typically, these sessions focus on individual children rather than on total program issues—such as activity programming; group dynamics; and, particularly, behavior modification—which may fall outside the psychoanalytically trained physician's core of expertise. Treatment programs should regularly evaluate the use of clinical consultants to see whether they are meeting current program needs. Consultants should be chosen for particular areas of expertise—not professional credentials—and should be assigned to well-specified, time-limited tasks under the direction of the executive or program director. At no time should clinical authority for an individual child, or for a group, be given to an outside consultant who has little or no direct contact with the child and whose contacts with the agency consist of a once-a-week visit.

In a related area, every staff member should receive training on a regular schedule, and adequate time and coverage should be provided so that all staff can attend training sessions. Outside consultants should be brought to these sessions only after considerable spadework has been done by staff. Too often, there is a temptation to "bring in the expert" before key questions have been formulated, or to search for prepackaged training materials that can be bought "off the shelf." I have often noticed that child care workers—particularly newer staff—learn a great deal vicariously from watching their executive director, chief social worker, supervisor, or consulting psychologist attempt to manage the real or simulated behavior of a child in the throes of a temper tantrum, or to maintain contact with a sullen and incommunicative adolescent just returned from a runaway, or to deal with a group of "program-weary" preadolescents who say, in unison, "There's nothing to do around here!" In short, much of the teaching that needs to be done in a therapeutic milieu—by child care workers, clinical staff, and consultants—is best achieved through modeling in real or simulated situations. Finally, all staff training should be regularly evaluated to see whether it is meeting the needs for which it was designed. Consumer feedback from all levels of staff should, therefore, be integral to the training process.

## A Concluding Note

One final issue that needs to be faced by all who work in group child care settings is that neither the children and youth we serve nor the programs with which we serve them rank high in the eyes of the general public. Unlike their mentally or physically handicapped counterparts, the troubled children and their families who make their way to residential or day treatment programs are generally seen as more responsible for their actions and less deserving of sympathy. Similarly, there remains in the public mind a sense of child caring institutions as less than desirable places for growth and development to occur. The fact that there is some truth in both of these sentiments makes even more difficult our task of convincing a skeptical public of the special needs of these children for services that may temporarily or permanently separate them from their families. It is, in fact, the reason that we must proceed with political advocacy on behalf of the right to services—especially for the group of troubled children who have no other natural constituency.

# 3

# Major Approaches to Residential Treatment

"How can these children be helped?" is a question that has vexed child welfare professionals and lay citizens for well over a century. While most nineteenth-century programs for troubled children stressed moral conversion as a necessary requisite for change, there was, even then, a recognition of the enormous power of the total living environment as a potent force in changing children's attitudes and behavior (Whittaker, 1971a). Exactly how one identifies all the powerful forces in a group living situation and redirects them toward therapeutic goals—in essence, creating a therapeutic milieu—is a question for which we still have no definite answer. That we continue to struggle after so many efforts by talented and dedicated theoreticians and practitioners is testimony to the complexity and difficulty of the problem. To understand our present situation a little better, this chapter will explore the seminal influences on the development of milieu treatment for the troubled child and

43

his family and critically review existing approaches to the therapeutic milieu.

## Psychoanalytic Approaches

In the early 1930s, a young autistic girl was brought to
Sigmund Freud for treatment; Freud referred the child to his
daughter, Anna, who specialized in child psychoanalysis. Anna
Freud determined that the child was in too regressed a condition for psychoanalysis and that what she really needed was a
total psychoanalytically oriented living environment. She suggested a young art student couple who had a burgeoning interest in psychoanalysis and education. The young couple agreed
and took the child into their family for what was to be a six-
year stay. Thus, the lifelong work of a pioneer in the residential
treatment of severely disturbed children—Bruno Bettelheim—
was launched. (Anna Freud continues her lifelong work at the
Hampstead Child Therapy Clinic in London.)

The group that was to have the most profound and last-
ing influence on the development of milieu treatment in the
United States included a large number of refugees from Nazi
persecution, who came to this country from Germany and Aus-
tria in the late 1930s and early 1940s. They were strongly influenced by psychoanalysis—particularly in its applications to
education—and by the power of the group association; and their
collective contribution literally *was* the literature on milieu
treatment for children from the 1940s through the 1960s.
These pioneers included Bruno Bettelheim (1950, 1955, 1967,
1974; 1948, with Emmy Sylvester); Fritz Redl (1959, 1966;
1957, with David Wineman); Susanne Schulze (1951); Gisela
Konopka (1946, 1954); Morris Fritz Mayer (1960; 1971, with
Arthur Blum); and Eva Burmeister (1960). While their adher-
ence to Freudian concepts varied in degree and while the children with whom they worked ranged from autistic to delinquent, they all attempted to apply basic psychoanalytic
principles to the child's total living environment. Of this distin-
guished group, two individuals—Bruno Bettelheim and Fritz
Redl—stand preeminent. Their work spans the continuum of

childhood disturbance from the solipsistic retreat of the autistic child (Bettelheim) to the acting out of the preadolescent delinquent (Redl). (No attempt will be made here to summarize the contribution of all the individuals mentioned here. The reader is urged to consult the original sources for a fuller explanation. Other contributions include Noshpitz, 1962; Goldfarb, Mintz, and Stroock, 1969; Cummings and Cummings, 1963.)

The two critical forces in the development of psychoanalytically oriented milieu treatment for children in the United States consisted of the contribution of the group already mentioned *and* the concurrent influence of the child guidance movement, with its emphasis on individual psychotherapy as the treatment of choice for the disturbed child and the psychiatric team as the preferred model of organization.

*Bruno Bettelheim.* Bettelheim's contribution to the treatment of severely disturbed children was molded by two major life influences: psychoanalysis and his experiences as a prisoner in the Nazi concentration camps of Dachau and Buchenwald. From psychoanalysis, he gained an understanding of the elaborate unfolding of the human personality, in all its vicissitudes; from his prison experiences, he discovered the resiliency of the human spirit in overcoming the most degrading environments.

From 1944 to 1973, he was director of the University of Chicago's Sonia Shankman Orthogenic School for emotionally disturbed children—a school that continues in the mold he cast. His books and articles cover a wide-ranging sphere of interests, including the concentration camp experience, prejudice, child development, and communal child rearing. Most pertinent to our discussion here are the volumes directly based on his experiences at the Orthogenic School: *Love Is Not Enough* (1950), *Truants from Life* (1955), *The Empty Fortress* (1967), and *A Home for the Heart* (1974). Bettelheim's (1974, p. 5) self-appraisal of this work is as follows:

> *Love Is Not Enough* was meant to suggest that a consistent therapeutic philosophy, with careful thinking, planning, and acting on it, has to underpin that tender care which is necessary if one

is to help a psychotic person gain mental health.
... The book illustrated this principle by describing big and small events alike as they followed each
other in the course of the day, in the life of those
whom the institution served.

The next book, *Truants from Life*, contained only a short statement on the overall treatment success as of that time; the essential content
consisted of four long case histories. It was hoped
that these would show how—and why—the person-
alities of these children unfolded during the years
they lived at the institution. From their quite different life histories and their various pathologies
(severe delinquency, anorexia, institutionalism, and
childhood psychosis), the reader could see how a
unified philosophy, and an institution based on it,
is helpful in restoring mental health. ... Many
years later, *The Empty Fortress* was to present a
more complete discussion of the therapeutic results
of the Orthogenic School for the most severe form
of childhood psychosis—infantile autism. *A Home
for the Heart* was written to make this particular
form of total therapy useful to others by detailing
what it consists of, and by telling the story of the
staff, because they are all important for its success.

It is difficult if not impossible to capture what is essential
in these volumes, for it is the anecdotes and images that remain
imprinted on the mind of the reader. For example:

- Bettelheim explaining that, in order to protect his child patients, no parent was ever admitted in the school's living area
  (1974, p. 210).
- Bettelheim cajoling an adolescent anorectic girl to drink a
  glass of milk and then securing her commitment to enter
  treatment (1974, p. 176).
- Bettelheim's gentle description of the disturbed child's slow
  transition from dreams to waking (1950, p. 83).
- Bettelheim's account of Paul, who progressed from "wild crit-
  ter" to university student (1955, p. 153).

- Bettelheim—who, it will be remembered, once described mothers of autistic children as "feral mothers" (1959)—passing off behavioral approaches to infantile autism as reducing children to the level of "Pavlovian dogs" (1967, p. 410).
- Bettelheim's uncanny sense of the effect of architecture on human behavior (1974, pp. 130-180).
- Bettelheim's detailed account of a staff member's living quarters—well organized in the northern half, disorganized in the southern half—as representative of her early unresolved years in the Deep South and her present well-integrated life in the North (1974, p. 299).

While there is much of value and sheer brilliance in Bettelheim's work, it is a difficult approach to operationalize. To be sure, his clinical accounts are fascinating descriptions of what disturbed behavior is like, though in my judgment many are based on false assumptions and sheer speculation about the origins of childhood disorders. Bettelheim's purposeful isolation of parents from the treatment environment—in the face of recent studies indicating the cruciality of the transition from institution to community (Allerhand, Weber, and Haug, 1966; Taylor and Alpert, 1973) and the potential for involving parents as full participants in the treatment process (Schopler and Reichler, 1971a)—indicates a rigidity of position apparent in other areas of his model; for example, in his refusal to analyze fairly the more recent behavioral approaches to childhood psychoses. I can still recall his response at a professional meeting some years ago to a questioner who asked (quite innocently) how the recent experiments in behavioral therapy with psychotic children should be "answered." Bettelheim responded: "Freud said it long ago—there will always be dogs barking at the wheels of the caravan, but the caravan rolls on." I can remember, as a young practitioner at the time, wondering if the dogs were, in fact, trying to communicate something to the caravan driver—perhaps a loose wheel—or a road missed? On a conceptual level, his model of milieu treatment is really no model at all but, rather, a collage of case vignettes, clinical observations, and descriptions of routine—fascinating to read in part, difficult to comprehend as a unified whole. In fact, there is such an inordinate amount of idiosyncrasy (and I intend no derogation here) in his work—for example, his extreme "protection" of the milieu against visitors and parents—that one is left wondering whether his methods could be applied successfully elsewhere.

On the positive side, Bettelheim's passion for detail is reflected in every clinical account. His respect for the individual is a theme that recurs throughout his work, and his attention to the therapeutic impact of the events of daily living—the rules, the routines, the games and activities, and the struggles—helped to turn an entire mental health profession's attention from the therapy room to the life space.

On the whole, however, a reader is forced to conclude reluctantly that the essential ingredient in Bettelheim's model of milieu treatment is Bettelheim himself. His is the omnipresent force—fathoming the depths of a child's behavior; challenging a staff member to look into himself; nurturing a frightened child in the night; stoutly defending his model against all who would challenge it. Arrogant, cryptic, challenging, engaging—in writing as in person—Bettelheim and his work stand permanently intertwined: exciting to experience, impossible to duplicate. Bettelheim concluded his last book on milieu treatment expecting and welcoming challenge: "I hope the reader will try to discover where I have gone wrong, but not be satisfied merely by registering a negative, but try to understand why and how it all could be done better. If he does this, he will have paid the author the highest compliment possible" (1974, p. 14). That is the challenge, the great stimulus, which Bettelheim's work presents: to find a better way. Whatever eventually becomes of his ideas, Bettelheim will always be viewed as a pioneering force in the development of milieu treatment.

*Fritz Redl.* What the contribution of Bruno Bettelheim represents for the psychotic child, the work of Fritz Redl represents for the delinquent. A psychologist and psychoanalyst, Redl came to the United States from Vienna in 1936, strongly influenced by Freud and by the work of August Aichorn (1935) with delinquent adolescents. He was keenly interested in the interplay between individual and group dynamics and in the group's potential as a medium for changing delinquent behavior. Redl settled in Detroit, where he was founder and director of the Detroit Group Project and Pioneer House—a small, community-based residential program for hyperaggressive, acting-out preadolescents. He also directed a special residential unit at the National Institute of Mental Health in Bethesda, served as consultant to several of the larger psychiatric children's hospitals in the country, lectured on an international scale, and was a professor of behavioral sciences at Wayne State University. His writings span nearly fifty years and cover the fields of child mental health, special education, group dynamics, and milieu treatment for behavior-disordered children. His two books on the Pioneer House project with David Wineman—*Children Who Hate* and *Controls from Within* (published as a single volume in 1957)—stand as singular classics in the literature of milieu treatment. His other books include *Mental Hygiene in Teaching,* with M. Wattenberg (1959), and *When We Deal with Children* (1966). Two of Redl's contributions to the theory of milieu treatment are his analysis of the essential ingredients in a therapeutic milieu and his development of the life-space interview.

In a brilliant synthesis of organizational, group, and individual dynamics, Redl provided the field of child mental health in the 1950s with a conceptual screen for viewing all the diverse elements in a therapeutic milieu. He also developed the various "tools" to be used in changing children's behavior. Central here was his concept of the *life-space interview* (LSI), a set of action-based interview strategies designed to help child care workers deal with real-life problems of children when and where they occur. *Life space* refers to the total physical, social, psychological, and cultural "space" surrounding an individual at any given point in time. The focus (and often the locus) of the interviews is the child's own natural milieu, and most deal with specific behavioral incidents. The strategies include "emotional first aid"—techniques designed to help a child weather a behavioral storm and return to the life space; and techniques for exploring a more chronic pattern of behavior in relation to the child's overall treatment goals. Basically, the life-space interview was developed for two reasons: (1) the inadequacy of the reality-detached, fifty-minute therapy session as a device for dealing with the problems of behavior disordered children living away from home; and (2) the need for a specialized set of techniques for child care workers and houseparents to provide what Redl called "therapy on the hoof." (The life-space interview concept has been expanded and applied to a variety of educational and treatment settings. See Long, Morse, and Newman, 1971, pp. 442-452, 473-491.)

The impact of Redl's work is difficult to assess. Though it opened its doors over thirty years ago, Pioneer House foreshadowed many of the innovations in community-based child treatment: low visibility, strong community ties, focus on teaching specific behavioral skills, and involvement of child care staff as on-line therapists (Redl and Wineman, 1957). I have suggested elsewhere (Whittaker, 1970a) several possible reasons why Redl's model was not widely adopted—generally having to do with its "folksy" terminology (some of the techniques are labeled "massaging numb value areas," "new tool salesmanship," "draining frustration acidity"), unlikely to appeal to the scientifically minded professional, and a falsely imputed view of the model as overpermissive. (For Redl's thoughts on this issue, see Redl, 1966, pp. 355-378.)

A third and more plausible reason has to do with the traditional structure of institutional facilities for emotionally disturbed children in this country. Many residential facilities are organized more around the needs of the professional groups who run them than around the needs of the children they are designed to serve. Thus, we have a "medical model" of residential treatment, which is usually just an extension of the psychiatric team from child guidance. In this system, child care workers are used to care for and often live with the children, but their function is not usually seen as "treatment" per se. A variation on the medical model is the "social work" model of residential treatment. Here the same kind of role rigidity is maintained, despite a shift in the status hierarchy. Typically, psychiatric social workers are responsible for the treatment of the children—usually in office interviews—though they may make use of psychiatric and psychological consultants. In the period 1950-1970, numerous specialties were elevated to professional status; but in some ways this practice worked to the detriment rather than the benefit of the children in care. In the course of a single week's time, the disturbed child might be expected to see his psychotherapist, group therapist, family caseworker, occupational therapist, recreational therapist, music therapist—and so on. The life-space model of treatment rejected such specific role definitions in favor of a far more generic approach. It was a model of treatment developed from the problems posed by the children in care and not from the needs of any single professional group. Herein probably lies a reason why the model has been adopted so infrequently: It wreaks havoc with the traditional notions of "who does what" in a residential treatment center. In addition, the life-space model contains a built-in threat to the therapist who is accustomed to working only in the sanctity of his or her office and in the context of the fifty-minute hour. Dealing with problems in the life space is akin to working in a fishbowl: both successes and failures are clearly visible to all.

Despite these and other problems in adaptability, Redl's work has contributed significantly to the theoretical development of milieu treatment in two important areas. His was the first and—at the time—most sophisticated attempt to provide a taxonomy of aggressive behavior in children. For Redl, there never was simply an "aggressive child"; instead, there was a complex interplay of personality factors and group dynamics located in a particular space-time context that combined to produce a specific behavioral result. In many ways, his work foreshadowed the efforts of Wahler, Patterson, and other applied behavior analysts in identifying the structural aspects of deviant child behavior (Wahler, House, and Stambaugh, 1976; Patterson and others, 1975). Second, his model stood nearly alone for many years as a testimony to the belief that success in milieu treatment is directly related to the ability of programs to incorporate child care workers as primary agents of therapy. While many clinicians paid lip service to the importance of child care staff, Redl built a model of treatment around them. He developed specific techniques—such as the life-space interview—for managing children's behavior as well as for teaching alternatives. He recognized the power of the peer group as a potential force for positive change and developed a conceptual scheme for observing and intervening with group behavior. His model recognized the importance of activities in a therapeutic milieu, and he helped to elevate program activities to the status of a "full-fledged therapeutic tool." His notions on the use of punishment and on preadolescents—contained in works written in the 1940s and early 1950s—remain valuable today.

In my opinion, Redl's work retains its viability because many of his concepts can exist apart from the psychoanalytic foundations on which they were originally conceived. Much of what Redl had to say about the techniques for the management of surface behavior in children can be translated without damage to a social learning framework (Redl and Wineman, 1957, pp. 395-486). The life-space interview material, although procedurally primitive, continues to provide a useful framework for organizing therapeutic conversations with children and can serve as an adjunct to individual behavioral programs designed to build new behavioral repertoires or extinguish old ones. Perhaps more than any other single theoretician of his time, he contributed to our understanding of what actually makes a milieu work.

*The Child Guidance Movement and Residential Treatment.* If the "life-space" model of Redl was slow to catch on in the children's institutional field, a more traditional child guidance approach, stressing individually oriented child therapy, spread rapidly. By the mid 1960s, nearly 70 percent of all child caring institutions provided individual treatment by psychiatrists, social workers, or other professionals; for institutions serving delinquent and emotionally disturbed children, the figure was closer to 90 percent (Pappenfort, Kilpatrick, and Roberts, 1973). Treatment typically consisted of ego-supportive casework provided by a therapist who was structurally unrelated to and often physically removed from the child's living space. This division of labor in child treatment has impeded attempts to change existing child care institutions and create new decentralized services. I have elsewhere (Whittaker, 1970c, 1971b) described the effects of the child guidance movement on the children's institutional field in the early part of this century and will provide only a brief summary here.

As early as 1920, the organizational requisites for the new mental hygiene technology were becoming clear: a psychiatric team composed of psychiatrist, clinical psychologist, and social worker operating out of a single clinic. This pattern of organization, with the subsequent addition of other clinical specialists, would constitute the basic pattern of service in child guidance for years to come. Soon the child guidance model—organized around the "psychiatric team"—became the paradigm for institutional treatment. It would be overstating the case to say that the majority of institutions for dependent and delinquent children incorporated the child guidance model in the 1920s—in fact, only a small minority would do so—but this particular form of organization for treatment did come to be recognized as the most appropriate one for the children's institution. What seemed to be working in the larger community should certainly be efficacious in the institution, so the logic ran. Just as the child guidance model provided a new organization for treatment, the growing popularity of Freudian psychology would provide a new technology for treatment.

By the end of the 1920s, certain institutions—among them, the Children's Village, Dobbs Ferry, New York; the New England Home for Little Wanderers, Boston; the Jewish Protectory and Aid Society's Hawthorne Cedar Knolls School, New York; and the Whittier State School in California—had developed their clinical programs to the point where they became models of how the new treatment organization and technology could be adapted for use in an institutional setting. These institutions roused professional interest throughout the country and attracted many visitors from children's agencies, who were anxious to see how the psychiatric team would function in an institutional setting.

One important drawback of the infusion of this new structure was the distance that was created between the members of the psychiatric team and the other members of the institutional staff. This fact may be demonstrated in the development of the role of the psychiatric caseworker. In the attempt

to establish social work as a scientific discipline, and to relate
the social worker's function on the psychiatric team to that of
the psychiatrist and the clinical psychologist, social workers had
to be disassociated from other—"nonprofessional"—health care
workers. Thus, in many institutions the department of social
service became something apart from the department of child
care. Social workers, like their professional colleagues in psychiatry and psychology, recognized the importance of the work of
cottage personnel but clearly saw them as operating on a different level. This sense of division comes through in descriptions of
various institutional staff training conferences held during this
period. The flow of information was downward from the professional staff (who presumably had the expertise in mental
hygiene and treatment concepts) to the line staff (who did not).
The social worker preferred to advise the psychiatrist of a "social knowledge and technique which he usually lacked" than to
·spend her time consulting with the line staff on matters of child
care and management (Taft, 1919).

Thus, toward the end of the 1920s a treatment structure
separate from the group living, or cottage, structure was developed in children's institutions. The separation was enhanced by
the fact that the treatment of choice for the newly classified
"emotionally disturbed" child took place mainly in a carefully
structured therapy session with a professional psychotherapist.
Cottage staff and other institutional personnel were viewed as
important supportive figures, but not as the primary therapeutic
agents. The fruits of this separation would be felt for many
years to come.

*Conclusions.* Psychoanalytic theory contributed much to
the early development of milieu treatment, both as a screen for
assessing disturbed behavior and as a framework for organizing
therapeutic interventions. The theory is of limited usefulness
today, however, for explaining the disturbed behavior of children or for treating it in the context of a therapeutic milieu. In
diagnosis, highly individualized explanations of disturbed or
delinquent behavior—which placed the blame on faulty superego or ego development—appear now to have little validity,
ignoring as they do environmental, sociocultural, and physio-

logical influences. In fact, the whole taxonomy of psycho-dynamic constructs adds little to our understanding of what specifically we mean by "delinquent," "emotionally disturbed," or "maladjusted" behavior. The vocabulary of psychoanalytic theory interposes a layer of confusing and vaguely defined terminology between the troubled child and his behavior and provides little practical help to the child care worker attempting to change the behavior; it also increases the likelihood of reifying internal, pathological personality states that have no empirical basis. Finally, the overwhelming predisposition of psychoanalytic theory toward functional or psychogenic explanations of disturbed child behavior places unwarranted blame on parents as the cause of their child's disorder and has tended to subordinate alternative explanations—neurobiological, sociocultural—in favor of the family etiology hypothesis.

In the area of treatment, a similar argument can be made. To the extent that some psychoanalytically based approaches to milieu treatment remain viable—the work of Redl, for example —they are useful *in spite of* their psychoanalytic underpinnings and not because of them. The structural implications of the infusion of psychoanalytic treatment into the therapeutic milieu have been particularly unfortunate. The concept of the role of child therapist as a professional separate and apart from the child's living space has had a profoundly retarding effect on the development of the milieu as a means and a context for therapeutic gain. Since the therapist was isolated from the actual behavior in the ward or cottage, his view of the child was derived from information collected in the artificial environment of the fifty-minute therapy hour. To compound the problem, the individual therapist was often the person responsible for directing the child's total treatment plan—including supervision of line child care staff, who had an infinitely greater knowledge of the child's behavior in a more nearly real-life context. Small wonder that the forces actually governing the course of a child's progress in residential treatment often had less to do with the formal structure of treatment authority and more to do with informal, covert systems. It is no accident that Polsky's classic *Cottage Six* (1962)—which showed that the dominant force in a treatment institution for delinquent adolescents was a powerful delinquent subculture, in part reinforced by the houseparents for purposes of control—was conducted in an institution where the psychiatric caseworker was both physically and functionally removed from the cottage culture. (As if to symbolically underscore this point, it has been disclosed that the actual "Cottage Six" was the most physically distant from the building where individual casework took place.) Equally unfortunate is the fact that the child's individual therapist was often the parents' only contact with the treatment center. Thus, critical information about the child's actual progress in acquiring skills for living was transmitted secondhand, if at all.

My intent here is not to impugn the motives of individual therapists or to question the efficacy of individual psychotherapy as a therapeutic tool appropriate for some children. Many therapists have been sensitive to the problems mentioned here, and there is a small but significant literature on the problems of adapting individual psychotherapy to a therapeutic milieu (Noshpitz, 1971; Brodie, 1972). These attempts, however well conceived, miss the major point: *A truly therapeutic milieu cannot be organized around the concept of individual psychotherapy as the central mode of treatment delivered by a therapist who is both physically and experientially removed from the child's natural life milieu.* This is the dilemma facing many existing child treatment programs today. Even when desirous of change, these programs find themselves saddled with an organizational structure that simply will not permit the decentralization of clinical authority from the therapy room to the life space. At the very least, an analysis of the structural and functional effects of the infusion of psychoanalytic concepts into the children's institutional field should forewarn us about the carte blanche acceptance of any theoretical system or pattern of organization until we have examined fully the possible unanticipated consequences of our actions.

## Behavioral Approaches

Behavioral approaches to milieu treatment are a relatively new phenomenon when compared to their psychoanalytic counterparts. In the children's field, as in the mental health field generally, behavior modification entered through the "back door" with those children for whom more traditional approaches had failed: notably, autistic children (Lovaas, 1967; Wolf, Mees, and Risley, 1964) and older, case-hardened delinquents (Cohen and Filipczak, 1971). In the early 1960s, pioneering work was undertaken by a group of psychologists and educators at the University of Washington, who attempted to apply the principles of behavior analysis in a natural setting—in this case a campus preschool. These early studies focused on the effects of teacher attention in maintaining problem behaviors in children. In a series of experiments, the investigators demonstrated that such diverse behaviors as regressed crawling (Harris and others, 1964), socially isolate behavior (Allen and others, 1964), excessive crying and whining (Hart and others, 1964), and excessive scratching (Allen and Harris, 1966) were directly controlled by their immediate consequences in the environment —in this case the attention of adults. Attempts to alter these behaviors through a selective process of withholding and dispensing social reinforcement were successful and acted as a catalyst for a series of research endeavors designed to demonstrate the practical value of a behavioral approach in a wide variety of child caring agencies: schools, residential treatment centers, juvenile courts, and group homes. As with the psychoanalytic approach, individual behaviorists differed in style and emphasis, but their efforts were founded on a commonly agreed-upon set of principles, from which their strategies evolved:

1. A child's psychological nature is his behavior; directly observable and measurable actions constitute the sum and substance of personality. The behaviorist rejects the notion of inner personality states such as id, ego, and superego.
2. Behavior is largely controlled by the environment and, in the case of operant or active behavior, is either strengthened, maintained, or diminished by its immediate effects on the environment. Therefore, if the reinforcers for any given behavior can be identified and brought under control, the behavior itself can be similarly controlled.

3. The symptom of the troubled child is the entire problem; it is not simply an external manifestation of some underlying disease process, psychoneurosis, or character disorder. If the acting out of the delinquent, or the bizarre behavior of the psychotic child, is stopped, then the basic problem of delinquency or psychosis has been solved.

From an etiological point of view, the behaviorist looks to the child's prior learning history for diagnostic clues: How were negative behaviors elicited? How are they being maintained? What sorts of reinforcers are operative for this particular child? Treatment typically involves four stages: (1) identification and specification of the problem behavior; (2) determination of the controlling conditions: patterns of reinforcement, learning history, environmental factors; (3) specification of prosocial behavioral goals; (4) application of any of a number of behavioral techniques, either singly or in combination, followed by a precise evaluation of progress.

These techniques often include the contingent use of both positive and negative reinforcers to simultaneously accelerate desired behaviors and decelerate undesirable ones. Behavioral treatment may occur as the result of an individual behavior modification program or a specially constructed learning environment. (For a programmed introduction to behavioral theory and technology, see Patterson and Gullion, 1968.) Some of the more important behavioral contributions to milieu treatment for disturbed and delinquent children are the Achievement Place project for juvenile court-referred preadolescents (Phillips and others, 1973a), the former National Training School program for adolescent delinquents (Cohen and Filipczak, 1971), and the work of Browning and Stover (1971) at the Children's Center in Madison, Wisconsin—a residential center for psychotic and behavior-disordered children.

*Achievement Place.* Achievement Place—a family-style, community-based treatment home for delinquent youths—grew out of the joint efforts of a group of concerned citizens, juvenile court professionals, and behavioral psychologists from the Bureau of Child Research at the University of Kansas at Lawrence. The goal is to teach youths the basic skills—social, academic, self-help, and prevocational—that will help them out of trouble with their families, their teachers, and the law (Phillips and others, 1973a). Central to the model is the teaching interaction created between the youths and their "teaching parents"—a professional couple, specially trained in the techniques of behavior analysis and intervention. Training for staff includes intensive classroom and practicum experience and may culminate in a master's degree offered through the University of Kansas. In Achievement Place, the youth progresses through a series of behavioral programs, which gradually allow him or her more freedom and privileges as behavior improves. Behavior is carefully recorded in school, in the living environment, and on home visits, and the progress of an individual youth is continuously monitored. The power of the peer group is tapped through a self-government system, including an "elected manager"; and a consumer review of program effectiveness is integral to the model.

An interesting finding occurred when the investigators attempted to replicate the initial Achievement Place project in a second home—and failed. Though they had recreated an identical point system, they had overlooked the subtle but extremely important social reinforcement that occurs between houseparent and youth around the dispensing of points. In fact, the point system could work at peak effectiveness only in the context of a warm, open, and giving interaction: "Many clinical colleagues have told us all along that 'relationship' is an essential component of any therapy. We are now convinced that they are right" (Phillips and others, 1973a, p. 107).

In contrast to earlier efforts at establishing behavioral programs for delinquents, Achievement Place attempts to describe and objectify the social processes that can enhance or inhibit the token economy: individual relationship, peer group process, and the specific teaching of social skills. The Achievement Place model has now been replicated in a number of communities, and adaptations of the model have been used in institutional as well as community-based settings. While results are far from complete, the positive aspects of the model appear to be these:

1. Achievement Place is a *communicable approach* to delinquency treatment; it represents perhaps the most precise and detailed behavioral model of community-based treatment for delinquents in existence today. Training and program development procedures are well articulated, and a number of specific training tools have been developed. (The model is currently being implemented and training materials developed in many sites around the country, but particularly at Boys Town in Nebraska.)

2. Achievement Place appears to work—at least insofar as a limited follow-up would suggest. On the criteria of recidivism, school attendance, and school grades, the early graduates of the program appear to be doing better than similar cohorts of youth exposed to probation or a traditional delinquency institution.

3. Costs are low when compared to those of institutions: $5,000-$8,000 (compared to $20,000-$30,000) for capital outlay, and $4,000-$5,000 (compared to $6,000-$12,000) for yearly operating costs (Phillips and others, 1973a, p. 106). Since the costs of institutional care are themselves low in comparison to the costs of private residential treatment, the savings may be even greater.

4. Achievement Place is a true community-based program—low in visibility, high in connectedness to other community systems: school, family, vocational, recreation, peer group— and could well be justified on humanitarian grounds alone.

Areas of continuing concern include the following:

1. While the initial results of the program are impressive, they are not based on a systematic comparison with other types of treatment. Since youths were not randomly assigned to the project, preselection factors may have favored those youths judged most likely to succeed in a community setting. Such a judgment—however sound clinically—would violate the principle of random assignment necessary for a true comparative study. Moreover, while the present comparison with a delinquency institution and probation makes sense—

both are traditionally used services for such youths—a more telling comparison might include other carefully specified community-based approaches—including nonresidential alternatives. Both of these concerns may be addressed in the more comprehensive external evaluation currently under way.

2. The teaching parent concept—while an exciting one—raises again the question of the enormous problems encountered in recruiting, training, and holding on to effective houseparents. Turnover is evidently a problem in the Achievement Place project, and alternate staffing approaches would warrant consideration.

3. Questions have been raised about the appropriateness of the Achievement Place model for other than small, semirural communities with fairly homogeneous populations and commonly shared life-styles. How successful the model would be in a culturally diverse, urban environment remains to be seen.

4. Cost comparisons need to be more fairly assessed. Phillips and colleagues (1973a) compare the cost of institutional care with an Achievement Place home, neglecting to control for the array of services contained in the institution's budget—school and social service, to name two—and provided free to Achievement Place by other community agencies. The whole cost of training the teaching parents and supporting the consultant staff—provided for on a National Institute of Mental Health grant totaling nearly $1,000,000—is not readily apparent in the budget figures. In fairness, these may reflect more start-up costs than ongoing program costs.

In sum, the Achievement Place model represents an innovative and exciting approach to community treatment which has managed to improve as a result of its failures. The commitment to comprehensive evaluation at all levels of the program significantly increases the likelihood that the questions raised previously will ultimately be answered.

*The National Training School Project.* Cohen and Filipczak (1971, p. xix) report on an experimental behavior modifi-

cation program for juvenile delinquents at the former National
Training School in Washington, D.C. Under federal grants, a
pilot program was established in the mid 1960s, the object of
which was to positively expand the academic and social repertoires of forty-one incarcerated adolescents through the use of a
specially designed learning environment. A point system—or
token economy—was used to deliver reinforcement for appropriate classroom and dormitory behavior. The goal of the program was to increase the academic behaviors of all students and
to prepare as many as possible for return to the public school
within one calendar year. Points gained in the classroom could
be redeemed for cash or used to buy a variety of privileges, including better food, certain program activities, and more comfortable accommodations within the program. Evaluation indicated significant gains in both IQ and educational behaviors
during the period of institutionalization. Data on recidivism of
the students indicated a slower rate of return to the juvenile or
adult justice system than for the group of National Training
School graduates as a whole.

The importance of the postinstitutional environment as a
support system is stressed by the authors as an important factor
in determining ultimate community adjustment. The crucial
nature of the postinstitutional environment was also stressed in
research conducted at the Robert F. Kennedy Youth Center
(KYC) in Morgantown, West Virginia—the federally sponsored
successor program to the old National Training School in Washington, D.C. There a sophisticated behavioral program developed by Herbert Quay at Temple University was used to type
delinquents into categories and to provide a total learning environment in the institution. An in-depth analysis of fifty KYC
releases revealed that the differential training program at KYC
was no more successful in promoting in-program success or
twelve-month postrelease success than were the programs at two
traditional training schools (Cavior, Schmidt, and Karacki,
1972). The analysis suggests that what happens to the delinquent adolescent following release is as much dependent on the
kind of support and assistance he receives in the community as
it is on the treatment he receives in the program. These findings

coincide generally with the conclusion of two other studies (Allerhand, Weber, and Haug, 1966; Taylor and Alpert, 1973), which indicate the enormous power of the postinstitutional environment in determining the ultimate success of residential treatment programs for emotionally disturbed children.

*The Children's Center.* The work of Browning and Stover (1971) at the Children's Center in Madison, Wisconsin, is significant because it introduced the concept of an experimental-clinical approach to milieu treatment for young disturbed children—based in part on the use of the single-subject design (see Chapter Eight)—and because the authors outlined the organizational barriers to implementing a behaviorally oriented treatment program in a residential setting.

The problems encountered involved program design and staff attitudes and reaction. Specifically, it proved difficult to design a program that was balanced (one that stressed equally the acceleration of desirable behavior and the deceleration of undesirable behavior), that offered continuous positive social reinforcement, and that elicited increasingly complex behaviors. Staff problems were even more numerous. First of all, they generally felt that behavior modification techniques were "unnatural." In addition, they did not always carry out the program's requirements. Sometimes they failed to reward newly acquired behaviors (so that the children lapsed into old behavior patterns to receive attention), or they had difficulty in "reading" correct responses and often reinforced the wrong response or delayed reinforcement, or they would settle for less than the agreed-upon criterion response (given their relatively low expectation of what the children were capable of). Again, poor interstaff communication was a real problem in effecting a successful behavior modification program. Finally, the authors found limitations to the generalization of effects and in providing a treatment environment that gradually approximated the home setting. They concluded that one should not assume generalization but, rather, should work to ensure that what is learned in one setting is elicited and maintained in another.

Browning and Stover's observations are similar to those of Repucci and Saunders (1974), who introduced a behavioral model into a state training school for delinquents, and form the nucleus of a growing literature on what might be called the sociology of behavior modification in residential settings. Other behavioral contributors whose work has significant implications for the development of milieu treatment are Lovaas (1967) and Kozloff (1975) with autistic children; Schopler and Reichler (1971a) and Johnson and Katz (1973) on using parents as developmental therapists for their own children; Rose (1972) on the behavioral treatment of children in groups; Goocher (1975) on a behavioral approach to child care work; and Wahler (1975) and Patterson and associates (1975) on behavioral interventions with troubled children in their own homes.

*Conclusions.* It is probably only a slight overstatement to say that the most significant advances in milieu treatment for troubled children over the last decade have come about as a result of the introduction of behavioral technology to the life space. The impact is not unlike that of psychoanalytic theory in earlier decades. Although it is too early to assess the overall impact of behavioral approaches on milieu treatment, the following observations appear to be justified on the basis of available evidence:

1. Behavioral approaches provide a systematic and effective means for teaching alternative behavior to troubled children.
2. The behaviorists have helped immensely in specifying such important but ill-defined treatment variables as relationship, role modeling, and teaching interaction.
3. The behavioral model is a communicable model—easily understood by line staff—which increases the probability of consistency in treatment between different staff members.
4. The behavioral approach has helped child care professionals focus on the specific behaviors that are causing the troubled child or his family difficulty and then devising equally specific strategies for dealing with them.
5. The behavioral approach does not assume an "illness model" of childhood disorders but, rather, focuses on specific steps that may be taken to "unlearn" old behaviors while adopting new ones.

6. The behavioral approach lends itself particularly well to comprehensive evaluation; goals are clearly specified in advance, and treatment procedures are explicit.

7. Individual behavioral programs are often difficult to establish—particularly for many of the complex interpersonal behaviors.

8. The organizational context is a critical intervening variable in determining the success or failure of a behavioral approach to child treatment. This is particularly true in residential settings.

9. Token economies apparently are subject to the same market forces as money economies and must be carefully monitored to avoid such things as inflation and recession.

10. Helping the child make the transition from the artificial environment of the behavioral treatment program to his home community is a difficult problem—particularly if control of environmental reinforcers is limited.

11. Behavioral programs are easily sabotaged—either unwittingly or purposefully—by staff members who may be unclear on or in disagreement with basic program objectives.

12. The early stereotype of behavior modification as "cold," "mechanical," and "Machiavellian" continues to exist in many communities and represents a problem of considerable magnitude for staff training and community acceptance.

While behavior modification is not a panacea for child treatment, as many of its earliest and most vocal proponents argued, neither is it the cruel and barbarous method that some of its early critics held it to be. Behavioral modification will most certainly play a prominent role in any future development of a model of milieu treatment for troubled children.

## Guided Group Interaction Approaches

Guided group interaction approaches stress the importance of the milieu as a total system in influencing behavior. As a social system, the child caring institution has held a particular fascination for social scientists. Jules Henry's (1957) description of the culture of interpersonal relations in Bruno Bettelheim's

Orthogenic School was followed by studies of the conflict between houseparents and social workers (Piliavin, 1963), socialization of residents in an institution for retarded children (Dentler and Mackler, 1961), and the interpersonal behavior of
children in a residential treatment center (Raush, Dittman, and
Taylor, 1959). Though its focus was an adult mental hospital,
Goffman's (1962) classic study of the "asylum" had major implications for the children's field in its description of how institutional structure and processes sometimes were at total odds
with the formally stated treatment objectives of the institution.

In 1962 the sociologist Howard Polsky published a small
book, *Cottage Six,* which directly challenged current notions of
what constituted quality residential treatment for delinquent
adolescents. As a participant-observer, Polsky joined a cottage
of delinquents in an institution that prided itself on the sophistication of its clinical services. In fact, "Hollymeade" had pio-
neered in the introduction of mental hygiene concepts in an
institutional setting. Each boy received frequent—sometimes
daily—individual therapy from a trained psychiatric caseworker
in an office physically removed from the culture of the cottage.
The remainder of the youth's day was supervised by a set of
cottage parents—largely untrained and effectively removed from
the clinical decision-making process in the institution.

Polsky concluded that the supposedly disorganized world
of the adolescent delinquent was, in fact, centered around an
elaborate diamond-shaped power structure, made up of the various subgroupings within the cottage: "leaders," "status seek-
ers," "con artists," "isolates," "bushboys," and "scapegoats." A
delinquent subculture—which stressed intimidation through
physical coercion, toughness, and a code of silence—flourished
within the cottage and endured, even though the central actors
changed periodically. In spite of the contribution of highly
skilled individual therapists, the critical force in determining the
individual youth's course of rehabilitation was the delinquent
subculture of the cottage. Cottage parents—largely untrained
and overworked—often bought into or tolerated the delinquent
subculture for the purpose of controlling the group. Because of
the house staff's inability to deal effectively with this delin-

quent subculture, individual boys felt abandoned to it. Polsky (1962, p. 149) explains: "In the family the child is not exposed to a father and a mother, but to their interaction, their 'family culture.' In the institution, the youngster is barred from extensive interaction with the professional staff culture, yet he is expected to achieve the latter's goals. In the cottage, hard-pressed cottage parents are outnumbered by delinquent youths. Many boys improve in spite of the negative peer culture; others fail because of it."

If the behavior of an individual delinquent is in fact maintained by a delinquent subculture, then effective rehabilitation should involve the peer group as an integral part of the treatment process. For example, the Achievement Place project has developed an elected manager system, which harnesses the power of the peer group toward positive ends. Another approach to delinquency treatment that focuses exclusively on the nurturance, development, and utilization of a positive peer culture is *guided group interaction* (GGI)*—a method of counseling developed after World War II for use with recalcitrant prisoners in army disciplinary barracks. Though they originated in total institutional settings, GGI groups have also been used in community-based day treatment programs and group homes (Empey and Lubeck, 1972; Flackett and Flackett, 1970). Pilnick (1971) defines guided group interaction as follows: "Guided group interaction is a process of group treatment which directs the dynamics and strengths of the peer group toward constructively altering and developing the behavior of the group members." According to Empey and Lubeck (1972), the basic objectives of guided group interaction are to question the utility of persistent delinquency, to provide behavioral alternatives, and to provide recognition for a youth's personal reformation and for his willingness to help reform others.

---

*Vorrath and Brendtro (1974) and others make a point of distinguishing their positively oriented peer approach (positive peer culture) from the original guided group interaction method. While the new emphasis on the positive aspects of the peer process is both understandable and laudable, the two labels describe, for all intents and purposes, the same phenomena and will therefore be used interchangeably.

In guided group interaction, the peer group acts as a positively reinforcing agent in helping the youth develop positive prosocial values; in addition, strong sanctions help to ensure conformity to group norms. In many institutional settings, for example, the group alone decides what privileges an adolescent may enjoy within the residence and when he is ready to return to the community.

The group itself is seen as the primary vehicle for change, and members are responsible for helping each other resolve problems both in and out of the group meeting. In addition to the highly structured group session—which occurs daily for a period of approximately one and a half hours—the members are usually together in work, school, and recreation as well. Through the process of group decision making and task assignments, many situations arise which require some members of the group to help others who cannot "handle the situation." This process builds the self-worth of the individual member and the confidence of the group as a positive force for changing behavior. Typically, groups are composed of seven to eleven adolescent members and an adult leader. The daily session begins with a reporting of problems by each member. While there is some variation among individual practitioners, the following list is representative (Vorrath and Brendtro, 1974, p. 76): low self-image, inconsiderate of others, inconsiderate of self, authority problem, misleads others, easily misled, aggravates others, easily angered, stealing, alcohol or drug problems, lying, fronting (trying to be something you are not: clown, tough guy, dumbbell).

Every aspect of the physical structure of the meeting room is arranged to provide for maximum eye contact: individual group members sit in a semicircle, and the group leader sits behind a desk or table, apart from the group but ready to influence the interactions as he deems necessary. The role of the group leader is pivotal; he alternately supports, confronts, interprets, and summarizes the interactions of the members and maintains a "presence" even when he is away from the treatment setting. For example, in an institutional setting the group leader may drop in at unexpected times and thus keep current on behavior that occurs outside of the group sessions. Vorrath and Brendtro describe the group leader's primary verbal behavior as "questioning," which serves the purpose of stimulating the group toward the solution of problems. Each session follows a strict agenda: reporting problems, awarding the meeting, problem solving, and leader summary.

Since many groups are formed in delinquency institutions, a primary source of reinforcement is the almost universal desire to return to the community. A central function of the group is to make it impossible for a member to leave the setting through delinquent means, such as "conning." The leader does not attempt to provide answers for the group but forces decisions back to the members. Final authority does rest with the leader, particularly with respect to discharge. Members therefore become dependent on one another, and "helping" is encouraged outside as well as within the daily group sessions.

The effectiveness of GGI remains open to question. Early experiments with GGI (McCorkle, Elias, and Bixby, 1958; Weeks, 1963) yielded no statistically significant differences in the recidivism rates of graduates of the GGI program and those of the regular reformatory. More recently, Empey and Lubeck's (1972) study compared graduates of a community-based GGI program with those of a traditional delinquency institution; again, there were no significant differences between the recidivism rates of the experimental and control groups. Although there was no assessment of long-term outcomes, the data suggested that the experimental program, which was much shorter and thereby less costly, was at least as effective as the control ·program (Sarri and Selo, 1974, p. 278). Stephenson and Scarpitti (1974), in a review of several institutional and community-based GGI programs, found that the GGI graduates fared somewhat better than the traditional reformatory graduates but not as well as youths on parole. Their overall conclusion (p. 189) was as follows: "Taken together, the evidence from these studies is not impressive with respect to the general efficacy of guided group interaction when compared with alternative programs of correction.

Vorrath and Brendtro (1974, pp. 150-151) report on an

unpublished study from the Minnesota Department of Corrections' Red Wing Institution (where the senior author initiated a GGI program), which purports to show a "success" rate of over 80 percent and a drop in recidivism from the previous 50 percent to 18 percent in a two-year follow-up of graduates of the program. What these results demonstrate is open to question, since a methodological comparison with several similar studies revealed that the Minnesota study ranked "poor" in four areas and "fair" in two others (Sarri and Selo, 1974, p. 268).

While generally inconclusive, studies of GGI as a treatment tool with delinquent youth suggest the following strengths and limitations:

1. For those older adolescents whose delinquent behavior originates and is maintained in the peer group, GGI presents a potentially powerful technique for going to the heart of the delinquent subculture and orienting it in a positive direction.

2. With its daily meetings, peer confrontation, and focus on present problems, GGI significantly lowers the probability of the delinquent's being able to "con" his way through the treatment program.

3. In an institutional setting, GGI can link school, cottage, and community behavior in a way that helps to ensure improvement across systems. It is a positive approach that stresses "growth" rather than illness and is, in many respects, a true "self-help group."

4. GGI is less expensive than traditional training school programs when used in a community-based setting.

5. Group leaders do not require extensive graduate professional education and are often selected for training from the ranks of line child care staff.

6. Some critics have argued that GGI is to a large extent based on personality rather than method. Some programs have centered around a single messianic leader, who brooks no compromise with the "rightness" of the model. Harstad (1976) suggests that GGI is not more widely used because its promoters have turned off prospective users through simplistic, overbearing, and insulting presentations.

7. Relatively little has been written about the method itself. The literature is sparse, and few formalized training programs for group leaders exist. Thus, agencies desirous of trying out the model often find that they have to buy into a long-term consulting contract to receive the necessary staff training.

8. GGI is presented as a total approach to youth treatment, and its use as an adjunctive therapy has been discouraged in favor of an "all-or-nothing" approach. This would seem to render useless the notion of differential diagnosis and treatment for the youthful offender.

9. As a way of organizing a total therapeutic milieu, GGI leaves much to be desired. With so much power invested in the group leader and so much action taking place in the group meeting, other staff—notably child care workers—can begin to feel that they are little more than caretakers.

10. The data—as with most total-treatment approaches—are at this point unclear. The present literature is particularly limited in two important areas: For what type of youthful offender does GGI appear to be most effective? What organizational structures provide maximum enhancement for the GGI approach?

11. GGI is less effective with the younger troubled child, for whom the peer group is less powerful, and for psychotic children or severely emotionally disturbed children.

### Educational Approaches: Project Re-Ed

Project Re-Ed (Hobbs, 1966) was designed to create a total living and learning environment for the troubled child and stresses the teaching of competence across the total spectrum of the child's development as the fundamental purpose of the helping environment. There is also in Project Re-Ed a theoretical eclecticism not found in the approaches previously discussed. While I am aware that many additional educational approaches to child helping exist—particularly in the literature of Western and Eastern Europe, the Soviet Union, and Israel—I believe that this particular approach has the most direct and immediate bearing on the development of community-based group care settings for troubled children in the United States. (For some additional examples of educational approaches, see Wolins, 1974; Makarenko, 1955; Guindon, 1970; Wolins and Gottesman, 1971.)

This pioneering program began as the result of a cooperative effort of the National Institute of Mental Health, Peabody College, and the states of Tennessee and North Carolina to provide a new kind of institution to help emotionally disturbed children. Re-Ed programs have been established in several locations in Tennessee, and there is one center in Durham, North Carolina. The critical influences on the program's originator, Nicholas Hobbs, and his associates have been described as follows: "Robert LaFon and Henri Joubrel of France introduced the staff to the idea of the *éducateur* and the small residential school. Catherine McCallum in Scotland provided the example of the "educational psychologist" trained on the job to work with disturbed children. Campbell Loughmiller's ideas on camping for disturbed boys profoundly altered the character of Re-Ed as did the Peace Corps and the Outward Bound Schools of England. The intellectual heritage of Dewey, Rogers, Wolpe, Skinner, and Barker (all together!) is apparent in the program (Bower and others, 1969, p. 9).

The Re-Ed model combines special education and group living in a small, community-based program. Staff consist of teacher-counselors—former classroom teachers with special training in program activities and life-space intervention. In his introduction to the project, Hobbs (1964) cites several governing assumptions and biases:

> *A learning bias.* The task of reeducation is to help the child learn new and more effective ways of construing himself and his world and to learn habits that lead to more effective functioning. We assume that the child is not diseased but that he has acquired bad habits. . . . Our effort is to initiate a learning process that will come to fruition in the weeks and months and years after the child's experience in a Re-Ed school. Reeducation is a problem in learning to learn.

*A time bias.* A child is most likely to get referred to a mental health facility at a time of crisis. ... Improvement thereafter may often be expected. ... To provide nothing more than a benign sanctuary for a child at a time of crisis is a worthy endeavor. The reeducation process claims time as an ally, not just as an effect to be bettered.

*A growth bias.* We do not assume some mystical growth force as an explanatory principle, but simply note descriptively that children (in the middle years) are still open to experience and change, with surplus energy to support the operation. A broken bone knits more rapidly at six than at sixty; we assume a comparable viability in the psychological domain.

*A social system's bias.* We are trying to move beyond concepts of individual adjustment, beyond concern for family-child relationships ... to a program of intervention that constantly assesses and tries to change in appropriate ways the child ... and all of the special people of importance or potential importance in his world.

*A bias away from "dynamic psychology."* With no clear advantage to be gained from the use of a therapeutic strategy (psychoanalytically oriented psychotherapy) that calls for a high level of psychological sophistication, we have chosen the simpler course: We are impressed enough by the complexity of the simplest seeming solutions to helping the disturbed child.

*An adiagnostic bias.* The formal psychiatric diagnosis is of little value in the process of reeducation. We have not been able to specify differentiated treatment procedures for differential diagnoses, nor have we observed thus far any relationship between diagnosis and responsiveness to the school program.

From this base, Hobbs identifies a number of core components of the reeducation process: developing trust, gaining competence, nurturing feelings, controlling symptoms, learning middle-class values, attaining cognitive control, developing community ties, providing physical experience, and knowing joy.*

In the Re-Ed model there are two teacher-counselors for each group of eight children housed in a community residence. Teacher-counselors have already taught in public school and have had additional training consisting of a period of course work and a practicum. One teacher-counselor is primarily a daytime formal teacher; the other is an after-school informal counselor who works with the group as a whole. All decisions concerning actions to be taken toward the child are in the hands of the teacher-counselor. The average length of stay for children is six months.

Evaluation consists mainly of parent and teacher ratings. While results were tentative, they generally showed favorable improvements in school performance and behavior at the time of graduation and an eighteen-month follow-up. Before Re-Ed, approximately 75 percent of the children were rated as having severe emotional or behavioral problems in school; after Re-Ed, approximately 75 percent of the children were rated in the normal range or as having mild problems (Bower and others, 1969). A follow-up study (Weinstein, 1974) indicates marked improvement in comparison with untreated controls, but further analysis is required before the effect of the project can be assessed with certainty.

Any assessment of the Re-Ed program must begin with an assessment of Hobbs himself. On rereading his work today, one is even more impressed with what he had to say in the early 1960s and the eloquence with which he said it. His conception of the philosophical base of Re-Ed preceded by at least a decade the most cogent and articulate arguments in favor of community-based services for troubled children. Re-Ed appears to capture in a single setting what is most desirable in those services: low visibility, a total-systems focus, strong linkages with school

*This last component appears to have been borrowed directly from the Maxim Gorky labor collective for delinquents, which existed in the USSR in the 1920s under the direction of Anton Makarenko (see Rhodes and Tracy, 1972, pp. 420-433).

and family, time-limited intervention, a "growth" perspective, and a simplified organizational structure. Moreover, Re-Ed has received accolades from its panel of consultants (Bower and others, 1969) and from the Joint Commission on Mental Health of Children (1970, p. 44), which gave unqualified endorsement to the program and urged its expansion nationwide: "Because of its proven effectiveness, in terms of both cost per child served and success in restoring the child to home, school, and community, the Commission recommends that the Re-Ed model be adopted and extended as one of the many needed kinds of services for emotionally disturbed children. Specifically, the Commission recommends that funds be made available to any state, community agency, or nonprofit corporation for the construction and operation of residential schools for emotionally disturbed children, patterned after the Re-Ed plan. Funds should be sufficient to establish at least 100 schools with at least one school in each state to serve as models for other programs."

With all this favorable publicity, it is puzzling that the Re-Ed concept has not made greater inroads into the fields of child mental health and juvenile corrections. While severe cutbacks in federal funding for children's programs and the vested interests of the existing mental health professions in maintaining the status quo in services must surely be counted as partial answers, there remain, on closer observation, some serious and unanswered questions about the Re-Ed model itself. First, although the model is detailed and eloquent on a philosophy of education for troubled children, it is woefully short on specifics: What specific skills must a teacher-counselor acquire in order to help children alter old behavior patterns and adopt new ones? What are the essential components in the group living process, and how do they relate to the major presenting problems of the children in care? While certain program elements— such as wilderness camping and program activities—are mentioned, it is not clear whether these are seen as primary or secondary formats for teaching or whether they apply equally to all children. Second, while I share Hobbs' bias about the inadequacy of psychoanalytic theory in explaining the behavior of troubled children and would second his strong emphasis on teaching competence, I part company with his "adiagnostic" bias. If his major point is the damaging effects of labels and the inadequacy of present diagnostic schemes (see Hobbs, 1975a, 1975b), then the answer must surely lie in the direction of devising *more precise* diagnostic criteria, which yield specific behavioral objectives. How does one operate "adiagnostically"? Does he ignore the complex array of bio-psycho-sociocultural forces in which the troubled behavior originated and through which it is being maintained? Does not an "ecological" approach demand a precise and systematic assessment of the child-in-environment? How does the teacher-counselor decide what will produce change in a given child and what particular response he should make, given a universe of possible choices? These are important questions for any demonstration effort to attempt to answer, and they are absolute prerequisites to the sort of nationwide dissemination envisioned by the Joint Commission on Mental Health of Children. In short, Re-Ed is, at the level of philosophy, entirely communicable and extremely compelling. At the level of actual practice, as reported in the literature, it is slightly better than primitive.

A related question concerns the selection, education, and duties of the teacher-counselor—patterned closely on the European model of *éducateur*. There is in the writings of Hobbs—as in many other proponents of the *éducateur* concept—an almost infinite optimism about the positive potential of bringing together "naturally" talented counselors and children with problems. For example, witness Hobbs' (1964, pp. 14-15) emphasis in the following description of the Re-Ed process: "Techniques are important but they are clearly not all, *nor are any particular procedures essential to the process of reeducation.* The heart of Re-Ed is the teacher-counselor, a decent adult; educated; well trained; able to give and receive affection, to live loose and to be firm; a person with private resources for the nourishment and refreshment of his own life; not an itinerant worker, but a professional through and through; a person with a sense of the significance of time, of the usefulness of today and the promise of tomorrow; a person of hope, quiet confidence, and joy."

This is a beautifully and simply expressed statement about the kinds of qualities one hopes to find in a child care professional. But is there something required beyond "joy" and "decency"? I am reminded here of the criticism that my late colleague Elton McNeil (1969, p. 17)—himself no stranger to the world of troubled children—offered in response to another version of the *éducateur* model:

> What is critically absent in the role specification of the *éducateur* is the "O" in the familiar S-O-R (stimulus-organism-response) formula of the learning theorists of a half a century ago. The *éducateur* stimulates the human organism via arts and crafts and vigorous activity, and, perhaps, he can subjectively sense positive response to these efforts. But this is a blind, mindless effort to gloss over the reality of the perceptual, motivational, emotional, and cognitive human transaction that occurs in the mysterious "black box" called psychic life. What seems lacking is a workable description of:
> 1. What kind of child with what kind of problem?
> 2. What developmental life conditions and experiences have produced this child-with-a-problem?
> 3. What life forces exist at this moment?
> 4. How is change produced in human beings, and what skills are needed to bring it about?

Other questions remain as well: What specific skill training does the teacher-counselor receive for working with families of troubled children? Does the Re-Ed model envision other professional pathways to the teacher-counselor role, or must all staff come from the profession of education? What is the turnover rate for teacher-counselors, and what organizational requisites are necessary to make this form of service delivery work at optimum efficiency? What sort of ongoing training, consultation, and ancillary support services are required by the teacher-counselor, and how are they woven into the fabric of the Re-Ed program? In short, while the concept of the teacher-counselor raises some exciting possibilities for the future development of community-based services, it also raises some important educational and organizational questions, which remain unanswered. At the time of its inception in the early 1960s, the Re-Ed program represented a bold and innovative departure from traditional child mental health services. Hobbs and his associates answered resoundingly in the negative to the supposition that emotionally disturbed children could not receive education for living in a short-term, noninstitutional, growth-oriented residential school staffed by specially trained teachers. The results of the first stage of their project are now available, and it remains for us to examine through future research and demonstration efforts what implications they contain for the future of residential child care.

The strengths and limitations of Project Re-Ed, then, can be summarized as follows:

1. At the level of philosophy, the Re-Ed concept—as articulated by its originator, Nicholas Hobbs—presents us with an eloquently written brief for the community treatment of troubled children, a brief that foreshadowed by at least a decade the arguments for deinstitutionalization.
2. Re-Ed proposed a bold restructuring of mental health services for troubled children in need of care away from home. Among the more significant aspects of the service package are its short-term nature, low community visibility, commitment to the development of the child, and educational emphasis.
3. Re-Ed's conception of the "teacher-counselor" represents a pioneering attempt to translate the European concept of the *éducateur* to the American scene.
4. At the level of program detail, the Re-Ed model is less fully developed. Procedures are not clearly apparent; indeed, one gets the impression that *no* procedures are critical to this approach—leaving an enormous problem when it comes to replication and evaluation.
5. The role of the teacher-counselor needs further amplification with respect to skill training, selection, professional background, development of a career ladder, and place on the mental health team.

These limitations not withstanding, the work of Hobbs and his colleagues in Project Re-Ed constitutes a bold and innovative approach to reaching troubled children in their home communities. As a theoretician, Hobbs was ahead of the field by at least a decade, and many of his ideas as embodied in Project Re-Ed deserve reexamination today.

### A Final Personal Reflection: The Other 23 Hours

Inevitably, the foregoing review led me to examine the seminal influences on my own thinking about the therapeutic milieu and, more specifically, the thinking behind an earlier collaborative effort, *The Other 23 Hours* (Trieschman, Whittaker, and Brendtro, 1969). That volume, written primarily as a practice manual for child care workers, attempted to provide a reasoned conceptual and practical approach to the care and treatment of emotionally disturbed children in residential centers during the hours of the day not spent in individual therapy. Our effort differed from Project Re-Ed and many of the other previously mentioned approaches to milieu treatment in two significant ways. First, the book reflects less a single demonstration effort and more the collective experience of the authors in a number of different treatment settings—notably the Walker School in Needham, Massachusetts, and the University of Michigan Fresh Air Camp. Second, we were not attempting to create a new model of service delivery for troubled children; rather, we were interested in examining how the events of daily living in a therapeutic residence—the rules, routines, games, and personal encounters—could be used to teach children something about the reasonable limits of their present behavior, while at the same time providing them with opportunities for growth and change. We hoped to develop a set of "lenses" for examining the events of daily life and a set of guidelines for managing them that would be useful for the line child care worker faced with tasks of nurturing, teaching, and disciplining the disturbed child in "the other 23 hours."

To this undertaking we brought a diverse array of professional experiences and theoretical biases; our backgrounds were in clinical psychology, social group work, education, and psychology. We pooled a collective experience that included child psychotherapy, behavioral modification, special education, and group treatment. The work of Redl and Wineman (1957) had a seminal influence on the development of the book and reinforced our common belief that the theoretical framework used in milieu treatment had first to be translated in terms that made sense to the child care worker operating alone in the life space with a group of disturbed children. In fact, our approach derived not from any single theoretical perspective—though psychoanalytic ego psychology—in particular, the later work of Robert White (1959, 1960) on "competence"—provided a unifying theme for much of what we finally developed. Rather, we used as primary data our own experiences and those of other child care workers in intervening with behavior in the life space. While we continued to be interested in the *why* of behavior, we were much more concerned with *what* to do about it—a concern that was continuously reinforced by child care staff who needed daily help in managing and redirecting the often noisy and troublesome behavior of the children in our care, as well as in providing them with constructive alternatives for the future. This essentially pragmatic approach to child care work yielded a result that was neither theoretically "pure" nor empirically tested and in no sense constituted a fully developed model of milieu treatment. We did produce a set of observations and suggestions that seemed to help child care workers and other professionals make some sense of the behavior of the troubled child in the "other 23 hours" while at the same time expanding their range of options for what to do about it.

Three central ideas emerge from the book. First, the therapeutic milieu is conceived of as a "living and learning" environment where the events of group living—the rules, routines, activities, and behavioral interchanges—become formats for managing disruptive, troublesome, and maladaptive behavior, as well as for teaching prosocial alternatives (Trieschman, Whittaker, and Brendtro, 1969, pp. 1-51). Because children learn in different ways, the milieu must incorporate many different teaching formats that accommodate to the different styles of learning: We believed that child care counselors, who work with the children around the clock, should be the major agents of therapy and that a therapeutic milieu should not merely help children gain insight, or manage their behavior, but should help them build competence (and confidence) in a wide range of areas.

A second contribution was the development of the concept of "relationship" as it informs the teaching context. In our scheme (p. 57), each element of a relationship—social reinforcement, communication, and modeling—facilitates a specific learning process: reward and punishment learning, insight learning, and identification-imitation learning, respectively. Using this framework, we offered suggestions for establishing "relationship beachheads" (see Brendtro, 1969) and for overcoming certain barriers to relationship formation. Our intention here was to identify the processes of social interaction that occur between child care worker and child and that can have a profound effect on the success of treatment—a fact graphically illustrated in the failure of the initial attempt to replicate the Achievement Place project mentioned earlier (Phillips and others, 1973a).

A third contribution of the book was its conceptualization and development of the various formats available for teaching alternative behavior: mealtimes, bedtimes, wake-up, and program activities. In each of these sections, we attempted to demonstrate the function of the routine, or activity, in developmental terms as well as its specific strengths and limitations as a format for teaching alternative behavior. The final section of the book dealt with understanding and dealing with temper tantrums, observing and recording the behavior of children in the life space, and avoiding some of the roadblocks to therapeutic management.

While *The Other 23 Hours* continues to provide a useful framework for understanding and intervening in the therapeutic milieu, certain shortcomings are more apparent today than they were at the time of publication.* First, while the theory base of the book is presented as essentially open and eclectic, it relies

*In the years since the publication of the book, I have benefited immensely from discussion of many of these issues with my colleagues, Albert Trieschman and Larry Brendtro. While their views, and mine, have changed since the book was published, I must, in fairness, take full responsibility for the following criticism.

far too heavily, in my opinion, on psychoanalytic ego psychology for its justification. The interposition of the term *ego* between the behavior that needs to be changed and the formats available for teaching reflects, I believe, the authors' classical training and the theory available at the time the book was written. I do not mean here to denigrate the function of cognitive process or to downgrade the enormous heuristic contribution of ego psychology to the development of a theory of human behavior. I do suggest that we are still far from having a coherent, unified theory of milieu treatment and should therefore avoid overreliance on any single theoretical schema, particularly one with such shaky empirical underpinnings. At another level, the book suffers from the same procedural primitivism for which I criticized other approaches to milieu treatment. This is a problem for residential treatment as a whole and is reflected in the available evaluative research, which, if it indicates change in the dependent variable at all, is unable to provide a precise definition of the independent variables responsible for the change.

A second and obvious flaw in the book is the absence of any clearly articulated procedures for evaluation of the individual case or of the total program. The evaluative component is critical to any approach to milieu treatment today, not only because it is the only way in which we will ultimately arrive at a theory of changing children's behavior but also because it may be necessary for the very survival of the program. Finally, the book suffers from an insufficient treatment of the important elements in the child's total life system. Notable here for their absence are sections on the importance of classroom education and the importance of working with parents.

Despite these and other shortcomings, I still agree with the essential conception of the milieu as a medium for competency acquisition that makes use of a variety of formats for teaching alternative behavior and which weighs equally the cognitive and affective as well as the behavioral components of the change process.

One can come away from a review such as this with the feeling that we really know nothing about what "works" in residential treatment. Such is not the case. Each approach to residential treatment has, in its own way, furthered our knowledge of one or another important aspect of the therapeutic milieu. We know, for example, more than we used to about the relative potency of insight versus behavioral approaches with particular levels of troublesome behavior. Research studies and painful experience have convinced us of the enormous power of the peer group as a potent intervening variable in changing individual and group behavior. We know that models of treatment organization that are functional in a clinic setting may not be at all appropriate when extended to a 24-hour-a-day program. Finally, we realize more than ever the critical importance of aftercare services as a follow-up to residential treatment and the notion of taking a total ecological approach to helping troubled children and their families. Future models of residential treatment will most certainly be built on the foundations laid by Aichorn, Bettelheim, Redl, Hobbs, and the many other contributors who have gone before. Perhaps the most important lesson to be learned from a review of this type is that no model of residential treatment should be based solely on theoretical presuppositions but should instead begin—as did the contributors cited above—with the real-life problems of the children coming into care.

# 4

## Group Living with Troubled Children

Our focus in this chapter is on the group living environment itself as a medium for growth and change. In my judgment, the major components of a planned group living environment are the incentive system, the program activities, and the group intervention system. Central to each of these components is the teaching relationship between the child care worker and the child and the focus on teaching basic social, emotional, and cognitive skills. Although the three components are separated here for purposes of analysis, there is considerable overlap between them. Minimally, they should not be antagonistic to one another; ideally, they should be mutually reinforcing.

### Organizing Principles

*The group living environment should constitute an arena for learning rather than a haven for intensive care.* The children we seek to help are not so fragile, "sick," or traumatized that they need to be isolated from the effects of their behavior on those around them. In fact, the group life environment should be so designed that it actively engages noisy, troublesome, acting-out behavior—as opposed to either simply suppressing it through punitive sanction or suffering through it in the belief that it is a requisite for therapeutic change. Our message in the milieu should be loud and clear: "We accept you as a person with rights, feelings, and individuality; we reject, totally, those things you do which make trouble for yourself or for others and which keep you from growing as a competent, autonomous individual." We seek to create an environment where all the participants—children and staff—are interdependent; care about one another; and are willing to challenge, support, and aid each other in the process of growth and change.

*A group life environment should provide the incentive to grow—and the freedom to fail.* The children and young people we serve in group care settings are experts in failing. They have done poorly in school, at home, and in other residential settings. Their self-image reflects a lack of competence and confidence, and their outlook on the future is often pessimistic if not fatalistic. Scores of caring adults have already "given up" on them, and they have something of an investment in maintaining their record of failure. After repeated such failures, some children really come to believe that they *are* uncontrollable, and a peculiar process is reinforced; that is, the agencies set up to serve the most troubled children are engaged in a constant process of "creaming off" only those who are most manageable —leaving the others to filter down to settings where admission cannot be refused and where all that can be reasonably provided is containment. Admittedly, there will always be some children who—despite our best efforts—have to leave the program prematurely. We should not, however, construct our helping environment in such a way that a young person knows that running away, or physical assault, or refusal to participate in school is a sure ticket to early departure. Misbehavior should be followed by clear consequences but also by equally clear pathways through which the child can regain his or her place in the program.

*The group life environment should provide numerous op-*

*portunities for modeling the kinds of behaviors we would like the children to adopt.* We should actively exploit all the opportunities available in the course of the day to provide real or simulated examples of behavioral alternatives. Models include staff, children, and various resources from videotapes, teaching materials, and other media. In addition to exposure to a variety of role models, the child needs ample opportunity to practice the behaviors being taught, to learn from self-correction and peer criticism, and to gradually gain confidence in his or her new behavioral skills. Modeling, particularly when coupled with role playing, provides a powerful tool for altering troubled and troublesome behavior. For example, Sarason and Sarason (1973) and Sarason and Ganzer (1971) have extended the use of modeling and role playing to institutionalized delinquents and low classroom achievers—and with impressive results. This focus on modeling and role playing reflects the basic purpose of the milieu: to teach practical skills for living.

*The group life environment should be capable of providing a graduated set of experiences which, over time, will approximate the community environment to which the child will return.* The group's life space should not be considered a static environment. It should be continually responsive to the changing needs of individual children for challenges in learning, meaningful rewards, and effective controls. If, for example, the new child requires heavy structure, clearly specified consequences for misbehavior, and limited degrees of freedom, the older, more competent child needs increasing amounts of responsibility, less frequent monitoring, and more independence. The balance between autonomy and control—with an individual child or with the group—is a delicate and ever changing one. Because the time spent in residence is limited, we need to constantly reassess whether we are expecting from individual children all they are capable of. Similarly, we need to ensure that, over time, the child's experiences will increasingly resemble those in the postplacement community. Precisely because they often are total institutions, children's residential centers sometimes err on the side of providing for too many of the child's needs in a manner totally foreign to the environment to which the child will return. Actually, the longer the child is in residence, the *less* attractive the group living environment should become. When a child is almost ready to leave the residence, things like program boredom and frustration with limits and routines should not be automatically answered by program change in the direction of more flexibility. Rather, at least part of our response should be: "You are right. This program has become too restrictive for you. You're ready to handle more on your own—and move on."

*The group life environment should be sensitive to subtle differences in social and cultural values and be clearly linked to the child's family, peer group, and neighborhood experiences.* Cultural relativity is perhaps the single most persuasive reason that an effective group life program cannot be simply "bought off the shelf" but must be molded, adapted, and modified to meet the particular characteristics of the population to be served. In short, both staff and children need to feel that they truly "own" the program—that it is not simply an artifact lifted from a book, research program, or demonstration project but a viable, changeable culture of which they are the creators and the stewards. If community-based programming is to work at all, it must take into account the peculiarities of the community it seeks to serve and also make use of whatever natural helping networks already exist in that community, in order to further the goals of treatment for an individual child. One indicator of the degree to which the milieu is culturally related is the extent to which children, parents, and other community agencies can describe with ease what the program is all about: whom it serves, how it works, and who "owns" it.

Finally, the milieu as a special helping environment should provide ways for graduates of the program and their families to visit and interact with the children in care. One striking impression I have from visiting scores of child caring facilities—including those newly constructed—is the absolute lack of pride of ownership or cultural tradition. There is often a sterility of atmosphere reminiscent of airport waiting rooms, an absence of art and artifacts, and a peculiar "unlived-in" feeling to many residential centers. Part of the enormous task of removing the stigma of placement means building a culture and a program that a child can be proud of—even after graduation. If the present array of facilities can in any sense be considered an experimental sample, bricks and mortar alone will not do the job.

Let us now consider the three major systems that make up the culture of group living.

### The Incentive System

As indicated earlier, the extension of behavioral modification procedures based on social learning theory has had a significant effect on residential treatment over the last several years. In some instances, individualized behavior modification programs make up part of a total treatment plan. For example, a program may be designed to increase task performance in a special education classroom, or to decrease self-injurious behavior, or to eliminate fire-setting behavior. (There are now many excellent clinical casebooks on the use of behavioral modification with children. See Graziano, 1971, 1975; Stedman, Patton, and Walton, 1973.) In other instances, all or part of the group living environment is designed to reinforce certain target behaviors across the entire group. Such interventions—variously called "levels systems," "motivational systems," or "incentive systems"—typically use some sort of point or token economy whereby the successful completion of certain behavioral assignments results in the accumulation of "currency," which may be traded for privileges such as free time, recreation, exemption from chores, home visiting, or trips to the community. Frequently, such group behavioral programs specify a series of levels—each with its accompanying responsibilities and privileges—through which a child may progress. For example, Meyer, Odom, and Wax (1973) describe a five-level incentive system in a residential institution for adolescents.

Kazdin (1977, p. 1) describes a token economy as a type of behavior modification program that relies heavily on the principles of operant conditioning: positive and negative reinforcement, punishment, extinction, reinforcement scheduling, shaping, chaining, prompting and fading, discrimination and stimulus control, and generalization. The pioneering volume by Ayllon and Azrin (1968) has now been supplemented by Kazdin's (1977) own extensive review of the literature on the token economy. In the children's field, there is a small but steadily growing literature on the use of incentive systems (see, for instance, Phillips and others, 1973a; Cohen and Filipczak, 1971; Meyer, Odom, and Wax, 1973). Davidson and Seidman (1974) cite over thirty studies involving the use of behavioral techniques with delinquents in both community and institutional settings. For other reviews see Braukman and others (1975) and Stumphauzer (1973). Other studies specific to residential programs include Bardill (1973); Fineman (1968); Jesness (1975); Karacki and Levinson (1970); Rice (1970); Seymour and Stokes (1976); and Scallon, Vitale, and Eschenauer (1976). Community-based applications include Carpenter and Carom (1968); Rose (1972); and Feldman and Wodarski (1975).

While there are many examples of incentive systems in the literature and in practice, no single agency or group of investigators has devoted as much time to systematically addressing the question of where the incentive system best "fits" into the total treatment program as has the previously cited Achievement Place project (Phillips and others, 1973a). From its beginnings in Lawrence, Kansas, this home-style, community-based treatment program has been extended to a variety of institutional and community programs for troubled children and youth. From the core project at the University of Kansas, satellite group home programs have been set up in many different communities around the country, and a major effort is presently under way at Boys Town in Nebraska to implement the model in a large institutional setting. The incentive system makes up only one part of the total Achievement Place model and is complemented by an elected manager system, a social skills component, and various other interventions. The following sequence occurs vis-à-vis the incentive system:

> When a youth enters Achievement Place he
> is introduced to the point system that is used to
> help motivate the youths to learn new, appropriate

behavior. Each youth uses a point card to record his behavior and the number of points he earns and loses. When a youth first enters the program his points are exchanged for privileges each day. After the youth learns the connection between earning points and earning privileges, this daily point system is extended to a weekly point system where he exchanges points for privileges only once each week. Eventually, the point system is faded out to a merit system where no points are given or taken away and all privileges are free. The merit system is the last system a youth must progress through before returning to his natural home. However, almost all youths are on the weekly point system for most of their nine-to-twelve-month stay at Achievement Place. Because there are nearly unlimited opportunities to earn points, most of the youths earn all of the privileges most of the time [Wolf, Phillips, and Fixsen, 1974, p. 235].

Table 1 lists the behaviors that gained or lost points in the Achievement Place project, and Table 2 lists the "costs" of various privileges. The project team is still updating and refining this point system, with less emphasis on the giving and taking of points and more emphasis on teaching "negotiation" skills between the youth and the family living teacher.

While the point system is viewed as the "work horse" of the Achievement Place program, its limitations are clearly recognized: "Point consequences provide immediate, concrete feedback to the youths each day and provide a powerful treatment tool. However, the world outside Achievement Place does not always provide systematic consequences for appropriate and inappropriate behavior" (Wolf, Phillips, and Fixsen, 1974, p. 422). The response to this particular problem with the point system in Achievement Place was the creation of a merit system that was not tied to a daily or weekly schedule.

*Problems in Implementing Incentive Systems.* Rhodes (1977), Repucci and Saunders (1974), Kazdin (1977), and Browning and Stover (1971) have outlined many of the difficulties involved in implementing behavioral modification pro-

Table 1. Behaviors and the Number of Points That They Earned or Lost

| Behavior That Earned Points | Points |
| --- | --- |
| Watching news on TV or reading the newspaper | 300 per day |
| Cleaning and maintaining neatness in one's room | 500 per day |
| Keeping one's person neat and clean | 500 per day |
| Reading books | 5 to 10 per page |
| Aiding houseparents in various household tasks | 20 to 1,000 per task |
| Doing dishes | 500 to 1,000 per meal |
| Being well dressed for an evening meal | 100 to 500 per meal |
| Performing homework | 500 per day |
| Obtaining desirable grades on school report cards | 500 to 1,000 per grade |
| Turning out lights when not in use | 25 per light |
| Behavior That Lost Points | Points |
| Failing grades on the report card | 500 to 1,000 per grade |
| Speaking aggressively | 20 to 50 per response |
| Forgetting to wash hands before meals | 100 to 300 per meal |
| Arguing | 300 per response |
| Disobeying | 100 to 1,000 per response |
| Being late | 10 per minute |
| Displaying poor manners | 50 to 100 per response |
| Engaging in poor posture | 50 to 100 per response |
| Using poor grammar | 20 to 50 per response |
| Stealing, lying, or cheating | 10,000 per response |

Source: Wolf, Phillips, and Fixsen (1974, p. 412).

Table 2. Privileges That Could Be Earned Each Week with Points

| Privileges for the Week | Price in Points |
| --- | --- |
| Allowance | 1,000 |
| Bicycle | 1,000 |
| TV | 1,000 |
| Games | 500 |
| Tools | 500 |
| Snacks | 1,000 |
| Permission to go downtown | 1,000 |
| Permission to stay up past bedtime | 1,000 |
| Permission to come home late after school | 1,000 |

Source: Wolf, Phillips, and Fixsen (1974, p. 413).

grams in group child care settings. Typically, these involve several different levels of problems, including improper assessment of target behaviors, failure to determine potent reinforcers, problems in implementation, problems of transition, and problems of staff communication and stereotypes. (See the section on "The Children's Center" in Chapter Three.) From the various reports, it seems clear that too little attention has been given to the question of the organizational requisites for the adoption of an incentive program. Many problems have to do with technical issues—for example, how to accurately assess complex behavior—but others are value questions. For example, should recreation and activity programs be seen as "givens" in a group living environment—offered noncontingently because of the learning opportunities they afford children—or should participation in them be made contingent on the accumulation of a certain number of points? As in the larger society, there needs to be a determination of what are the "basics" to which any child is entitled—regardless of behavioral achievement. For example, Browning and Stover (1971) encountered real resistance in a state facility to the use of food as a reinforcer. Once these central questions have been answered for any particular program, there remain a host of problems centering on the staff's perceived flexibility in interpreting and implementing the program. Rhodes (1977) identifies several potential pitfalls with incentive systems: allowing children privileges not appropriate to their level; not following through on consequences set forth in the incentive program; giving privileges to a child not because of his level but because these privileges are seen as mandatory—that is, educational and therapeutic; arbitrarily withholding privileges that a child has earned; policing the privileges that a child has earned; changing a child's level between grading sessions; providing reinforcers that have not actually been identified as such for the individual; providing competitive privileges not included in the incentive program dispensed now contingently.

In addition, I have encountered several problems that arise with the establishment of an incentive system in a residential setting. The first problem might be labeled the *adoption of an incomplete model* or, more accurately, the *dilemma of the half-baked approximation*. This problem is almost invariably signaled by the following: "Oh, we tried a behavioral program in our agency last year—it didn't work." Typically, when one goes back and identifies exactly what *was* implemented, it appears as an incomplete, poorly conceptualized system, usually "cribbed" from someone else's program. Proper staff training in behavioral methods was lacking, and adequate behavioral consultation was not available. Unfortunately, after such an abortive and unsuccessful attempt to implement an incentive system, some agencies are disinclined to look at anything even vaguely resembling a behavioral program. One proximate cause of this particular problem is the overwhelming need that exists among child care practitioners for models that work. In a practically oriented field such as group child care—where time and financial resources are limited and service pressures are great—there is a tendency to adopt models of care and treatment prematurely or incompletely, without proper understanding of their strengths and limitations.

A related and serious problem—*guilt by association*—concerns the extent to which incentive systems, token economies, and other behavioral interventions are seen as tinged with a Machiavellian-Orwellian aura. Some common descriptive adjectives reflecting this point of view include "cold," "mechanistic," "dehumanizing," "artificial," and "simplistic." The problem in countering these stereotypes is precisely the fact that they contain some grain of truth: behavioral interventions *are* manipulative; to a staff unfamiliar with behavioral principles the procedures *can* seem "unnatural"; and much of behavioral theory *is* concerned with the mechanics of how behavior is acquired and extinguished. And possible counterarguments—the fact that all therapies are, to one extent or another, designed to manipulate behavior; or that all programs, wittingly or unwittingly, reward and punish certain behaviors; or that a theory about the mechanics of behavior does not have to be applied mechanistically—are not exactly compelling, particularly when the debate is laced with emotion about what is "right" for the troubled child. London (1972) suggests that we have achieved the "end of ideology in behavior modification." I think not—at least, not in the child care field. That is why we desperately need to define and agree on a set of basic purposes for group child care settings; otherwise, technology or, rather, misperceptions of technology will govern program design. We need to go beyond the stereotypes and look at the realistic contributions that behavior modification can make in a group living environment, where all helping technologies should be used in a humane, sensitive, and caring manner.

Another problem, *technological preoccupation,* reflects a kind of clinical myopia. It occurs when child care staff begin to see the incentive system as an end in itself rather than a single tool for changing behavior. Entire staff meetings sometimes are devoted to discussions of what level a particular child is or should be on or what privileges should be given at a particular level. These *are* valid questions—but not the only ones that need to be asked. The incentive system is, after all, an artificial and contrived program designed for a specific purpose: to bring behavior rapidly under control and to teach some prosocial skills. The problem occurs when staff and children begin to "see the world" totally through the artifact of the incentive system and not in terms of the real-life contingencies the child will encounter in the posttreatment environment. There really are two parts to this problem, involving *time* and *breadth of coverage.*

With respect to time, most authorities agree that a child should move as quickly as possible from a tightly controlled point system to a merit system that draws much more on social reinforcement for its potency and more nearly approximates the real world. Therefore, we need to avoid the trap of designing ever more complex levels systems and spend more time thinking about how we can move youngsters to a more natural— albeit educationally oriented—environment.

The issue of breadth of coverage involves, essentially, a value question: Do we wish to involve the entire group living environment in the formalized incentive system—or not? Simply on the grounds of consistency and efficiency of operation, a strong case can be made for involving the total group life culture in the incentive system. I would argue the contrary and for two important reasons—one practical, one philosophical. First, there is always the danger of designing an incentive system that is so complex and so pervasive that it simply will collapse under its own weight. The more variables we try to fold into this one format for teaching, the more probable this collapse becomes. Such recognition argues for a group life environment that uses multiple formats for teaching alternative behavior and does not overuse any particular one. Second, I would not want to design or ask staff and children to participate in a culture that is uni-dimensional—where every behavior and every response must be weighed in terms of points, tokens, and the like. I would much prefer a culture where children could, on occasion, look forward to the noncontingent dispensing of rewards—just because life isn't always terribly predictable or maybe just because it seems a decent thing to do at the time. Similarly, I believe that children need to learn—in addition to a basic consistency to the routine—that adults *are* different in the ways they respond to behavior. Finally, the culture of group living should, I believe, be sensitive to those facets of human existence that are not always readily measurable on a daily behavioral rating—facets such as thoughts, feelings, and attitudes. My own preference therefore would be to limit the scope of the incentive system to the major routines of group living (wake-up; mealtime; bedtime; household chores), with some provision for an individual behavioral rating (see McInnis and Marholin, 1977). The child's progress in other major sectors of the environment—for example, in the classroom—can be recognized in the daily or weekly review. This need not mean a formal tie to the incentive system but could consist of verbal or written feedback from teachers or other persons with whom the child is involved.

The *pay-as-you-go-problem* is reflected in the statement "Don't bug me, I've already paid my fine." That is, the child can endure the secondary pain of giving up points in exchange for the privilege of not having to talk about what might be a chronic problem in behavior. A related problem involves the "straitjacket effect" on child care staff, who may feel limited in the range of responses they can offer to a particular behavior: "I feel that all I ever do is punch cards [or dispense points]; if only I had a chance to talk to these kids." Although these problems are not the inevitable result of implementing a levels system (Achievement Place, for example, has structured times for staff-child conversations), they can create real morale problems for child care staff, who begin to feel as if they are working for the system rather than vice versa.

The *problem of second-class citizenship* occurs in traditional settings where behavioral intervention is accepted only in clearly prescribed and limited areas. There is a clear hierarchy of treatment, which is reflected in clinical authority, staff distribution, and consultation time. Typically, one-to-one-therapy is seen as the primary treatment; all other modes are seen as "ancillary," "supportive," or "adjunctive." As one behaviorally oriented child therapist put it: "They say, in effect, you handle the encopresis, fire-setting, and physically assaultive behavior. We'll handle the core problems in psychotherapy." In group care settings, such an attitude might translate into a limited acceptance of an incentive system as a tool for managing surface behavior, with the "real" work of treatment to occur in individual child therapy sessions. This lack of recognition not only makes for ill feeling on the treatment team but obscures the fact that behavioral interventions are primary interventions, which cannot be relegated by fiat to second-order status. A related phenomenon that occurs in settings where one-to-one therapy is still seen as the primary intervention could be characterized as *The Helping Hand Strikes Again.* Here the therapist unwittingly reinforces the very behaviors that staff are attempting to eliminate or suppress through the incentive system. In their classic study, Ayllon and Michael (1959) report that such "bootleg" reinforcement provided by a social worker in individual casework sessions caused the reemergence of psychotic talk in a patient—after the behavior had been almost totally extinguished by the nursing staff. In children's residential centers, this kind of problem speaks to the wisdom of involving all professional staff in the process of case planning and informing all supportive staff—cooks, housekeepers, maintenance persons —of the goals and plans for an individual child.

## Contributions of Incentive Systems

Given these and other problems, what contribution can an incentive system make to the group life environment?

The first and most obvious strength of the incentive system is that it can rapidly bring behavior under *control*. To children and youth whose major presenting problems often include disruptive, acting-out behavior, the incentive system provides a clearly defined set of expectations regarding behavior in the life space. This control function is particularly critical in the early days and weeks of placement, when relationships are not yet formed and when the living group is at an early stage of development.

A second major advantage of the incentive system is that it works to ensure a *consistency* between staff members in dealing with the same behavior. For the child who habitually "tests out" the adults in the system to see where the weak links are, or who is prone to playing off one adult against another, the incentive system, with its clearly specified expectations and consequences, constitutes a formidable obstacle to manipulative behavior.

A third advantage of the incentive system is its *clarity* about behavioral expectations for an individual child and the group. Particularly when it is displayed in some visual form—on a chart, for example—the incentive system helps to make the culture of group living a visible culture and one in which the consequences for behavior are determined not by individual staff whim but by group consensus. Ideally, the incentive system should tell the new child in residence: "Here is how we expect you to behave, and here is what you can expect in return."

As a format for learning, the incentive system provides an excellent medium for teaching the most basic social skills, including self-care and hygiene, care of property, management of daily living routine (mealtimes, wake-ups, bedtimes), behavioral management, and basic interpersonal communication. The child learns how to manipulate the immediate environment of the cottage or group home to meet his or her own needs. In the discussion of points, privileges, and levels, he learns something of the art of negotiation and is provided a relatively safe and structured experience in dealing with an adult.

The incentive system also provides the child with a

clearly visible *measure of progress* in the program and does so in a time frame that is compatible with his or her presenting problems—which often include a focus on the immediate situation and a difficulty in dealing with vague concepts about future improvements. Early in the program a daily point tally or daily behavioral rating provides regular feedback to the child about progress in the program as well as immediate reinforcement for doing well. The incentive system can help with the task of taking some overall goals and breaking them down into more proximate and attainable objectives.

*Conclusions.* The incentive system is a potentially powerful tool for changing children's behavior. As such, it constitutes an important building block in the group living environment. Its placement in the life space of the cottage, ward, or group home should be preceded by a full staff discussion of both the problems in implementation and the positive features previously cited. Whatever particular variant of the incentive system is ultimately adopted should reflect the values, norms, and special concerns of the helping environment into which it is being introduced. As with all new interventions in the life space, the environmental impact of the incentive system should be as fully explored as possible—*before* implementation. Basic questions should include: What do we want from the incentive system? How does it further the basic purposes of the caring culture? What are its likely limitations in our program? To what extent will we have to modify existing paradigms to meet our special needs? How will it "fit" with the rest of the program? Because, as we have seen, not all consequences can be anticipated, a full evaluation of the incentive system should be built into the program design.

### Program Activities

As we saw in Chapter Two, many children entering group care settings have a limited range of play skills. The reasons for this deficit are numerous but may include lack of exposure to adequate modeling of play behaviors; aggressive or withdrawing behaviors that make it difficult for a child to enter into the play situation; and a whole range of motor, cognitive, and perceptual problems that complicate the learning of the structure of activities as well as participation in them. (Richard Small and Robin Clarke describe some of these learning blocks in Chapter Seven.) Whatever the specific reason for the deficit, the effect often is that the child is removed from meaningful contact with peers and deprived of the sense of confidence that comes from successful mastery of games, crafts, sports, and other program skills. (For contributions to the literature on program activities see Gump and Sutton-Smith, 1955; Redl and Wineman, 1957; Churchill, 1959; Maier, 1965; Trieschman, Whittaker, and Brendtro, 1969; Herron and Sutton-Smith, 1971; VanderVen, 1972; Vinter, 1974.)

Activities have many functions in a group life culture—of which, perhaps, five are preeminent.*

*Program Activities as Aid in Assessment.* Games and activities provide a rich medium for assessing the child's general developmental level as well as exploring specific behavioral deficits. The staff can determine, for example, the child's general response to program activities (bored, excited, enthusiastic) as well as the particular activities he or she may be attracted to or seek to avoid: individual or group, "high risk" or "safe," verbal or nonverbal. In addition, the child care staff can learn which activities the child typically turns to when bored, angry, sad, or elated. Finally, a child's response to a particular activity may provide clues to his handling of tasks in other group situations:

> Today I introduced model racers to my group of eight-year-olds. I told the youngsters they could work individually on their cars, that they could take them home when finished, and that I would come around to help them individually as needed. Billy immediately asked that I put his

*An earlier version of the following discussion appeared in Whittaker, 1976b. The quoted statements are taken from case examples provided by child care workers and other clinical staff in various training workshops that I have conducted over the past ten years.

racer safely away, so that he could take it home later. He never opened the box and spent the rest of the session reading a comic book. Karl demanded that I help him first and suggested I put the parts together as I could do a "neater job." Bobby and Joe sat together in a far corner of the room and carried on an animated conversation while working on their projects. Eric wanted to know how much the models cost and whether his mother would have to pay. He seemed uneasy about his ability to glue the parts together. Finally, Sam—who had gotten right to work with his project—suddenly thrust it angrily to the floor, said it was "ruined," and wanted to know when we were going to have snacks.

Free-form activities—like swimming—may elicit clues to the kinds of issues individual youngsters are dealing with, as well as the kinds of controls they respond to most readily:

On our first visit to the "Y" today, Tim—a husky ten-year-old—managed to fall off the deep end of the pool when clowning near the edge. He was immediately pulled out by one of the guards and told to return to the shallow area. Most of the other youngsters thought this enormously funny— except for Jerry, who told me in quite an agitated manner that Tim should be punished because a boy in his camp had almost drowned last summer when fooling around on a dock. He didn't buy my suggestion that we discuss the matter later in group and stayed on the sidelines for the rest of our session.

Much behavior observed in activities may be equally a function of the group developmental level or the physical setting of the group living environment. For example, a crafts room littered with half-completed projects invites distraction if not destruction. Staff should be clearly in charge of program planning—particularly early in the group's development—and should settle on a small number of games and activities, which, over time, will yield an accumulation of group responses against which to measure an individual child's behavior. (For a compilation of activities appropriate for diagnostic purposes, see VanderVen, 1972, pp. 244-257.)

*Program Activities as Specific Treatment Intervention.* Games with high-powered "It" roles (Gump and Sutton-Smith, 1955)—Red Light, Statues, Simon Says—may enable the low-powered, low-status child to experience the feeling of mastery that comes from leading the group. Conversely, low-powered "It" games—Tempo, Dodge Ball, Hide and Seek—may show the high-powered members what it is like to be on the lower end of the totem pole. Subsequent group discussion of activities like these can provide the basis for an analysis of the child's feelings of inclusion or exclusion. On a more intensive level, Garland and Kolodny (1972, p. 235) suggest programmatic ways of dealing with the group scapegoat by "playing out" the scapegoating process in a safer, more controlled context. It is, in fact, possible to structure activities to help individual children deal with particular themes that are current in the group's life or are consuming the energies of certain members. Fear of "newness" and change, anxiety over presumed incompetence (in academics, sports, social interaction), or feelings of exclusion from the peer group are all themes that may be safely played out and then discussed in the context of activities.

> Today each of the children contributed an "embarrassing" hypothetical problem from school —a problem faced by an imaginary child who was new to her school and neighborhood. Some examples were: having to talk in front of the whole class and forgetting what you had to say; taking a shower in gym and having the other kids laugh at you; being asked a question by the teacher and not hearing everything she said; and being the last kid picked for team sports. The group then used props and role-played the embarrassing situation; we all worked to identify specific behaviors which she could employ to lessen the embarrassment and

humiliation. Later we talked about how real these situations were, and I was surprised at how many of the members volunteered their own "most embarrassing moment"—usually having to do with perceived physical or academic incompetence.

VanderVen (1972, pp. 208-215) talks of the importance of using activities in four critical areas of development: perceptual ability (particularly, the ability to process stimulation from the environment), the recognition and expression of feelings, the development of self-esteem and positive self-concept, and the development of socialization skills. These developmental issues may be approached via the treatment goals for an individual member or for the entire group. One such group issue, mentioned earlier, has to do with building in the requisite skills for solitary play. One group handled this issue in the following manner:

> Working from a list of suggestions from the group (as well as from past experience), I compiled a list of things to do "when you are alone": reading, playing with matchbox cars, block building, and "Legos." Several of these activities were made available during regular periods following group athletics; children were urged to choose whichever activity they wanted—the only condition being that they had to play by themselves. In discussion in subsequent weeks, the idea of playing alone was positively reinforced—necessary in the staff's judgment because "being alone" often had negative connotations. Reports of fantasy play—with toy figures or cars—were also reinforced, and each child was asked to list his or her three favorite activities for being alone. Parents' aid was enlisted (most enthusiastically) to provide a space—usually the child's bedroom—and some simple activities for being alone. Cues were developed so that the child could go off alone without a lot of questions, and parents were urged to reinforce successful "away times."

Activities that elicit high expressive content—puppets and dolls, for example—may be used to model a particular behavioral problem and its resolution. Patterson (1965) employs a most creative combination of play therapy and behavioral modification in working with an individual school-phobic child. Such techniques may also be used in a group context. For instance, a continuing story might be played out by puppets over the period of several group sessions; the "story" in this case would again have to do with a particular developmental issue or behavioral problem being faced by the members.

*Program Activities as Positive Reinforcement After Discussion.* Most latency-age children and early adolescents find it difficult to attend to prolonged group discussion—particularly when it focuses on personal issues. Groups handle their discomfort (anxiety, boredom) by acting silly, distracted, or aggressive or simply by "tuning out" the staff leader. Since discussion is an important medium for learning in a group life culture, it is well to consider how program activities may be used to enhance discussion time. According to the behavioral psychologist Premack (1959), a pleasurable activity can be used to reinforce a less pleasurable one if it is made contingent on it. Focused group discussion—often a less pleasurable activity—may be increased if a range of more pleasurable activities (including table games and snacks) are made available after a predetermined period of discussion. Such contingencies are strengthened by strong positive social reinforcement directed to the group as a whole: "You kids have really worked hard on some difficult problems. Now let's have a break." Such comments also help to define the culture of the group as a place for both serious discussion and pleasurable activities.

*Program Activities as Aid to Behavior Management.* Many child care staff become frustrated at their inadequate efforts to control misbehavior during the group's meeting time. Such low-level behavior may include silliness, overexcitement, physical and verbal "poking," hyperactivity, and inattention. Long, Morse, and Newman (1971, pp. 397-491) have identified many behavioral techniques for managing the behavior of young children in such situations. In addition, simple activities may be used to focus the total group on the leader or a central task. Trieschman, Whittaker, and Brendtro (1969, pp. 107-108) and VanderVen (1972, pp. 204-242) have written of the importance of these short-term activities. Especially helpful are games which become a part of the group culture and assist the children in the transition from outside to inside the group. Word games like "20 Questions" or simple paper-and-pencil games like "Hangman" often provide a bridge into the culture of the group. With latency-age and younger children, gross motor activities—tumbling or climbing—provide an important release after long hours in a classroom. Most important is that the activity becomes a group ritual—a "something" we all participate in prior to the next scheduled event. Such short-term activities consistently used provide a structured set of expectations which will cut down on the need for behavioral management. For example, a continuing story at the end of each group treatment session brings the group back to the central focus on the leader and provides a ritual bridge back to the group life program. Activities also may be used to disperse the group quickly ("Hide and Seek") or bring them together ("Follow the Leader") as a means of blocking troublesome group behaviors during a session.

*Program Activities as Aid in Skill Building.* Project Re-Ed and other community-based programs have made use of wilderness camping and survival training techniques similar to those used in the Outward Bound program. In a focused way, such activities seek to build self-reliance and confidence through a series of graduated experiences designed to teach resourcefulness and/or group interdependence, as well as to expand physical endurance. In a broader sense, the children and youth who enter group care programs are deficient in many areas and can benefit from a wide variety of activity programs which focus on the teaching of specific skills. In the group life environment, members of the supportive staff (clinical or maintenance), as well as the volunteers, often have special skills and could take one or more youngsters for a short-term skill session. Areas of interest to a group of adolescents might include auto maintenance, small-engine repair, photography, dance, ethnic cooking, or rock climbing. One benefit of using nonprofessional staff as activity leaders in skill-building sessions is that children are exposed to new and different role models in a semistructured but delimited area of their choosing. Another form of skill teaching includes activities that provide a sense of mastery over the immediate environment. For example, an "information hunt" (similar to a treasure hunt except that participants bring back answers to a series of questions) can be effectively used to familiarize a group of adolescents with a new environment.

Today, by prearrangement with school officials, I arranged an information hunt for the youth who would be entering junior high in the fall. Two teams of four members were given identical lists of questions which related to the physical spaces, history, and personnel of the school. After a brief introduction, each team was off on its search—with members ranging far and wide in and around the building. Sample questions included: How many doors are there on the third floor? What is the principal's favorite food? For whom was the school named? What hours is the library open? I had briefed school staff about the purpose of the activity and alerted them that they would be approached with questions. During the hunt, one staff member circulated throughout the building to monitor progress, and I remained in the main entrance to answer questions. After the hunt was over and a winning team determined, we adjourned for hamburgers and a discussion of what we had learned of the school and the people who work there.

The information hunt gives youngsters a legitimate reason to explore an environment and talk to key persons in a "nonofficial" way. Similar activities can be derived around transportation systems or sectors of the city that the young people will be using for recreation, school, or work. Activities such as dramatics, charades, and film making—as well as larger-scale projects such as car washing—also can be used as vehicles for teaching such basic social skills as conversation, team work, and the use of humor.

*The Process of Program Planning.* Typically there are three major stages in program planning: *analysis of purpose, structure of the activity,* and *individual differences.* Each stage suggests a number of key questions:

1. What is the major purpose of the activity: specific treatment intervention, behavioral management, positive reinforcement after group discussion, assessment, skill building, or some special purpose (for instance, to introduce new members into the group)?
2. What is the precise nature of the activity, and what special requirements will it impose on participants? What rewards does it contain? How restrictive is it? How much does someone need to know to be able to participate? What is the rule structure, and how is it enforced?
3. What do we know about the participants as individuals (their skill, motivation, and on-tap control) and as a group (the general level of development, communication, and the like)?

Another factor to consider is the *physical setting* for the activity. In planning an activity, we are creating an atmosphere; and in this respect no factor is more important than the physical space in which the activity will occur. Last-minute room changes on a regular basis connote a sense of impermanence and unimportance. A regular meeting place and time for group activities is crucial, as is the physical appearance of the space itself (see Churchill, 1959). The children's right to privacy also must be respected; if they are to be observed, either directly or on videotape, they must first agree to such procedures. Similarly, we need to define spaces in the group living environment where solitary play can occur legitimately and uninterruptedly.

The most critical intervening variable in the successful implementation of program activities is the child care worker's own level of comfort. The worker must feel free to really enjoy playing and should be aware of activities that may be threaten-

ing or unfamiliar to him or her. Playing *with* children demands
full involvement, and this may mean a psychological shift away
from the other "adult" activities which the worker has just
come from—activities such as staff meetings, home visits, or case
conferences. Children are quick to sense adult discomfort at
participating in games and activities through subtle nonverbal
cues, such as clothing that says "I don't want to get messy,"
even when the verbal message is to the contrary.

Since much of program planning is done on the run, the
work of activity analysis often occurs after the session has been
completed. Staff meetings and supervisory conferences can be
fruitfully used in developing an *activity profile* for the total
group as well as for individual children. Key questions include:
For which of the five major purposes are activities being used in
the life space? Are there additional areas in group living where
activities could be used effectively? Typically, one finds overreliance on a single favorite activity, or activities used only for a
single purpose, or a conspicuous absence of activities during
times of the day when they might be most useful (for instance,
during transition times). Similar questions can be raised from
the point of view of the individual child's activity preferences,
dislikes, reactions to large-group and solitary play, and the like.

The result of the planning process should be a common
understanding of the group's likes and dislikes in activities and a
working knowledge of activities that can, variously, bring the
group together, take it apart, generate enthusiasm, "put a lid on
troublesome behavior," teach specific social skills, facilitate discussion, and further the specific learning goals of individual children. One useful outcome of the planning process is the
creation of a card file organized around some of the variables
previously listed and citing not only the particular requirements
of various activities but the reaction of both the group and individual children to them.

*Problems with Activity Programs.* Despite the best efforts
at planning, problems with activities can occur—and should be
anticipated. One such problem is *boredom with the program*:
"There's never anything to do around this crummy place." "We
did that activity last week." "What are we going to do today?"

Comments like this from the group—particularly when they come at the beginning of a long weekend shift—are likely to send even the most seasoned of child care staff into mild depression. The fact is that groups *do* get into a rut—either by overusing a favorite activity until it is no longer reinforcing or by gradually pushing all responsibility for program planning onto child care staff. As in a family, the living group periodically needs to rearrange its "furniture" by altering the physical, social, and psychological spaces within the environment—for instance, by periodically infusing new activities into the milieu, by increasing group responsibility for program planning, or by modifying the time in which favorite activities are expected to occur. If certain activities—television or certain board games, for example—are being overused to the point of frustration, perhaps they could be put "on the shelf" for a period in favor of outside activities. Longer-term projects—for example, camping or gardening—which may be seasonal in nature provide a new focus for program planning and involvement.

Program boredom—or frustration or behavioral upset—can also result when activities or materials are inappropriate for the age or developmental level of participants. Young latency-age children, for example, probably will not be responsive to activities that require a high degree of interaction; and a group of psychotic adolescents, who are socially immature and dependent, will be more like late-latency children in their program preferences.

There is also the related and difficult problem of *work*. Finding a meaningful place for work in a program for children or adolescents—particularly one in which other people tend to the care of facilities and equipment and in which program materials abound—is a difficult and challenging task. Young people sense immediately the difference between recreation, make-work, and meaningful work and give the lie to the notion that "a child's work is its play." It is not. Child's play is child's play. Interestingly, Wolins' (1974, pp. 267-291) study of successful group care programs in several countries indicated that the provision for meaningful, productive work was a variable associated with all successful programs. There is clearly a strong argument to be made for involvement of the total living group in the tasks that need to get done on a daily basis—if for no other reason than that everyone needs to participate in making the culture work. Beyond this, I have a strong intuition that programs which regularly manage to involve the group in some larger work project—building a cabin, clearing a campsite, refurbishing a group home, or putting food by—have few problems with program boredom.

Another major problem is *staff participation*. To shift, as suggested earlier, from one set of professional activities (meetings or conferences) to a play situation is a difficult and complicated process. Sometimes staff just don't feel much like playing with a group of youngsters whose behavior they may have been managing all morning. The activities—particularly with younger children—are undoubtedly different from those that the staff would choose for their own enjoyment. Sex-role stereotypes may make it difficult for male and female staff to participate in certain activities. Confidence in one's ability to carry out an activity competently may get in the way of participation. Finally, there is the feeling "If I join the game as a participant, what happens when I have to step back into my role as group leader?" The problem of perceived authority loss is a real and vexing one.

Difficult as these problems are, the alternative—nonparticipation—is worse. Nothing contributes more directly to program boredom than the unenthusiastic response of the child care worker who stands on the edge of the group—waiting for the activity to happen. While recognition of one's own limitations is important—not everyone should feel compelled to do all the activities—the prime determinant of program participation should be the group's needs and not the staff's desires. Therefore, the staff must occasionally participate in games and activities that are less than totally stimulating and show enthusiasm when they do not really feel it. Activities can and should be pleasurable, but their implementation often involves hard work and a staff norm that values participation in and planning of programs. A full range of resources—including time for planning, adequate supplies, and regular opportunities for skill building—should be available for child care staff. Of these, time for planning activities should be integral to the child care function—and not relegated to off-duty free time. On the question of potential loss of authority through participation in activities, there are no easy answers. It is true that participating on the level of a child *can* make it more difficult to move into the role of disciplinarian when the need arises. At the same time, full and enthusiastic participation as an adult may be precisely the thing that reduces the need for behavior management around activities.

A major unanticipated result of program activities is their *environmental impact.* For example, if the wildly successful game of "Capture the Flag" is scheduled in the evening, bedtime may have to be postponed for a few hours until the group "comes down." Similarly, the weekend staff may find themselves scheduled for a physically taxing activity, such as an all-day hike, at a time when there are few back-up staff on call to deal with potential problems on the group's return and when cooking help is also lacking, meaning an added set of tasks for the already weary staff. The point is that each major activity should be accompanied by an environmental impact statement, which looks at its potential effects on subsequent programming and assesses its costs and benefits with respect to group management, resource availability, and staff emotional reserves.

Another problem has to do with *community programming.* Few programs have the resources (or the desire) to carry out all activities on campus. The move to community recreational facilities creates a separate set of problems, which are potentially very beneficial for learning but which require staff attention and group discussion *before* moving off the campus. Typically, these problems include separate rules for "on" and "off" campus, the potential for overstimulation, the problem of waiting, behavior in vehicles, relationships with outsiders, and fear of labeling ("There are those kids from the institution"). Staff also must resolve logistical problems of where and how to obtain back-up help if necessary and how to handle loss of group control in a strange environment. Nowhere is the staff member on more public display than when he or she is managing a temper tantrum in the middle of the shopping mall. A clearly defined set of rules and expectations for off-campus programming is a cornerstone in the overall activity structure.

A final problem concerns *strings-free activities*—activities offered noncontingently instead of as privileges for acceptable behavior. Such activities, when they are offered immediately after troublesome outbursts, *can* be interpreted by the child as a reward for misbehavior. At the same time, activities constitute a powerful medium for teaching appropriate behavior; and when they are withheld "pending good behavior," we are, in effect, depriving the child of a potentially helpful medium for learning. Although there is no single right "answer" to this dilemma, the solution must surely lie in a closely monitored relationship between the incentive system and the activity structure, so that group rules are respected. You don't automatically get to go roller skating after back talking to staff all day and refusing to do school work, but discretion is permitted in the use of activities with individual children. As with the incentive system, staff need to feel that they truly "own" the activity structure and be clear exactly what they wish to get from it. To view all activities as totally contingent on acceptable behavior greatly reduces staff discretion and the possibility for individualized programming.

### The Group Intervention System

The final building block of the group life culture involves the systematic use of the small group as both a "means" and a "context" for effecting behavior and attitude change in children (see Vinter, 1974, pp. 3-34). In one sense, *everything* we do in the life space involves some manipulation of the group process, and a basic understanding of group dynamics is critical to all phases of child care work practice: designing incentive systems, planning program activities, developing routines that teach, managing behavior and teaching skills. Our focus in this section will be a more limited one: What specific uses may be made of small-group intervention in a planned living environment—and to what ends?

Table 3. Differential Approaches to Group Treatment of Children and Adolescents

| | Psychodynamic | Behavioral | Guided Group Interaction |
|---|---|---|---|
| Assumptions | Existence of unconscious, Freudian model of personality structure. Behavior connected to inner states. Conflicts revealed through play, social relationships. Group as corrective experience. | Personality best understood as the sum of observable behavior. Behavior largely controlled by environment. Troubled behavior is the whole problem, not a symptom. | Delinquent behavior elicited and maintained by negative peer culture. Helping others increases self-worth. Each youth responsible for own behavior, capable of change. Delinquent skills redirected in the group. |
| Purpose | Personality and behavior change through free interaction in a carefully structured social environment. | Behavior change in individual and in group as a whole by application of principles of social learning. | Use of dynamics of peer group to constructively shape behavior of group members. |
| Client population | Children 4 years through adolescence. Usually primary behavior problems—not psychotic, psychopathic, withdrawn. | Behavior-disordered children; no particular problems ruled out. | Primarily older delinquent adolescents, often in institutions. Not psychotic, schizophrenic. |
| Group composition | Groups usually 6 to 10 in number. Careful balance of problem types important factor. | Usually small group, homogeneous for presenting problem. | Groups usually 7 to 11 in number. Common experiences with delinquent acting out. |
| Knowledge/theory base | Psychoanalytic theory/ego psychology. Neo-Freudian developmental theory. | Social learning theory. | Still developing. Connected to intensive interaction techniques (Lewin, Rogers, and others). |
| Leading theoreticians | S. R. Slavson, Haim Ginott, Mortimer Schiffer. | S. Rose; the combined contributions of many applied behavior analysts. | H. Vorrath, L. K. Brendtro, S. Pilnick; L. T. Empey. |
| Role of therapist | Varies from totally permissive to strong role model. Generally nondirective, neutral, parental figure. | Therapist identifies antecedent reinforcers, determines new contingencies. Monitors, models, teaches, controls contingencies. | Pivot of group process—controls contingencies, supports, confronts, summarizes. |

(continued on next page)

Table 3 (Continued)

| | Psychodynamic | Behavioral | Guided Group Interaction |
|---|---|---|---|
| Role of client | Child seen in terms of inner conflicts, distorted or absent ego skills. | Child seen in terms of some dysfunctional behaviors and/or need to learn new behaviors. Self-reporting, self-reinforcement encouraged. | Adolescent confronted with responsibility for own behavior. Defenses challenged. Encouraged to seek and give help within group. |
| Intervention strategies | Activity, play, multiple interaction as basis for behavior change and/or working through conflicts. | Use of behavioral contracts; contingent reinforcement, with group taking large responsibility. Transfer to community group reinforcement emphasized. | Daily group sessions, highly structured. Peer group set up as reinforcer for prosocial values. Decisions forced back to group. |
| Strong points | Strong theory base. Focus on child as individual. Emphasis on interaction, educative power of group environment. | Nonillness model. Emphasis on specific behavioral objectives. Easily communicable method. Considers differential behavioral environments. | Emphasis on growth, self-help. Use of peer group as positive force. Redirection of delinquent social skills to positive goals. Relatively inexpensive. |
| Limitations | Expensive; serves limited population. Therapist training lengthy. View of family as pathogenic. | Difficult to apply to complex behavioral phenomena. Generalization of learning effects to natural environments limited. Role of group process unclear. | Overemphasis on personality of therapist rather than method. Limited to selected older adolescents. Weak theory base. "All-or-nothing" approach. |
| Empirical validation | Weak. Problems with validating key assumptions. Little strong evidence indicating effectiveness in producing behavior change. | Strong. Many studies show effectiveness in producing behavior change. Long-term generalization remains a problem. | Weak. Paucity of reported studies. Little strong evidence indicating effectiveness in producing behavior change. |

Note: For an elaboration of these concepts see Whittaker and Small (1977).

There has long been a recognition of the power of small-group intervention in residential treatment. In much of his pioneering work, Redl (1966; Redl and Wineman, 1957) developed the conceptual framework for understanding the group process in residential care. The analysis of such variables as "group emotion and leadership," "contagion," and "group composition" was central to this contribution. Morse and Small (1959) and Morse and Wineman (1957) extended Redl's concept of the "life-space interview" to a small-group context in a summer camp for delinquent youth. Konopka's (1954) classic volume delineated multiple uses for the small group in a child caring institution. Maier (1965) explored group work as a part of residential treatment. Other significant contributions were made by Schulze (1951), Mayer and Blum (1971, pp. 72-93), and Polsky and Claster (1968). In addition, each of the three major traditions in milieu treatment—psychodynamic, behavioral, and guided group interaction—contributed to our understanding of how to use the group as a vehicle for growth and change in a therapeutic milieu. Within this literature, the contributions of guided group interaction ("positive peer culture") contain the most prescriptive and detailed plan for group intervention (see, for example, Vorrath and Brendtro, 1974, especially pp. 85-116). Table 3 summarizes these diverse approaches to group treatment of children and adolescents.

Whatever particular theory informs group intervention, two key elements that need to be understood are *group composition* and *group development*. The subject of group composition has been addressed by Paradise (1968), Paradise and Daniels (1970), Shalinsky (1969), Bertcher and Maple (1974), Rose (1972, p. 21), Feldman and Wodarski (1975, pp. 72-75), and Redl (1966, pp. 236-253). In many smaller settings—for example, group homes—the composition of the group is predetermined by the population in residence. Thus, the leader may have few choices in this area—given the reality of a limited client pool. However, if group members are too dissimilar in age or developmental level or degree of disturbance, the choice of activities available to the group will be greatly narrowed. Similarly, on the question of size, anything much beyond six or eight members becomes something other than a small-group experience. One also should consider the adult participants. Some children's treatment groups wind up with an almost equal number of adult observers and coleaders, with the result that roles become confused or behavior gets out of hand. Coleaders can be effective, however, in programming for subgroups and in dealing with particular interpersonal issues, such as the child's manipulation of one parent against the other. In any case, children should be aware of who shall be in attendance at each session and what their role will be.

Of somewhat more practical value—to both the leader involved in a specific group intervention and the child care worker who "works with" the group in the life space—is an understanding of the ways in which small groups typically develop. While much has been written on the subject of group development, one model, in my judgment, is particularly relevant for understanding the group process in a group living environment and is rich in implications for child care practice. (For a fuller elaboration of models of group development, see Whittaker, 1970d; Sarri and Galinsky [in Glasser, Sarri, and Vinter, 1974, pp. 71-89; Feldman and Wodarski, 1975, pp. 13-38].) Garland, Jones, and Kolodny (1965) developed a five-stage model of development applicable to child treatment groups. Derived from an analysis of group-process records at a children's agency over a three-year period, the model is solid in its theoretical underpinnings, well articulated, and richly exampled with group-process materials. The five stages—preaffiliation, power and control, intimacy, differentiation, and separation—represent the kind of framework presently available to child care workers for understanding elements of the group process:

1. *Preaffiliation.* "Closeness" of the members is the central theme in this stage, with "approach-avoidance" as the major early struggle in relation to it. Ambivalence toward involvement is reflected in the members' vacillating responses to program activities and events. Relationships are usually non-intimate, and a good deal of use may be made of rather stereotyped activity as a means of getting acquainted.

2. *Power and control.* After deciding that the group is potentially rewarding, members move to a stage during which issues of power, control, status, skill, and decision making are the focal points. There is likely to be a testing of the group worker and the members, as well as an attempt to define and formalize relationships and to define a status hierarchy. Issues suggested by the power-struggle phenomena include rebellion/autonomy and protection/support.

3. *Intimacy.* At this stage personal involvement is intensified, group members are more willing to bring into the open their feelings about other members and the group leader, and there is a striving for satisfaction of dependency needs. Sibling-like rivalry tends to appear, as well as overt comparison of the group to family life. There is a growing ability to plan and carry out group projects and a growing awareness and mutual recognition of the significance of the group experience in terms of personality growth and change.

4. *Differentiation.* The members now begin to accept one another as distinct individuals and to see the social worker as a unique person and the group as providing a unique experience. Relationships and needs are more reality based, communication is good, and there is strong cohesion.

5. *Separation.* The group experience has been completed, and the members may begin to move apart and find new resources for meeting social, recreational, and vocational needs. The following reactions have been observed repeatedly in groups in the process of termination: denial, regression, recapitulation of past experiences, evaluation, flight, and pleas from the members that "We still need the group."

Garland, Jones, and Kolodny also have developed strategies for leader behavior—particularly activity programming appropriate to the various stages of development.

Use of knowledge from research in group development—or any other phase of group dynamics—is relative to the purpose of the group. In the context of the group living environment, small-group intervention may serve multiple purposes, including management of daily living, problem-oriented discussion, program activities, and transitions.

*The Daily Management Group.* Whatever their particular presenting problems, children in group care share one problem: they must learn to live, work, and play with one another and with the "other" group—the staff—in a complex, interdependent, planned living environment. Some of the problems they must learn to deal with are problems precisely *because* of the setting. Learning to coexist with a roommate, "share" a key adult with six other children, or take your turn on the dishwashing machine are not unique to group care settings but are typical of the kinds of situations with which a child in residence must learn to deal. They illustrate why the milieu can be a rich medium for learning through living.

The daily management group—as its name implies—meets briefly each day to work out the common concerns of staff and children around the major tasks and routines of the day. It provides *information* to children about changes in program and staffing, upcoming special events, requests from kitchen or maintenance staff, "special news" from children or staff and a variety of other things. It also serves as a vehicle for *scheduling* the various chores, program activities, community visits, and field trips that take place in a group care setting. In this context children learn to deal with each other around the things that simply have to get done in order to make the culture "work": washing the dishes, making the beds, settling problems of disputed ownership, and figuring out who needs a haircut this month. Much like a family meeting, the daily management group provides a focal point for all who live in the setting to plan together—to live together.

The management group also functions as a forum for *arbitrating* minor disputes, airing *griefs,* and sharing *positive feedback* with the people who make the milieu work. Accordingly, a session might include discussion with the cook about a change in menu, a message from maintenance staff about care of the bathrooms, or a group negotiation around later bedtimes in the summer. Though the results of the management group may be clearly therapeutic, it is not viewed as a treatment group per se. Its focus is on the tasks that need to get done in the cottage or group home and the normal stresses and strains that accompany any group living venture. The central message should be, "This is the way that people who live with each other come together to plan how to make it all work." Sessions can be brief, thirty-forty minutes, and slotted into a transition time; for instance, immediately following lunch or after school. Membership should include all children from a living unit, all child care staff present, and other supportive staff who may wish to attend and who have an item for the agenda. Given a certain level of maturity and group development, leadership may rotate among children or be handled by child care staff. (Phillips and associates, 1973b, made interesting use of an "elected manager" whose function extended beyond the actual group meeting.)

*The Problem-Oriented Discussion Group.* The members of a living group or a subgroup may come together to deal with a particular problem of one of the members or an issue that concerns the entire group. The problem might involve an ad hoc session around a crisis (such as a group runaway) or a regularly scheduled session around a long-standing concern (such as the group's scapegoating of a particular member). Problem-oriented discussion is designed to explore feelings, develop behavioral alternatives, and provide group support and encouragement as well as criticism. The following incident illustrates the type of problem handled in the problem-oriented group:

> Blackhawk Cottage—part of a larger residential center for adjudicated delinquents—scheduled a roller skating party with a girls' cottage from the same institution. Since the boys would be host for the activity, they met in their management group to plan the evening, including music, games, and refreshments. One of the members, Jerry, was considerably less mature and sophisticated than the rest of the group. He was more impulsive, gregarious, and at times provocative. During the planning session, a concern arose as to how Jerry would "come across" at the party—whether he would

"act funny" or dress properly. Several members
chorused that Jerry should stay back in the cottage, despite the entreaty from the group leader
that this was a total group activity. Jerry responded in two ways to this mounting criticism—
by acting humorously (playing the buffoon) and,
finally, with anger. Eventually he stormed angrily
from the room. The other members seemed to
greet his exit with a mixture of guilt ("We sure
took care of him") and relief ("Now let's get on
with the planning"). The group leader briefly
looked for Jerry to rejoin the group, but he had
gone to his room sobbing and refused to come out.
She returned to the group and, after expressing disappointment in the group's behavior, called an end
to the planning meeting and scheduled a special
group session to discuss the incident with Jerry
after supper.

Here the focus of the group clearly shifted from the task
of planning to some basic issues concerning the group's way of
handling one of its members. The staff member will seek Jerry
out and support his coming to the evening session to explore
the problem, which, in his case, is long standing. The focus of
the meeting will be on developing positive ways of providing
criticism—so that Jerry can get a handle on what he does that
upsets the group. Additionally, the group leader will explore
why these kinds of concerns—about dress, behavior, and appearances—occurred in the first place and how they might relate to
some larger concerns of the group, which they conveniently laid
on Jerry.

Leadership for this type of group always resides with the
staff member and requires a considerable knowledge of group
dynamics—as well as clinical skill. Groups may have coleaders—
for instance, a child care staff member and a social worker—or a
single leader.

The problem-oriented discussion group is the most "offi-
cially" treatment-like in its character. It should meet regularly,
at least weekly, and as special circumstances warrant. The cen-

tral rationale for this group is not simply that "things have to get done" but that each of the members shares a responsibility for helping the others deal with real-life problems. "Treatment," or help, comes not just from the clinical and child care staff but from the group itself. In some modalities (for example, positive peer culture), the problem-oriented group session, held daily, constitutes the major treatment intervention. However often it meets, this type of group should be somewhat more private than the management group. Staff should sit in only at the pleasure of the leader—in consultation with the total group.

One important function of the problem-oriented group is to provide positive feedback to individual members on progress made toward change goals. The living group is a support group—perhaps the most important resource available to the child or adolescent—and should be used as such. For instance, the leader might elicit positive feedback about some area of functioning prior to criticism. He or she may also model the desired behavior by praising individual members and the group as a whole for hard work on difficult problems and by offering support and encouragement to members who are facing particularly difficult life situations—for example, dealing with the fact that they will not be returning to their natural families but to a foster home.

*Activity Groups.** The rationale for the use of activities in a group living environment has been covered in the preceding section of this chapter. The planned use of activities in a small-group context constitutes a powerful tool for teaching basic physical and social skills. While simple games and activities may be used to achieve basic purposes in any of the four types of groups, here they are a central focus and constitute the primary teaching medium. They afford an opportunity for programming for subgroups of children with special needs. Such groups often take the form of special-interest clubs that meet on a weekly basis. For example, a cluster of three or four lower-status group members may meet with a leader weekly for an off-campus

---

*I am specifically not referring here to the method of group treatment—activity group therapy—developed by Slavson (Slavson and Schiffer, 1975).

activity: bowling, roller skating, beachcombing. The focus is simply on facilitating friendships, providing some protected time with a special adult, and having a good time. Other groups, mentioned earlier, may focus more on skill acquisition in a particular area: photography, guitar playing, or citizens' band radio. The focus here is on broadening interests and developing marketable peer skills. Membership may be self-selected, or a staff member may invite a small group to form a special club. Leaders may be drawn from child care and other professional staff. This type of activity group also allows staff members to share their particular skills and interests in a less pressured context. In an environment where discussion of problems is quite properly the order of the day and where individual needs must often be subjugated to the desires of the total living group, the activity-focused club provides a break from the major routines of the day and the opportunity for a close relationship with a smaller, more select group of peers and a helping adult.

*Transition Groups.* Small groups also may be used as a bridge to the child's home community. The passage from residence to community is often troublesome. The child must get used to a new set of routines, make new friends, master a new school environment—and, sometimes, a new family. One way to aid in this transition is to compose a group expressly for the purpose of preparation for community life. Membership could include one or more individuals who are scheduled to leave the residence at approximately the same time and, perhaps, program graduates who have successfully mastered the community environment. Or a group may be composed of several neighborhood peers and a youngster who is getting ready to leave the residence. Here the focus is on activities that provide an opportunity to learn about community resources: playgrounds, recreation facilities, libraries, and the like. Such groups sometimes can be facilitated through local youth-serving organizations—boys' clubs, YWCAs, girls' clubs—with the child care worker or social worker providing group leadership.

The transition group provides a context for discussion of feelings about leaving and recapitulation of important experiences. For older adolescents, the group's focus might be on emancipation—with the small group providing continuing support to members who for the first time are living on their own. Such groups may begin in the agency and continue to meet in the community long after the young persons have left the residence. Crucial to such groups is the inclusion of some positive role models—in this case, graduates who have made it on their own and are successfully living independently. With so much attention given to the child-in-residence, transition to community living remains one of the more neglected areas in the field of group child care.

## Other Formats for Helping

The incentive system, program activities, and group intervention are not the only tools available in a group life culture—though they are the most important ones. Other useful strategies include the life-space interview (Redl, 1966), various behavior management schemes (Redl and Wineman, 1957; Patterson and others, 1975), and the therapeutic use of routines (Trieschman, Whittaker, and Brendtro, 1969; Beker, 1972; Foster and others, 1972; Redl, 1966). Most of these strategies may be used in the context of the three major systems. For example, the incentive system provides a useful framework for organizing the tasks involved in the major routines of wake-ups, mealtimes, and bedtimes. The life-space interview may be used in a group context, in an activity, or in negotiating with an individual child about his or her daily point total.

Some practitioners conceive of social skills as a separate component of the group life program, rather than a set of techniques subsumed under one of the other teaching formats. However they occur, the teaching of basic social skills is an important part of the total group life program. Typically, children are taught to handle aggressive behavior in others, deal with frustrating or provocative situations, and get along with others in a work situation. Werder, Stenson, and Carlson (1976) have devised a "survival skills" program for adolescents in a delinquency institution; the program provides behaviorally-specific training materials on communication, assertiveness training, and school problems. Other important contributions have been made by Wolf, Phillips, and Fixsen (1974, pp. 678-725). A promising development in social skills teaching involves the use of cognitive restructuring, as well as the traditional techniques of behavioral rehearsal, modeling, and instructions.

One format for helping, which does not "fit into" the three major systems, is psychotherapy. Whittaker and Trieschman (1972) have provided an orientation to the uses of psychotherapy in a therapeutic milieu. Despite the previously identified problems with incorporating psychotherapy into a group life culture (see Chapter Two), this particular format for teaching is still appropriate with certain youngsters—particularly those whose learning profile reflects a predisposition toward insight. Two things are critical. First, the milieu cannot be organized around the psychotherapeutic relationship. Psychotherapy should be seen as an important intervention but one that is clearly *supportive* to the basic teaching core of the program. Second, the therapist should be an integral part of team decision making about the child's overall case plans. The dangers of working at cross purposes are great. My hope for the future is that we can get away from the ideological debate that has surrounded the uses and abuses of psychotherapy in a therapeutic milieu and get down to the basic contributions of insight learning to the child's total education for living. In this respect, the recent work in cognition and behavior modification, reported by Mahoney (1974) and Meichenbaum (1977), shows much promise.

Finally, the group life environment does not exist as a closed system, separate and apart from the other major spheres that affect it—notably, the school, the family, and the community. The building of linkages to the "real world" is crucial. The group life environment must be seen not as an island unto itself but as a functioning part of a larger community environment.

# 5

---

# Developing
# Community
# Linkages

The need for a close relationship between agency and community is underscored by data presently available from a variety of sources. For example, the landmark study on the effectiveness of residential treatment by Allerhand, Weber, and Haug (1966) suggests that, except for those children at both extremes of the continuum (those so resilient that they can overcome the effects of a less than desirable postinstitutional placement and those so disturbed as to mitigate the effects of even the most positive environment), the greatest determinant of successful community adjustment will lie in the postplacement experience. Other studies of residential care appear to confirm the critical nature of the community experience in determining success (Cavior, Schmidt, and Karacki, 1972). Interestingly, Wolins' (1974) study of group child care facilities in four countries strongly suggests that social integration within the larger community is positively correlated with success. Support for the notion of building strong ties between communities and group care programs also comes from the recently completed national study of group care conducted by the Child Welfare League of America, which places considerable emphasis on the development of a linkage system (Mayer, Richman, and Balcerzak, 1977, pp. 155-192). The work of Garbarino (1977a, 1977b) suggests that many of the families of troubled children are isolated from potent support systems and require a fair amount of advocacy in mustering needed community services. This would be particularly true of a family attempting to reintegrate a child recently returned from residential care. There is a small but growing literature on building community support systems for troubled children. Apter (1977) describes a multidisciplinary program involving problem-oriented summer camping and follow-up community advocacy for behaviorally disordered children. Dokecki and Hutton (1977) describe the "liaison specialist" role—an outgrowth of the liaison teacher role developed in the Re-Ed Project (discussed in Chapter Three). Gatti and Colman (1976) describe "community network therapy" with families of troubled children, and Collins and Pancoast (1976) present a strategy for identifying and utilizing "natural helping networks."

Another major reason for building community linkages is organizational survival. Quite apart from the kinds of community support needed to increase the likelihood of success with any particular child, group care agencies themselves require a certain amount of what Wolf (1976) has called "social validity" or Bronfenbrenner (1977), in a larger sense, refers to as "ecological validity." As group child care programs move toward a community orientation—group homes, day treatment, community outreach—their need for community integration increases. The whole thrust toward the "normalization" of children's services—including the provision in many special education statutes (and sure to extend to other areas of services as well) that service must be offered in "the least restrictive environment"—means that child caring programs will have to have much more involvement with the communities that support them (Wolfensberger, 1972).

For structural and historical reasons, the need for community linkages presents a formidable challenge to the group care agency. As mentioned earlier, funding tends to follow children in full-time care; day treatment, aftercare, and community work with families enjoy considerably less support. Such policies can have the effect of maintaining children in residence longer than they need be, simply because that is the only way to maintain a level of funding adequate to provide services to children and families. More fundamentally, child caring institutions have, by design, been separate from their host communities—an arrangement which served both the need for isolation from presumed pathogenic community influences and also provided a measure of obscurity from community vision: out of sight, out of mind. One commentator described the problem as follows: "The institution is threatened by its tradition of isolation. It may tend to remain, as it has so often been in the past, a collection of social outcasts, juvenile and adult, who for reasons of their own or of others have been brought together to live under highly artificial conditions euphemistically described as "family life" (Coleman, 1940, p. 8).

Clearly, in nearly forty years things have changed. Residential treatment centers are more closely related to their host communities than previously. Also, the traditional notions of what constitutes a family have broadened to include other than two-parent, intact units, making it easier for group care settings to justify themselves as child rearing environments. It is well to remember, however, that, in building bridges between the group care program and its surrounding environment, one is going against what for a great many years was a mutually beneficial arrangement. Left alone, child caring institutions could develop their own culture of treatment designed to insulate the child from the influences of the community. All needs could be met in the milieu, making for ease of institutional operation. At discharge, the hope was that the child had been properly strengthened and immunized sufficiently to survive the environment to which he or she was to return. At the same time, the community could point with pride to its clearly segregated and encapsulated institutions, which stood as irrefutable evidence that something was being done about the problem of troubled and troublesome children. Whatever the logical and obvious flaws in such arrangements—and they are numerous—one can scarcely overestimate the degree of emotional commitment on the part of both institution and community in maintaining things as they were. The task, therefore, of building community linkages and community support may well be the most difficult task of all.

### Community Resistance to Group Child Care Programs

Coates and Miller (1973) outline some of the problems encountered in developing community-based group homes for delinquent youth. Many of these problems plague existing residential treatment programs as well. While certain of these problems are idiosyncratic and neighborhood specific, there do appear to be some common themes in the community resistances to group child care programs. Following are some of the major difficulties described by the authors, as well as others that I have found in the field.

Many communities attack the basic assumption of localized treatment by simply stating that the problem of delinquency, or emotional disturbance, or drug use does not exist in their locality. Therefore, the argument goes, why should they have to provide treatment space for those "other" children. In addition, many community residents fear the problems that will arise from having delinquent, disturbed, or mentally retarded children in their midst—problems such as physical violence, petty theft, vandalism, and sexual molestation. Somewhat similarly, many community residents are swayed by the argument that the development of a group care facility with its negative image will lead, inevitably, to a decline in property values. Fears of increased traffic, parking problems, and uncared-for grounds tend to bolster this conviction. Many neighborhoods also react negatively to what they feel will be the intrusion of structures that are out of proportion to the residential environment. With new construction or remodeling of existing facilities, compliance with multiple licensing regulations often raises costs to a point where the group care facility appears larger on paper than in reality.

Furthermore, since many community-based group child care programs—particularly those newly incorporated—lack community recognition and acceptance, the new program is often labeled as the work of "outsiders." Local community sponsorship, when well thought through, is a decided asset. Too often, however, local institutions (churches, for example) pledge community sponsorship but really have no clear-cut responsibility for the program other than provision of space. In such cases, the sponsor is tagged as simply a "front" for the outside agency.

Coates and Miller (1973) found also that successful community-based programs use simple, clear, and straightforward language to describe their mission. Vague and difficult-to-define terms like "halfway house" or "therapeutic milieu" may stand in the way of community understanding and support. The use of provocative acronyms such as BURN, SCARE, SMACK also serve to stir up community concern (Coates and Miller, 1973, p. 79). Other symbols that may cause problems include staff and resident dress and use of language. Hardly reassuring also is the fact that many staff members are young and inexperienced; may come from areas other than where the facility will be located; and appear not terribly different from the residents they will supervise, so that they seem unlikely to exert authority.

In sum, the group care program faces a number of formidable obstacles, both in facilitating community ties for its graduates and achieving its own legitimacy and integration in the community of which it is a part. These two objectives—successful integration of graduates and organizational integration—suggest a certain overlapping of tasks and are mutually reinforcing: when a group child care program is linked with its constituent communities, its graduates will be more readily integrated into the community; when the treatment of an individual child is socially validated by parents, neighbors, schools, and other referring agencies, the agency will be more readily accepted and integrated into the larger community.

As with designing the internal program, the pattern for

establishing external linkages must fit the particular community and group child care program it is intended to serve. To extend Bronfenbrenner's (1977, p. 516) recent definition of "ecological validity" from research to the realm of services, a group care program is ecologically valid when its various strategies of intervention actually fit the environments toward which they are directed.

## Group Care in Context: Toward Community Integration

Figure 1 (in Chapter One) illustrates some of the major systems that influence the group care program and are, in turn, influenced by it. Each provides an opportunity for a program linkage; taken together, they constitute a bridge between agency and community. Such a bridge should be large enough to accommodate two-way traffic: new ideas coming into the program and new graduates seeking to find their place in the larger community.

*Family.* The child's family—natural or foster—constitutes the single most important influence on postresidential adjustment. The degree of agency investment in the development of family linkages should reflect this fact. No other system has as great a potential payoff or as diffuse a relationship with the child in care. Because of the critical nature of the family relationship, Chapter Six will focus exclusively on the problem of developing linkages between the family and the group child care program.

*School.* With the exception of the family, the school represents the most powerful institution with which the returning child will have to deal. In addition to problems of formal learning, the child and his or her family have to learn how to negotiate the complex organization of the school; develop a variety of relationships with teachers, counselors, and other helping persons; and make the system work for them. As with the family, the school provides opportunities for a variety of linkages with the group living environment. For instance, child care workers can participate in the classroom, consult with teachers, form transition groups oriented to school-related problems, and

engage in educational advocacy. Again, because of the importance of the topic, I have devoted an entire chapter to the relationship between the school and the group living environment.
Chapter Seven will deal with the question of helping staff and
parents develop an understanding of the special mission of the
school program—whether it exists on campus or in the community—and its relationship to the child's total treatment program.

*Peer Groups.* The peer group provides a major socialization experience for the child. For the adolescent, it becomes the
primary source of support and social validation. Influencing the
peer group to which the child or youth will return constitutes
an important task in community reintegration. The kind of
transitional group described in Chapter Four can facilitate this
reintegration by gradually exposing the child to the environment to which he or she will return and also by directly influencing the character of the neighborhood peer group. Feldman
and his associates (1972), used traditional community agencies
as a setting for developing recreation groups composed mostly
of "normal" peers and a few antisocial children. This creative
and innovative project enjoyed widespread community support;
the children were "mainstreamed" with few difficulties. Such a
project has obvious implications for the child returning from
residential care. Vorrath and Brendtro (1974, p. 149) describe
an aftercare project in which former students from a "positive
peer culture" program, working under trained group leadership,
help youths returning from residential placement to achieve a
successful reintegration into their home community. Other possibilities for peer linkages include identifying afterschool activity groups, church groups, and community center groups where
the child can continue to pursue activities enjoyed in the residential center. In addition to formal group treatment, one residential center provides a variety of short-term, skill-focused
activity clubs from which the children are free to choose. Such
groups provide valuable learning opportunities for the child in
need of some marketable peer skills, as well as an opportunity
for staff to pursue particular recreational interests. Such group
experiences often help the child define interests and make a better adjustment to the postresidential environment.

*Juvenile Justice System.* Rosenheim (1976) suggests that the police be involved at some level of policymaking for group care, since they presently provide an enormous transportation service to juveniles—though one may disagree with where they are taken or how they get there! The point is that many outside of the human services mainstream have a powerful effect on what happens to children returning from group care arrangements. Notable for its influence is the whole of the juvenile justice system—police, courts, juvenile judges, public defenders—which has a great deal to do with where children and youth end up in the continuum of group care services, how long they stay there, and what happens to them when they leave. A community group home for delinquent youth may often be the first place visited by police when there are acts of theft or vandalism in their neighborhood because that is where the known delinquents reside—an example of why residential centers need to be in touch with the juvenile justice system before problems occur. For programs serving younger and more disturbed children, police may often be involved in dealing with runaways (or walkaways) from the program. To lay the groundwork for such circumstances before the crisis occurs, staff and police might meet to discuss the goals of the program and to establish lines of communication and procedures for emergencies. In a similar vein, it is to the benefit of the group child care agency if juvenile court judges, public defenders, and court staff know intimately the character of the program, the type of youngster it is designed to serve, and its limitations. Such sharing of information can make for more informal placement decisions. Some possible linkages include development of a court liaison relationship, shared consultation and training with court staff, informational sessions with juvenile court judges and law enforcement agencies, short-term staff exchanges between the group care program and juvenile court, and the use of shared volunteers. One program that uses volunteers creatively in the case-planning process is the guardian ad litem project of the Seattle-King County Juvenile Court in Seattle, Washington. Here, volunteers take on major responsibilities for assessing all of the community supports available to a child and his family and for making appropriate recommendations to the juvenile judge.

*Recreation System.* Traditional agencies such as YMCAs, YWCAs, boys' clubs and girls' clubs, scouting programs, and community centers provide a rich opportunity for resocialization of the newly returned resident from the group care program. They contain a variety of prosocial role models, and they provide a normalizing experience in a nonstigmatizing environment. Feldman and associates (1972) have demonstrated that antisocial children can be blended into traditional youth-serving recreational agencies. Such resources are particularly important for the child whose home situation is somewhat shaky but who can survive if programmed out of the home for most of the after-school hours.

*Other Systems.* Other particularly helpful community systems include churches, the business community, and local public service associations, all of which can supplement the contributions to aftercare made by public social and health services. Collins and Pancoast (1976) suggest the importance of identifying natural helping networks in the child's neighborhood, or of creating support systems using indigenous community residents. The projects they describe which appear to have considerable relevance for group child caring programs include peer counseling, use of the elderly in working with children, and use of "natural neighbors."

## Unresolved Problems

Arguing for the development of community linkages is like arguing for "improving mental health": it is a difficult goal to fault, but no one is quite sure what it actually means, much less how to achieve it. For group child caring programs, the problems are considerable.

*The Problem of Scope.* The arguments for the development of community linkages expose the inadequacies of the present service system. We do not presently have an integrated continuum of family and children's services—much less an adequate family incomes policy to support it. The group care program is therefore presented with a dilemma. It can carefully shepherd resources in order to do the best possible job with children while they are in care—at the possible expense of aftercare and community liaison. Or it can disperse resources throughout a larger area for the purpose of ensuring community reintegration at the possible expense of a sophisticated group life program. If it chooses to emphasize community integration, it may be unable to handle the most difficult, acting-out child because of a shortage of residential staff. If it chooses the more limited scope, it might be unable to maintain such a child in the community—for want of aftercare staff—once he has been helped in the group life program.

No one is more aware of the consequences of either choice than the executives and boards of directors of voluntary child caring agencies, who are ultimately charged with the responsibility for fiscal stewardship and program accountability. I am convinced that much of what gets dismissed as professional conservatism and resistance to change on the part of group care executives and boards is, in fact, a desire to conserve scarce financial and human resources and a fear of overextension into program areas that have little hope of garnering continued support. There is clearly a need for a clear statement about what can and cannot be reasonably expected from each program— types of children served, length of stay, and adequacy of community follow up.

*The Problem of Incomplete Theory.* If the theory behind constructing a therapeutic milieu is in its early adolescence, the theory of developing community linkages has just been born. To be sure, all the work mentioned earlier is promising, and countless other examples of creative linkage systems exist in child caring programs throughout the country. But we still have not developed precise methods for assessing communities, identifying natural helping networks, or selecting appropriate linkage mechanisms. The empirical and theoretical contributions toward understanding the total ecology of communities contained in the work of Bronfenbrenner (1977) and Garbarino (1977a, 1977b) and the model developed by Litwak and Meyer (1974) for linking public school and local community point the

3

direction for future work. But the most promising experiments
of all are undoubtedly being carried out by pioneering group
care programs that are resolving by trial and error the question
of what constitutes an effective linkage system. Such efforts
need to be collated and "mined" for testable hypotheses concerning the development of ties between the group child care
program and the various systems that support it.

   *The Problem of Duration.* Just as the breadth of service
presents dilemmas to the group child care program, so does the
length of service. When is a child's case "closed"? What is a
reasonable period for community follow-up? What can be done
about the child who achieves a certain plateau in adjustment
and then has a recurrence of troubled behavior? Such questions
do not yield easy answers and are especially difficult to resolve
when needed services are a scarce commodity. Legitimate pressures for specialization by age and type of disorder may weigh
against reinitiating service for the child who has graduated. Yet
the fact remains that no single agency knows the child and his
family as well as the residential program that cared for him on a
daily basis over an extended period of time. Similarly, does the
residential program have any continued role to play as a kind of
"parental force" long after the child has left the program? While
such a role might well be in the child's best interests because it
would provide continuity of care, in many programs such community involvement might mean a diminution of service to the
children presently in care.

   *The Problem of Staff Allocation.* Where within the staff
should the responsibility for building community linkages lie?
At the level of the individual child, there is merit in the appointment of a "liaison specialist" to help muster community services and act as an advocate on the child's behalf. But the staff
who know the child's needs most intimately—and are able to
communicate them to others—are those who work directly in
the group life culture. There is also the question of whether
family work and community liaison should be handled by the
same person. For the smaller agency not given the luxury of
highly specialized staff roles, the problem is in determining with
whom the responsibility for community work lies—social

workers, child care staff, community volunteers—and how much time should be allocated to it. The executive in most agencies performs the outside role of raising money, establishing ties with appropriate government funding agencies, and generally selling the program. The difficulty is determining what is a reasonable balance of inside and outside activities, as well as how other resources—for example, the time of board members—can be effectively used in building community linkages.

*The Problem of Professional Boundaries.* Even if sufficient resources were instantly available to fund a group child care program for establishing community linkages, considerable problems of implementation would remain unsolved. Disputes over agency "turf" or the proper role and function of various professional groups constitute a formidable obstacle to the development of effective community ties. The resistance to the Re-Ed program, which offered a new model of service delivery, separate from traditional child mental health services, illustrates the kinds of problems attendant on redistricting professional boundaries. Even within programs, a juggling of roles—as in family work or community outreach, for example—can occasion considerable dissension and resistance. Tradition dies hard, and it is simply good judgment—before initiating any new program—to assess who in the professional community is likely to be threatened by it, or obstruct it, and how their resistance can be effectively neutralized.

A final point concerns coordination of services. Despite the fact that service coordination is logical and economical, in the absence of an overall service structure there really are few incentives for the various agencies to become involved. Thus, the group care agency attempting to coordinate a community follow-through program for a particular child may well find schools and other agencies less than eager to cooperate. They may, for example, see only the added work that comes from individualizing the child and providing staff time for coordination. While its resources are clearly limited, the group care program should think in terms of a quid pro quo to increase the likelihood of commitment. For example, free consultation to classroom teachers around problems of behavior management,

free use of campus facilities to community groups, and participation on governing and professional advisory boards are all
ways of providing incentives to community agencies to work together with the group child care program.

## Conclusion

Successful child helping does not end at the point of
graduation from the residential program. No matter how powerful the culture of group living, it cannot overcome the effects of
a harmful community environment. A child's later experiences
in school, family, and neighborhood will largely determine
whether gains achieved in the group life program are maintained. For this reason alone, the group care program needs to
link itself with those powerful community institutions that will
have an impact on the returning child: family, peer group,
school, and others. On another level, the group care program
needs a certain social validation from key community agencies,
parents, and citizens if it is to survive and be effective.

If the argument for ecologically sound child treatment is
compelling, then the models for how to achieve it are few in
number and incomplete. Boards and executives must decide
where to allocate scarce resources, and a more rigorous community follow-up will inevitably lead to arguments over agency
boundaries and professional roles. Such difficulties are well
worth the effort, however, if they serve the basic purpose of
bringing the group care agency into the community—and the
community into the agency.

# 6

## Parents as Partners in Helping

"Success" in treatment depends substantially on our ability to involve parents or parenting persons as full and equal partners in the helping process. What, then, accounts for the failure of group child care settings to develop dynamic and effective methods of working with parents and other caring persons? That such a gap in services exists is evidenced by the relative lack of literature on family participation in residential care. (For a sampling of the literature that does exist, see Koret, 1973; Finkelstein, 1974; Magnus, 1974; Dimock, 1977.) The recently published Child Welfare League of America report on group care (Mayer, Richman, and Balcerzak, 1977, pp. 114-123) cites several promising prototypes for family participation in residential treatment, but, in general, family work remains—like the school program—an underdeveloped area.

## Family Involvement in Residential Care: Some Problems

*Economic Disincentives.* The cost of family work, particularly aftercare, often must be borne by the residential center. Many agencies are thus prevented from providing the kind of family outreach work—including work with siblings and neighborhood peers—that they would like to.

*Geographical Isolation.* Since many centers draw on a far-reaching catchment area, some extending across state lines, families are often inaccessible for regular involvement. A related difficulty is that many of the large institutional settings are located in rural areas at considerable distance from their clients' communities and often without public transportation.

*Sociocultural Differences.* In his study of adolescent delinquents in a large institution, Polsky (1962) notes some of the problems that occur when the goals, cultural values, social class, and life experiences of the therapist are not shared by the client population. Such a lack of correspondence may extend to other areas as well—ethnic and minority heritage, for example—and may act as a barrier to full family participation.

*Limited Definition of Parental Involvement.* Many programs offer parents a single role—that of client or patient—if they are to be involved in the process of their child's treatment. Such a conception is based on the belief that the parents themselves are troubled, disorganized, and in need of treatment—all of which may be true. In fact, recent studies (Bernstein, Snider, and Meezan, 1975; Fanshel, 1976; Fanshel and Shinn, 1977) indicate that a high percentage of children entering placement do so primarily because of parent-related difficulties. But even if one accepts the "family etiology hypothesis," programs that offer parents only a single vehicle for involvement (clinical treatment) may overlook the numerous other possibilities for growth and change available to them—for example, parent education and family support groups. Furthermore, even the most troubled families are not incapacitated all the time and may, on occasion, participate in other aspects of the program as volunteer parent supporters. In short, parents may require extensive professional help in individual or conjoint treatment; but they also may be quite able and willing to help the program—in spite of their difficulties.

*Guilt over Causation.* Many parents feel that they alone are responsible for their child's difficulties and may be reluctant to enter into a relationship with a professional for fear of being judged or criticized. In some ways, as Schopler (1971) has suggested, parents of troubled children have become "scapegoats"—perhaps because the specific factors that cause a particular child to have problems are still largely unknown.

*Fear of Failure.* In most instances, the parents have tried to alter their child's troublesome behavior and have failed. Their feelings of helplessness and frustration are often rekindled as they view their potential involvement in a helping relationship— particularly if they are required to be the teachers, therapists, or mediators of reinforcement for their own child. In such cases, we may be asking parents who already feel overburdened and defeated to take on yet another responsibility for their child's care—with no meaningful adjustments in other parts of their lives. A related problem concerns the parents who have made an accommodation to their child's bizarre, disruptive, or withdrawing behavior and—despite their realization of the necessity of change—may be reluctant to alter old coping patterns.

*Overwhelming Life Circumstances.* Many families of children entering group care are beset by a host of problems: family disorganization, absence of a parent, inadequate finances, poor health, legal difficulties. Such multiproblem constellations affect families across class and socioeconomic lines, but the poor have fewer resources available for adequate coping. No amount of skilled treatment can make up for an absence of the basics: adequate income, health care, decent housing, and education. Thus, the residential center must adopt new formats for family helping, including social brokerage and advocacy.

## Formats for Parental Involvement

*Parent Support Groups.* The greatest single support for the parents of a handicapped child often comes from other parents who share a common experience. No amount of professional education or clinical training can provide the kind of insight and empathy that comes from having a troubled child of one's own. The collected wisdom of parents who have "been through it" represents a most important source of practical knowledge for other parents as well as for professional staff. One useful way of sharing this knowledge is through a parent support group—the purpose of which is to provide a relaxed atmosphere in which parents can get to know one another, share experiences, and receive support and encouragement. While professional staff can act as facilitators for such a group, it is the parents themselves who set the tone and agree on the topic for discussion. Since a relaxed atmosphere is helpful, each session should include time for informal socialization and refreshments. One useful technique for initiating such a group is to have each parent tell the story of their child's difficulty, how they have managed to cope with it, and what changes it has made in family life. Since many parents will initially feel reluctant to share experiences, for fear of being blamed or judged, the leader can model encouraging behavior by positively reinforcing the parents for telling their own story. Informal social ties and communication links may be encouraged, helping to overcome the isolation that many families of troubled children experience (Garbarino, 1977a, 1977b). For the parent who feels frustrated in the middle of a weekend visit, or angry after a school conference, the chance to talk with another parent on the telephone may be more beneficial than a formal session with a professional. Parents can begin to form a supportive network, which they can monitor and activate and which draws on their own resources.

While support groups have not been common among parents of delinquent or behaviorally disordered children, they have, particularly in recent years, been quite visible in organizations among parents of mentally retarded, physically handicapped, and autistic children. Their growth among parents who have abused or neglected their children (Parents Anonymous, for example) suggests that even where there is the greatest societal assumption of parental culpability, parents can come forward and provide a powerful mutual support system for one another. This augurs well for the development of support groups for parents of delinquent and behaviorally disordered children.

In residential treatment, where parent involvement—to the extent that it exists at all—has consisted mainly of work with individual families, there is a clear and pressing need to find ways for families to come together and support one another. The residential center can provide valuable expertise in staff leadership—at least initially—as well as a place to meet and possibly other resources as well, such as child care for siblings during group meetings. It can also encourage the notion that parents, as consumers, have an active role to play in the program and a need to know one another in order to recognize common concerns. Such support groups may eventually form the nucleus of a parent organization with more diverse goals and a wider-reaching involvement in the program. Initially, however, the focus should be on the provision of support through shared experiences, the development of informal helping networks, and the opportunity for socialization. Perhaps the most important message that can be conveyed—particularly to parents whose child is new to care—is that someone else besides themselves and the professional staff knows about their child, cares about his or her progress, and shares an intimate understanding of what it is like to live with and care for a troubled child.

*Parent Education: Content and Context.* Parent education should not only be harmonious with ethnic, class, and neighborhood values but should fit with the particular family's culture. Parents need techniques that work in the environments they inhabit—not in the rarified atmosphere of the therapeutic milieu. Thus, wherever parent education occurs, its ultimate test should be in the home or foster home to which the child will return. Any failures experienced should be seen as failures of the educators to come up with techniques that work in the real-life environment of the home and neighborhood, rather than as failures of the parent in applying them.

Parents and foster parents need to feel that they can actively and enthusiastically support the strategies of child rearing being taught and the choice of problem behaviors to which they are directed. Therefore, the professional should seek those areas of child management that are giving the parents the most pain and strain and help to devise strategies to alleviate them. Furthermore, parents and child should be afforded regular channels for feedback not only on *what* is being taught but on *how* it is coming across.

Many approaches to child management present a whole series of tasks to parents, with little apparent sensitivity to the fact that they have often experienced frustration and failure in parenting or that they have special needs of their own. Such individuals will not automatically become successful parents by reading and following programmed texts in behavioral methods or "cookbooks" on child management; they will benefit only if a careful assessment of total parent-child needs is made and strategies of helping carefully introduced. Parents need strong reinforcement for the job they have done, as well as for the new tasks they will assume. There is no communication more meaningful to the parents of a handicapped or troubled child than that from the professional which says, in effect, "We are in this together. Although I can never really know what it is like to be a parent of a child with problems, I care about you and your child and am going to stick with you and see what can be done." The notion that someone else—separate from family —knows intimately and cares about their child may constitute the most potent incentive of all for parents fearful of giving up old and dysfunctional—but comfortable—methods of child rearing and trying out new ones.

Approaches to parent education are many and varied. Some focus on developing effective communication, while others teach specific behavioral techniques to handle problems in daily living. Parent education programs also make use of a variety of educational methods, including small-group discussion, short courses, in vivo training, role playing and modeling, and programmed self-instruction. Though the various approaches differ considerably, most develop the notion of parents as teachers as well as learners and encourage sharing of information and knowledge. Discussion may focus on such topics as active listening, effective communication, monitoring and managing disruptive behavior, play and activities, sexual awareness, sibling rivalry, and the development of responsibility and discipline.

While no attempt will be made here to summarize the various approaches, the following are representative. Ginott (1965) and Gordon (1971) emphasize the development of effective communication and are eclectic in orientation. Dreikurs (1964), Dinkmeyer and McKay (1973), and Dreikurs and Grey (1968) develop the principles of Adlerian psychology with respect to parent education. There is also a growing literature on behavior modification for parents, including Patterson and Gullion (1968), Patterson (1971), and Becker (1971). In addition, separate curricula have been developed for foster parents, parents of handicapped children, and single parents. Most of the books and programmed texts are designed to be self-contained, but many practitioners prefer to draw teaching materials from a variety of sources to fit the particular values and life-styles of the parents they are serving. As in all other areas of group child care, professionals should try to develop or modify the teaching materials and not rely simply on prepackaged curricula. In this regard, the group life environment itself provides perhaps the most potentially valuable source of information for parents of children in care. Few other settings afford such a real-life view of the child grappling with the major routines of daily living: wake-ups, mealtimes, bedtimes, schooltimes, chores, games, and activities. The specific insights gained by child care workers and other professional staff constitute just the kind of targeted information that is most useful to parents.

Equally important as the content of parent education is the context in which it occurs. In fact, these two variables are interactive: the closer the teaching environment approximates the child's natural life milieu, the more likely the focus will be on the kinds of problems that are most stressful to parents, teachers, and other care givers. Costurn (1978) has developed a "bug in the ear" program in a child care center where parents, while working with their children on a specific task, receive prompts from a professional through a small "hearing aid" device. This procedure allows for immediate feedback to the parent in a real-life encounter. Home visiting by child care and other professional staff is another strategy employed by many group child care programs to bridge the gap between residence and home. Some agencies have even experimented with having staff live with families for brief periods of time in order to provide on-the-spot feedback and encouragement in trying out new parenting skills.

The residential setting has a unique role to fill in providing parent education to the community at large. Information garnered from a specially designed total living environment with the most troubled and troublesome children has much to offer parents, foster parents, day care providers, teachers, and other community care givers. Such services, whether they take the form of parent education classes or consultation sessions, help to change the image of the residential center away from that of a highly specialized setting, providing services only to a small and select number of children, to an agency that has a valuable service to provide to the community. One latent function of offering such community-based parent education is to "normalize" the image of the services provided: a parent is not necessarily "sick" or "crazy" just because he needs help with the difficult task of child rearing. Over time, such a broadened concept of what the residential center has to offer and to whom it can be of help will lessen the stigma of placement and make easier the task of community reintegration.

*Parent Involvement in the Life Space.* For many child care staff, visiting day has traditionally been a difficult day to work. There are the predictable upsets revolving around the parent who couldn't come or the pain of the family's rejoining briefly and then separating again. Equally troublesome are the tasks of managing siblings, talking with parents, intercepting contraband items, and helping families find a quiet place to come together. Whatever the rationale for family visiting, the staff—and often the children—may feel that their life space has been invaded and that they are on display. Even though there are numerous problems to work through, everyone is usually relieved when the last family leaves the residence. For parents, too, the situation is often awkward, since they remember past inadequacies and are afraid of being judged or observed. There is also a role ambiguity about who is in charge during the visit—the parents or the staff. In short, there is a certain artificiality about visiting day, as two different sets of parenting persons—child care staff and parents—come together briefly, perhaps with a social work intermediary, with the goal of catching up on the child's progress and the family's recent history. Because visiting day has become so ritualized, many programs are experimenting with more frequent home visiting, or five-day-per-week programming.

A larger issue, however, concerns the role that parents should play in the life space. As noted in an earlier chapter, some have argued for the benefits of more and not less separation from family; in fact, the traditional rationale for residential treatment centered on the need for a temporary separation. There are other barriers as well. Many centers which would welcome fuller parent involvement find that they cannot achieve it because of uncooperative parents or parents who are so caught up in their own life problems that they do not have time or energy left over for outside involvements. Many families live at great distances from the residential center, making frequent visits a hardship, and many programs lack the space and staff time to permit anything but the occasional parent visit. Finally, some professionals are not used to meeting with parents in other than structured family sessions held in the therapist's office.

The rationale for involving parents more fully in the life space is twofold. First, since families that produce troubled children appear to be socially isolated from key support systems (Garbarino, 1977a, 1977b), they are acutely in need of a family support system. Second, there is no better classroom for learning the skills of parenting than the culture of group living. Parents are presented with hundreds of situations in which caring and competent adults are managing the behavior of their child and others and teaching basic life skills. Even "failure"—as when a child care staff loses his temper or fails to control a misbehavior—can have positive benefit in that it demonstrates to the parents that inadequacy is not theirs alone. Parents can come to respect child care workers for the skills they do possess and see them as partners in helping. For the child care worker and other professional staff, greater parent involvement means, at least initially, a loss of "superperson" status. Parents come to see that child care workers, social workers, and other clinical staff do not have all the answers, do have problems dealing with difficult behavior, do make mistakes, and, at times, lose their cool with children. In short, they come to see them as more human—more like themselves. Finally, the closer working together of staff and parents reduces the "we/they" feeling that can develop in residential programs and helps to ensure that whatever differences exist between the culture of group living and the family culture are at least understood.

Specifically, how can parents become more fully involved in the life space? One fairly simple and easily activated linkage consists of a regular telephone contact (weekly, or even more frequently if the parent desires) between staff and parents. The purpose of the call should be seen as making contact and sharing information. Staff need not feel that they must come up with answers to family problems but simply that they are being a help by listening. Parents need reassurance that their child is being well cared for; most important, they need to feel that they are still involved, if only vicariously, in that care. Such contacts should not take the place of regular telephone conversations between parent and child but may coincide with them.

Parents also can be encouraged to observe treatment sessions, in order to learn techniques for use in the home (Schopler and Reichler, 1971a) and to experience the feeling of support that comes from knowing that someone else is actively concerned. Such observation times best fit with on-campus school programs, particularly when one-way glass is available. They also provide an opportunity for parents to visit with each other informally. A simple sign-in sheet can alert teachers to who has been observing, so that they can follow up if need be. Marcus (1977) cites some of the benefits that accrue from such collaborative arrangements. Clearly, such observations have less applicability for older children, where questions of confidentiality between therapist and child are more centrally involved.

In some programs (for example, the "bug in the ear" program), parents are involved directly as coparticipants in the life space of the cottage, classroom, or day treatment program and receive on-the-spot coaching from staff in methods of effective parenting with their own child. On occasion, parents and siblings also can participate in the culture of group living by sharing a meal and by joining in special group activities, such as birthdays, field trips, or sporting events. Again, the implicit message is that parents are part of the overall agency culture and have a place in some of the pleasurable activities as well as the more formalized structures of family therapy and parent education. Some agencies even plan one special event—usually a picnic—where all staff, children, and families come together. Child care workers, with their intimate knowledge of the child's likes and dislikes, can also be helpful to parents in planning for individual activities on weekend or holiday visits.

Large group projects—painting, fall cleanup, opening or closing a summer camp program—provide opportunities for parents to provide some meaningful help to the agency. Many parents also have special skills that can be useful in the group life program. They can, for instance, serve as active consultants to many aspects of group life programming: menu planning, furniture buying, site selection for group homes, and the like. Parents, too, need to feel a pride of ownership in the program and some degree of control over what happens. Too often we overlook these opportunities for parent involvement, either because they are not organizationally efficient or because we do not think of relating to parents in other than traditionally defined ways.

Other avenues of parent involvement include public speaking and related activities before legislative and other community groups. Parents are often the best spokespersons for the program and provide a social validation of program effectiveness that cannot be supplied by the professionals. Such efforts also provide an opportunity for parents to be involved in a project that does not focus on their particular child. Thus, they can experience some success and mastery, even when the family situation does not seem particularly bright.

In sum, parents can and should be sought out to participate in virtually all areas of agency programming. Some will not
participate whatever the strength of the invitation; others will
require help in effective involvement. Parental involvement does
suggest a more complex, less "tidy" program and also a new set
of problems for child care and other professional staff to deal
with. In my judgment, the effort is justified in that these are
precisely the kinds of problems the parents will be forced to
deal with, once the child returns home.

   *Conjoint Family Treatment.* Conjoint family treatment is
a form of therapy that includes all family members in a therapeutic encounter. The family system itself, as well as individual
members, is seen as a target for change. The central notion behind most conjoint family treatment is that the pain and difficulty experienced by one family member—in this case, the child
in placement—will in some way affect the total family functioning and also that successful treatment of an individual member's
problem will ultimately require alterations in the family's total
pattern of functioning. The family therapist presents a model of
effective communication to family members by reacting to,
clarifying, and interpreting what family members say to him or
her and to each other. Family members are urged to share feelings with each other in the treatment session, and each family
member's contribution, including that of the youngest child, is
listened to with respect. The tremendous growth in knowledge
of how to work with whole families is reflected in the considerable literature on the subject—much of it written in the last decade (see MacGregor and others, 1964; Whittaker and Trieschman, 1972, pp. 383-425; Finkelstein, 1974; Berkowitz and
Graziano, 1975; Patterson and others, 1975; Gatti and Colman,
1976; Stein and Gambrill, 1976; Wahler, House, and Stambaugh, 1976). The recent work of Reid and Epstein (1972, 1977)
with its focus on task-centered, problem-oriented, and time-
limited intervention is an exciting development in the field with
clear implications for family work in residential treatment.

   Many of the specific issues surrounding the use of conjoint family treatment in residential settings have already been
identified: parental guilt over causation, the "we/they" feeling
that can develop between staff and parents, the problem of cul-

tural relatedness, and the problem of geographical isolation. Another potentially troublesome issue concerns the divided loyalties a child can develop between home and residence. In particular, the child who had resisted forming relationships but has come to like the child care staff, the program, and the other children may feel apprehensive about returning to a less than ideal home situation. Also troubling is the child's realization that he has been receiving special help but his family has not—or has not been able to make use of it. In such instances, family sessions may help all family members accept the fact that while the parents still love their child, he or she will need to remain away from home for an indefinite period.

Another issue concerns the locus of family treatment. As with parent education, the content of family sessions must reflect problems that are real for the family in the natural environment. While the agency provides a common meeting ground, home-based family treatment is also a useful format for engaging family problems and one that lends itself to cooperative efforts by social workers and child care workers. The basic point is that communication between parent and professional is a two-way street; it should ideally involve staff participation in the family environment as well as parental involvement in the group life culture.

## Conclusions

The relationship between family culture and the culture of group life is crucial to the successful transition of the child from residence to community. Family work should be broadly conceived to include parent education, family support groups, conjoint family treatment, and parent involvement in the life space. Other avenues for involvement—including volunteer participation and parent help with fund drives and legislative presentations, as well as the development of formal parent organizations such as the PTA—should also be encouraged. Parents must be made aware of their potential for participation, and professionals must come to understand what it is like to be the parent of a handicapped or troubled child. With this in mind, I offer the following suggestions developed by Kathryn Gorham and her colleagues and included in the volume *Issues in the Classification of Children.*\* Though developed for parents of mentally handicapped children, they have considerable relevance for parents of troubled children in residential treatment.

## Suggestions for Professionals

1. Have the parent(s) involved every step of the way. The dialogue established may be the most important thing you accomplish. If the parent's presence is an obstacle to testing because the child will not cooperate in his presence, the setup should include a complete review of the testing procedure with the parent. (Remote viewing or one-way windows are great if you are richly endowed.)

2. Make a realistic management plan part and parcel of the assessment outcome. Give the parents suggestions for how to live with the problem on a day-to-day basis, with the needs of the child, the capacities of the family, and the resources of the community all considered. Let the parents know that you will suggest modifications if any aspect of the management plan does not work.

3. Inform yourself about community resources. Give the parents advice on how to go about getting what they need. Steer them to the local parent organization.

4. Wherever possible, make the parent a team member in the actual diagnostic, treatment, or educational procedures. It will give you a chance to observe how the parent and the child interact.

5. Write your reports in clear, understandable, jargon-free language. Professional terminology is a useful shortcut for your own note-taking; and you can always use it to communicate with others of your discipline. But in situations involving the parent, it operates as an obstacle to understanding. Keep in mind that it is the parent who must live with the child, help him along, shop for services to

\*Reprinted here by permission of author and publisher. (See Hobbs, 1975, pp. 284-289.)

meet his needs, support his ego, give him guidance. You cannot be there to do it for him. So the parent *must* be as well informed as you can make him. Information that he does not understand is not useful to him. The goal is to "produce" a parent who understands his child well enough to help him handle his problems as he grows up.

6. Give copies of the reports to parents. They will need them to digest and understand the information in them, to share the information with other people close to the child, and to avoid the weeks or months of record-gathering which every application to a new program in the future will otherwise entail.

7. Be sure the parent understands that there is no such thing as a one-shot, final, and unchanging diagnosis. Make sure he understands that whatever label you give his child (if a label must be given) is merely a device for communicating and one which may have all kinds of repercussions, many of them undesirable. Make sure he understands that it says very little about the child at present and even less about the child of the future. Caution him about using that label to "explain" his child's conditions to other people.

8. Help the parent to think of life with the child in the same terms as life with his other children. It is an ongoing, problem-solving process. Assure him that he is capable of that problem solving and that you will be there to help him with it.

9. Be sure that he understands his child's abilities and assets as well as his disabilities and deficiencies. What the child can do is far more important than what he cannot do, and the parent's goal thereafter is to look for new abilities and to welcome them with joy when they appear. Urge him to be honest and plain speaking with his child. Tell him that the most important job he has is to respect his child, as well as love him, and to help him "feel good about himself." Tell him that blame, either self-blame or blame of the child, has no part in the scene. *It is no one's fault.*

10. Warn the parent about service insufficiencies. Equip him with advice on how to make his way through the system of "helping" services. Warn him that they are not always helpful. Tell him that his child has a *right* to services. Tell him to insist on being a part of any decision making done about his child.

11. Explain to him that some people with whom he talks (teachers, doctors, professionals of any kind, other parents) may dwell on negatives. Help train the parent not only to think in positives but to teach the other people important in his child's life to think in positives.

### Suggestions for Parents

1. You are the primary helper, monitor, coordinator, observer, record keeper, and decision maker for your child. Insist that you be treated as such. It is your *right* to understand your child's diagnoses and the reasons for treatment recommendations and for educational placement. No changes in his treatment or educational placement should take place without previous consultation with you.

2. Your success in getting as well informed as you will need to be to monitor your child's progress depends on your ability to work with the people who work with your child. You may encounter resistance to the idea of including you in the various diagnostic and decision-making processes. The way you handle that resistance is important. Your best tool is not the angry approach. Some of your job will include the gentler art of persuasion. Stay confident and cool about your own abilities and intuitions. You know your child better than anyone else could. You are, obviously, a vital member of the team of experts.

3. Try to find, from among the many people whom you see, a person who can help you coordinate the various diagnostic visits and results. Pick the person with whom you have the best relationship, someone who understands your role as

the principal monitor of your child's progress throughout life and who will help you become a good one.

4. Learn to keep records. As soon as you know that you have a child with a problem, start a notebook. Make entries of names, addresses, phone numbers, dates of visits, the persons present during the visits, and as much of what was said as you can remember. Record the questions you asked and the answers you received. Record any recommendations made. Make records of phone calls too; include the dates, the purpose, the result. It is best to make important requests by letter. Keep a copy for your notebook. Such documentation for every step of your efforts to get your child the service he needs can be the evidence which finally persuades a program director to *give* him what he needs. Without concise records of whom you spoke to, when you spoke to him, what he promised, how long you waited between the request and the response, you will be handicapped. No one can ever be held accountable for conversations or meetings with persons whose names and titles you do not remember, on dates you cannot recall, about topics which you cannot clearly discuss.

5. Make sure that you understand the terminology used by the professional. Ask him to translate his terms into lay language. Ask him to give examples of what he means. Do not leave his office until you are sure you understand what he has said so well that you can carry the information to your child's teacher, for instance, and explain it to her in clear, understandable language. (Write down the professional terms too. Knowing them might come in handy some time.)

6. Ask for copies of your child's records. You probably will not get them, but you *could* ask that a tape recording be made of any "interpretive" conference. It is very hard to remember what was said in such conferences.

7. Read. Learn as much as you can about

your child's problem. But do not swallow whole what you read. Books are like people. They might be offering only one side of the story.

8. Talk freely and openly with as many professionals as you can. Talk with other parents. Join a parent organization. By talking with people who "have been through it already," you can gain a perspective on your particular problems. Besides, you will receive moral support and will not feel quite so alone. Get information from parent organizations about services available, about their quality. But bear in mind that a particular program might not help your child even though it has proved helpful for another child. Visit programs if you have the time and energy to do so. There is no substitute for firsthand views.

9. Stay in close touch with your child's teacher. Make sure you know what she is doing in the classroom so that, with her help, you can follow through at home. Share what you have read with her. Ask her for advice and suggestions. Get across the idea that the two of you are a team, working for the same goals. Make your child a part of that team whenever possible. He might have some great ideas.

10. Listen to your child. It is *his* point of view that he is giving you, and on that he is an expert.

11. Work hard at living the idea that differentness is just fine—not bad. Your child will learn most from your example. Help him to think of problems as things that can be solved if people work at them together.

# 7

## Richard W. Small
## Robin B. Clarke

# Schools as Partners in Helping

$A$t first glance it seems obvious that any discussion of specialized helping environments for children would be incomplete without a section on the school. After all, a large portion of each child's day is spent negotiating some sort of formal classroom experience, either within the program or in the community. Moreover, many of the dramatic advances in the education of children with special needs (Mann and Sabatino, 1974) are relevant to children in residential care:

*Note:* The authors wish to thank the staff and students of the Walker School, Needham, Massachusetts, for making this chapter possible. We owe a special debt to Albert E. Trieschman, whose inspiration to child care workers and teachers extends well beyond the confines of one treatment program. James Whittaker and our colleagues Christian Gruber, Jr., Robert Gass, and Donna Townsend contributed immeasurably to the final form of this chapter by their insightful comments throughout the course of manuscript preparation.

155

- Piaget (1970) and Montessori ([1912] 1964, [1939] 1973), among others, have influenced the growth of teaching methods based on the child's interaction with the physical environment in all learning situations. Some of the practical approaches derived from their work are directly applicable to activity programming outside the classroom (Schwebel and Ralph, 1973; Silberman, 1973).
- Cruickshank (1971; 1975, with G. Johnson), Frostig (1973, with P. Maslow; 1976), Kirk (1966), and Bangs (1968) are just a few of the educators who have contributed to the growing knowledge base in the difficult area of developmental learning disabilities. The insights into the remediation of learning difficulty suggested by these and other practitioners are increasingly useful outside the classroom as treatment programs work with multiply handicapped youngsters.
- The development of behavior modification techniques in the special education classroom has kept pace with similar advances in the wider field of child care. This literature is a rich source of pragmatic suggestions for all staff working with children: Bijou (1971) offers a number of teaching ideas for exceptional children based on operant techniques; Bradfield (1971) applies behavior modification to the remediation of learning disabilities; Homme (1969) and Meisels (1974) offer examples from a range of approaches to contingency contracting in the classroom; and Hewett (1969) provides a classic description of a token economy in a structured classroom for emotionally disturbed children.
- Special education has devoted a great deal of attention to the management of surface behavior in the classroom. Swift and Spivack (1974) have compiled a comprehensive review of the many contributions to this literature. The practical approaches which they cite are especially relevant to child care workers.

But despite all this potential for common ground, special education as an element of the helping environment has been largely neglected in the literature of residential treatment in the United States. The early formulations of the milieu as a powerful tool for helping troubled children (Bettelheim and Sylvester,

1948; Bettelheim, 1950; Redl and Wineman, 1957) deliberately moved away from the language of the school to emphasize treatment. If love was not enough for these children, neither was ordinary education: "In a therapeutic milieu . . . the child's development toward increasing mastery must be facilitated. Training in skills and achievement, specialized program and activities, are of peripheral importance only. They are therapeutically justified solely if they originate from the central issue of the therapeutic milieu" (Bettelheim and Sylvester, 1948, p. 192). The *central issue* of treatment was always the repairing of ego disturbances and the promotion of ego skills. Undeniably, such detailed focus on the child's psychological capacity to interact with the physical and interpersonal environment contributed enormously to the whole field of caring for children with special needs. But this same emphasis on ego function and dysfunction also tended to oversimplify the nature of the learning process. Specifically, it promoted a rather narrow view of the etiology of learning problems—a view that has had a remarkably persistent influence: "Traditional education goals that emphasize mental acquisition and cognitive operations in learning have not worked with these children, mainly because early disturbances in personality development impaired their capacity to engage in the kind of learning most children have acquired in their homes before they start school" (Davis, 1972, p. 49).

In fact, with the notable exception of Hobbs (1966), the recent literature of residential treatment describes the school (if it considers the school at all) as a clinically separate or supportive entity, even when it is a physical part of the treatment program (American Association of Children's Residential Centers, 1972; Adler, 1976); more frequently, however, the classroom gets completely overlooked in otherwise detailed discussions of the therapeutic components of the milieu (Whittaker and Trieschman, 1972; Weber and Haberlein, 1972; Mayer, Richman, and Balcerzak, 1977). A striking example of this latter phenomenon was the publication of the book *The Other 23 Hours* (Trieschman, Whittaker, and Brendtro, 1969), which, despite its hopeful title, nevertheless neglected five and a half of those hours by omitting any mention of the children in school.

Fortunately, the increasing development of what Whittaker (1975) has termed the ecology of child treatment, suggested in part by Hobbs (1966), provides an opportunity to take another look at the traditional distinction between "going to school" and "being in treatment." From the ecological perspective, the school can be broadly considered as a significant influence on the child and on family life. More specifically, the classroom can be reconsidered as an integral part of the total treatment program, with its own sophisticated technology and its own legitimate therapeutic goals—namely, to teach competence skills so that each child's special needs for learning are met.

### Teaching Competence Skills: The Concept of Individual Learning Style

In attempting to structure the total environment as a curriculum for teaching competence, we are faced with the problem of connecting the goals and unique teaching methods of the child care worker with those of the classroom teacher and other key staff. In many ways, this is really a question of finding a language that all staff can share. What exactly do we mean when we talk about competence skills in different contexts? Is it possible to identify concrete skills involved in the various kinds of learning that take place outside the classroom as well as in it? Is there any connection between the way that the individual child learns to read and the way that he or she learns how to climb a tree or to get along in a group of peers?

In considering the child's capacity to learn in any situation, the teacher needs to make a conscious effort to deal with functioning in the present, avoiding diagnostic conclusions that emphasize difficulty in one area of development as the cause of learning problems. Emphasis on dealing with the cause of learning dysfunction may lock a teacher into an unproductive struggle with the past:

> As the psychodynamic approach leads a teacher to substitute [for academic goals] work on deep underlying conflict, the learning disabilities

approach pushes him to treat deep-seated (and still hypothetical) neurological problems. If a teacher permits this kind of goal substitution, he courts the very real risk of failing to help the child learn skills vital to feelings of self-worth and essential to achieving a meaningful life in society. The question of what a teacher can use in his work with an emotionally disturbed and/or learning-disabled child is left disturbingly open. . . . The conceptual purists offered me approaches that clashed at their most basic level. The "psychodynamic approach" suggested an absolute reliance on meeting the child's emotional needs and avoidance of creating reciprocal demands on the child. The "learning disability approach" set up vigorous perceptual training sessions whose justification was so abstract that demands needed to be handled quite bluntly as demands. What I needed were tools to handle a specific situation whose focus was in the present, not in the psychological or neurological past. And I needed tools which would make our efforts contribute toward reaching a preselected academic goal, not ones which would force us to select among divergent new goals [Gruber, 1975, p. 5].

From this point of view, the initial strategy for effective teaching throughout the therapeutic environment should be to disregard—at least temporarily—the labels and stereotypes which the children bear, so that all staff are free to analyze observable behavior and come to some conclusions about what is likely to work best with each child. In making such assessments, we can begin to build a common vocabulary of teaching by looking at the child's *individual learning style*. By learning styles we mean something more comprehensive than acquisition rate or overall temperament. We mean to suggest that *the level of competence each child brings to learning is based on a particular balance of developmental strengths and weaknesses which can be observed, recorded, and augmented by various teaching strategies.* Implicit in this notion is a view of the learning process which considers the child as a *whole*—as a unique system receiving, associating, and expressing through the constant interaction of five developmental modalities: perception, cognition, affective/emotional organization, language, and motor functioning.

Whatever the task, mastery is rarely the result of the discrete involvement of any one of these modalities. In order to catch a ball or write one's name, one needs visual perception and motor facility. Speaking involves language, cognition, and motor functions. Playing a group game demands cognitive understanding, motor skills, perceptual coordination, and complex affective control. At the same time, each functional modality is comprised of identifiable and individually variable skills. It is the particular mix of these skills that determines learning "style." For example, the child with relatively superior motor skills will be most comfortable when he or she can manipulate objects or otherwise engage in bodily activity in the learning process; the child with primarily visual perceptual strength will tend to rely on an image of the problem even in abstract task situations; and so on. In the therapeutic environment—as the experienced child care worker, teacher, or therapist already knows —successful programming for the individual child involves taking into account a number of factors unique to each child as he or she interacts with the environment.

### Functional Skills in Individual Learning Style

In Table 4 we have listed some of the readily observable functional skills that determine individual learning style. By setting things up graphically in this way, we do not intend to represent a comprehensive theory of learning but simply to indicate one way of understanding the child. In the interest of making this model a usable tool, we have admittedly made many arbitrary categorical distinctions and deliberate simplifications. We hope that the risk of dealing too briefly with extraordinarily complex areas of human functioning is justified by the value of stressing a more inclusive understanding of the child's competence, which can be shared by all staff in the therapeutic environment.

**Table 4. Functional Skills in Individual Learning Style**

| Perception | | Cognition | Affective/ Emotional Organization | Language | Motor Functioning |
|---|---|---|---|---|---|
| *Visual-Spatial* | *Auditory* | | | | |
| Laterality | Figure-ground | Abstraction | Self-image | Phonemics | Gross motor |
| Directionality | Discrimination | Categorization | Impulse control | Vocabulary | Fine motor |
| Figure-ground | Sequence | Generalization | Social perception | Grammar | Eye-hand coordination |
| Discrimination | Closure | Time sense | Social judgment | Auditory reception | Balance |
| Closure | | Number concepts | Delayed reward | Visual reception | Posture |
| Position in space | | Arithmetic reasoning | Foresight | Auditory association | |
| | | | Motivation | Visual association | |
| | | | Adaptability | Verbal expression | |
| | | | Body image | Manual expression | |

← INTEGRATION →

*Perception.* Perception—the way in which the brain interprets stimuli received by the sense organs—depends on the integration of previous sensory experience and individual neurological organization. Perception skills critical for learning can
therefore be highly variable for each child, based on the overall
progress of development. The children most often referred for
residential care are notorious misperceivers—certainly of human
interactions but probably also of basic sensory data in many
situations. Table 4 presents some of the basic skills involved in
both visual and auditory perception.

Visual perception is subdivided into the following elements:

1. *Laterality.* The ability to see oneself as the center of space
   and to distinguish right side from left side, top from bottom,
   and front from back; necessary for such tasks as moving
   through crowded space (the forest, an obstacle course, a city
   street) or discriminating right and left body parts.
2. *Directionality.* The ability to orient the body in relation to
   the space outside oneself; necessary for such tasks as map
   reading or following directions from place to place.
3. *Figure-ground.* The ability to perceive objects in the foreground while at the same time blocking out background
   stimuli; necessary for such tasks as focusing on one word on
   a page or finding a utensil in a drawer full of utensils.
4. *Discrimination.* The ability to pick up fine visual detail in
   differentiating one similar form from another; necessary for
   such tasks as discriminating an *f* from a *t* or a smile from a
   frown.
5. *Closure.* The ability to fill in the missing parts of an object
   when only some parts are shown; necessary for such tasks as
   identifying *br-t* as *brat* or for "seeing" objects through the
   window of a speeding car.
6. *Position in space.* The ability to discriminate among objects
   which have the same form but vary in their spatial position;
   necessary for such tasks as differentiating *b* from *d* or comprehending geometrical patterns in art or building design.

Competence in the visual-perceptual area greatly affects how well the child can "tune in" to any learning situation. Some children are extremely oriented to visual experience, learning most effectively through visual-perceptual channels. But a child seriously lacking in these skills may constantly lose his place when reading, be unable to find things when they are right in front of him, or become disoriented in familiar surroundings. If a child is unable to judge distances and spatial relationships with confidence, he may exaggerate his footsteps in moving up or down stairs or otherwise move awkwardly. Many of the symptoms commonly associated with the rather vague syndrome dyslexia seem primarily related to visual-perceptual confusion. The program's emphasis on structure and on helping the child organize his day is especially important for these children.

Auditory perception is the interpretation of stimuli sent from the ear to the brain. Auditory perception may be subdivided into the following elements:

1. *Figure-ground.* The ability to focus on foreground sound and block out background sound; necessary for such tasks as hearing the teacher in a noisy classroom or paying attention to the instructions of the adult at the dining room table.
2. *Discrimination.* The ability to discriminate among auditory stimuli; necessary for such tasks as hearing the difference between *sat* and *sad* during a spelling test or between *no* and *now* in adult directions.
3. *Sequence.* The ability to interpret auditory stimuli in correct order of presentation; necessary for such tasks as hearing the difference between *bets* and *best* or for remembering whether one is supposed to get dressed first and then come to breakfast or to come to breakfast and then get dressed.
4. *Closure.* The ability to fill in missing parts of a whole word or meaningful sequence of sounds; necessary for such tasks as understanding syllabification rules or for knowing that your bicycle was fixed when all you heard before the car went by was "bi____ ."

Some children are "all ears" as they make sense out of their environment, learning most efficiently through the auditory channel. In contrast, the child with weak auditory perception may say "Huh?" as a first response to most questions and directions, though he has no problem with hearing acuity. He may forget instructions or follow them in the wrong order. During the science lesson, the teacher may be speaking and he may be paying attention to the motor sounds of a jet far in the distance. When he is asked to bring a pen to class, he brings a pan. As with problems in visual perception, the end result can be frustration and poor self-image for the child. He may become withdrawn or stubbornly "deaf" to verbalizations of which he is unsure. In dealing with such behaviors, the adult should resist quick interpretations of emotional conflict or resistance (though, of course, they may be there) until simple accommodations in the environment are attempted. These accommodations can include providing a quiet place for the child to work, presenting tasks one at a time, using pictures of words in the environment, emphasizing hand movements, and insisting on eye contact so that the child can read lips in "hearing" what is being said.

*Cognition.* It is tempting for the educator to dwell on *cognitive* functioning as the most important determinant of individual learning style. Certainly cognition plays a part in all areas of physical and social development. At the same time, the precise meaning of cognition in terms of specific behaviors and as distinct from other areas of developmental competence can be very unclear to the practitioner. In an effort to avoid this kind of imprecision, the model represented in Table 4 makes an arbitrary distinction between language and cognitive functioning and focuses on critical, measurable skills in the cognitive area.

The ability to think clearly, to move beyond concrete events to abstract ideas, to form complex concepts, and to categorize are a few of the cognitive skills necessary for learning. As with language, the exact manner in which the brain develops and carries out these operations is not completely understood. The best evidence suggests that cognitive skills are partly constitutional but are also based on the relative depth and variety of sensory experiences in early childhood (Piaget, 1963; Piaget and Inhelder, 1969). Actual opportunities to manipulate, touch, smell, or otherwise experience concrete objects can aid concept formation throughout life. Some of the key cognitive operations related to learning are the following:

1. *Abstraction.* The ability to discern, within a framework of concrete events, elements, characteristics, and relationships; necessary for dealing with the idea of *home* as different from the concrete reality of *house* and for logical inference in general.
2. *Categorization.* The ability to group experiences and objects into classes, based on similarity of concrete representation or function; necessary for understanding basic geometry, dealing with tools, or just separating the laundry.
3. *Generalization.* The ability to infer causal or phenomenological relationships among discrete events; necessary for understanding the laws of physics or for figuring out that hitting the baby will make mother angry every time.
4. *Time sense.* The ability to be oriented as to time; necessary for planning ahead or for matching available energy to the duration of a given task.
5. *Number concepts.* The ability to count and use simple numbers to represent quantity; necessary for fully understanding most aspects of the environment.
6. *Arithmetic reasoning.* The ability to deal with such concepts as equality, inequality, commutation, and distribution in everyday experience; necessary for such tasks as shopping, making change, and estimating.

A child with noticeable cognitive confusion may seem far more a puzzle than other youngsters in the group. He may have persistent trouble with "simple" tasks such as grouping, counting, or sorting objects by category. He may become confused when asked to list everything he can think of that is furniture, or he may be unable to predict adult responses from repeated episodes of interaction. He may count on his fingers or be unable to give change or tell time. In many ways the therapeutic milieu is uniquely set up to deal with cognitive difficulty by its potential for restructuring and reinterpreting the environment for each child. The task of the teacher and child care worker in this context can be seen as promoting the child's *inner* organization by building outer environments which "make sense" for the child and which become the basis for his mastery of future environments.

*Affective/Emotional Organization.* Affective or social-emotional competence is a broad category of skills involved in the learning process. Mastery in this area includes the skills necessary to manage the internal turmoil of emotions, thoughts, and feelings; it also includes skills that are important for the effective presentation of the self as a part of the interpersonal environment:

1. *Self-image.* Accurate and positive thoughts and feelings about the self; necessary for meaningful social interactions and for such tasks as tolerating one's own mistakes and learning to be assertive.
2. *Impulse control.* The ability to monitor and control thoughts and actions; necessary for sustained attention, for example, waiting one's turn in line.
3. *Social perception.* The ability to "read" the affective productions of others and to "hear" the natural voice of a social setting; necessary for learning to make friends, for becoming part of a group, or avoiding getting kicked out of the library.
4. *Social judgment.* The ability to weigh alternatives and probabilities in social situations; necessary for such tasks as knowing when to be aggressive and when to walk away from a fight.
5. *Delayed reward.* The ability to postpone gratification for future gain; necessary for such tasks as saving one's allowance to buy an expensive toy or for fully comprehending the value of rewards in a token economy.
6. *Foresight.* The ability to consider the future in the midst of current behavior; necessary for planning ahead and for fully conscious control of behavior.

7. *Motivation.* The ability to take pleasure in (and derive energy from) autonomous achievement; necessary for overcoming difficulty in learning to read or to ride a bike and for self-programmed learning.
8. *Adaptability.* The ability to remain oriented and stable in the face of change; necessary for mastering the anxiety involved with transitions.
9. *Body image.* Visceral (internal/physiological) awareness of the body and body parts, as well as the conscious awareness of the body in space and time; necessary for modifying impulses to dangerous behavior and for knowing that you will not break apart if you fall or explode if very angry.

Efficient learning clearly is hampered in the child who is crippled by anxiety, rage, or distorted self-image or who is unable to give affection. Less obviously, learning also is hampered in the child who cannot deal with sadness, joy, or excitement or who constantly falters in social situations because he misreads emotion and affect in others. A child lacking in emotional competence may be heedless of danger or paralyzed by anxiety. He may be unable to think ahead, to know when the teacher is really angry, or to understand why the other children avoid playing with him. In facing specific academic tasks, he or she may be unable to risk making the mistakes that are a part of learning.

*Language.* Many children learn to manipulate language early in life. Word games and the nuances of meaning are a continual delight to them. For some children, however, language development may be slow. For these children, words and the use of words may be less a tool than a perplexing barrier to seeing into the life of things. We have subdivided the process of language functioning into the following elements:

1. *Phonemics.* The ability both to discriminate among and to produce individual sounds correctly; necessary for learning letter sounds and for pronouncing words correctly.
2. *Vocabulary.* The ability to understand the meaning of words, including the comprehension of different meanings in different contexts; necessary for the correct interpretation

of written and spoken communication and for fluency of speech.

3. *Grammar.* The ability to understand both surface and depth structures of sentences; necessary for determining when a collection of words is a sentence, when a sentence has meaning, when sentences with different word order have equivalent meaning, and how the arrangement of words in a sentence indicates their relationship to each other.

4. *Auditory reception.** The ability to derive meaning from verbally presented bits of information; necessary for grasping the complexities involved in a question such as "Did you hit Michael or did he hit you?"

5. *Visual reception.* The ability to derive meaning from visually presented bits of information; necessary for understanding the action in a comic strip or for interpreting a person's response on the basis of facial expression.

6. *Auditory association.* The ability to understand the relationships between objects or concepts when presented orally; necessary for such tasks as understanding, on the basis of an oral description, that sugar and salt look alike.

7. *Visual association.* The ability to understand the relationships between objects or concepts when presented visually; necessary for such tasks as categorizing pictures or for anticipating what comes next when you see a child heading for a fire and a mother running toward the child.

8. *Verbal expression.* The ability to express simple and complex meanings vocally; necessary for such tasks as describing the "big fish that got away" or for communicating which tool is needed when you cannot remember the name.

9. *Manual expression.* The ability to express simple and complex meanings without the use of speech; necessary for complete communication in almost all social situations.

Emotionally closed-up youngsters who *also* have distinct language disabilities may refuse to speak or may use mostly

---

*The definitions of receptive, associative, and expressive categories of language functioning used here are based on the comprehensive work by Kirk (1966).

single words and simple sentences in their speech. Incorrect use of pronouns, possessives, plurals, tenses, adjectives, and adverbs may confuse the meaning of the sentences they do use. In dealing with these children, the teacher needs to be aware not only of the difficulty of language exchange from the point of view of the child but also of the possibility of distorted meaning as a result of such difficulty. In order to be sure that a meaningful exchange is taking place, the adult must be able to determine whether the child cannot understand what is being communicated or whether he understands but is unable to express himself in response. If the child cannot understand what he hears, the teacher can help him by allowing him more time to respond, by simplifying the sentence, or by using pictures or gestures as aids to meaning. If the child has trouble with expression, the teacher can help by asking questions that elicit more specific responses. For instance, if the question "What would you like to play today?" elicits no response, "Would you like to play tag?" may be more productive.

*Motor Functioning.* The general area of motor functioning can be looked at as the integration of large and small muscle activity. Within this area, there are the following elements of performance:

1. *Gross motor.* The ability to utilize and coordinate the large muscles of the body; necessary for such activities as running, jumping, or climbing.
2. *Fine motor.* The ability to utilize and coordinate the small muscles of the body; necessary for such activities as drawing, writing, or cutting with scissors.
3. *Eye-hand coordination.* The ability to control the eye and the hand at the same time for one task; necessary for such gross motor activities as catching a ball and such fine motor activities as drawing from a model.
4. *Balance.* The ability to coordinate both large and small muscles to maintain balance equilibrium; necessary for such activities as riding a bicycle or hopping on one foot.
5. *Posture.* The ability to hold the body erect; necessary for such activities as efficient and comfortable standing, sitting, or walking.

An accurate evaluation of a child's motor abilities is critical for teaching. Many children function best only when motorically involved in the learning task. Movement and activity will be a hallmark of their "style" in any situation. For the child with strong motor competence, the program needs to provide positive ways to exercise skill as well as to focus on the control of excess or inappropriate activity. The child with weak motor skills may be able to read but be unable to write legibly. For this child the classroom teacher may need to provide a tape recorder in order to avoid struggles which are connected more to problems in shaping words on the page than to emotional blocks to expression. Similarly, the child care worker may need to arrange private or small-group motor skill practice sessions before exposing the child to competitive play situations, where he or she may experience failure and humiliation.

Motor skills are important for adaptation to every part of the environment. This area is an excellent one for pointing out how curriculum goals in the life space can complement curriculum goals in the classroom. Providing appropriate motor skill training in the recreation program not only helps the child in athletics and in developing marketable peer skills; it also helps improve body awareness, self-confidence, and even specific handwriting skills in the classroom.

*Integration.* In Table 4 we have used the term *integration* to underscore the dynamic nature of the learning process and to indicate the constant interaction of different modalities with each other. More global functional abilities which contribute to learning style—abilities such as attention and memory—are highly influenced by this integration of developmental skills within the individual. *Attention* can be defined as the complex ability to remain organized within the network of visceral (inner physiological) and environmental stimuli, and to consciously order and direct stimuli in a purposeful way for short and long periods. In many ways the ability to "pay attention"—or, more accurately, to pay *selective attention* when involved in a given task—is the most delicate of developmental competence skills. Every teacher and child care worker knows from bitter experience that it is also the most situationally variable. Each child's attentional strength as it varies in different learning situations is therefore an important aspect of learning style. Many children referred for residential treatment who are labeled impulsive or hyperactive can be more usefully looked at as lacking in attentional strength. They may be unable to process the stimuli presented to them in an orderly fashion and have little control over competing messages received through the senses. External aids such as individual study carrels, earphones, and carefully structured living spaces—provided first by the adult and later approximated by the child in programming his or her own learning—may be necessary for efficient learning. They may also help reduce the incidence of behavior problems.

Long- and short-term memory is involved in all efficient learning. Memory is also a highly variable capacity in each person. Some children may have trouble with specific recall of words and names, while others are perfectly at ease reciting the alphabet backward; some may have an uncanny ability to remember details of physical space, while others need to keep asking directions to the park. Subtle differences in learning style can be a result of variations in visual as distinct from auditory memory as well as of variations of retention interval depending on whether the child is motorically active or quiet. Of course, the teacher in residential treatment will also see youngsters whose learning is hampered by memory distortions or blocks as a result of affective/emotional disorganization.

## Program Implications:
## Learning Style and the Learning Environment

The value of looking at the whole child and stressing observable skills is that we can be theoretically eclectic in our approach to teaching. We can draw upon views of development that stress ego organization, cognitive and neurological organization, and the primacy of social learning. More to the point, the emphasis on individual differences in learning style rather than on individual pathology can be the basis for building teaching "tools"; we can use learning style as a way to make practical sense out of our assessments of children *and* as a way to start

formulating mutually understandable goals in the whole program of teaching competence. Most important, since we can see
that each child—as a whole person with a consistent learning
style—approaches unrelated tasks in the curriculum of residential treatment in identifiably consistent ways, the *methodological emphasis* of the program as an intervention can be redefined. That is, in helping each child acquire competence skills
in any or all areas of functioning, we will emphasize individual
strengths and will only secondarily attempt to remediate individual weaknesses. This is an important technical and clinical
shift. Although we will not avoid the child's weak areas or ignore real problems when they exist, we will first look for existing competence skills which can be exploited (and which the
child can learn to use on his own) in any new learning situation.
The whole program thus becomes a comprehensive *learning
environment* which is responsive to the functional strength of
individual learning style as well as carefully structured to focus
on individual special needs.

   *Assessment Versus Diagnosis.* In setting up the classroom
as an effective learning environment, the teacher first must
assemble as much information as possible about the individual
learning style of each child. This initial step must be understood
as a process of overall assessment rather than diagnosis. This is a
fine (and arbitrary) distinction, but we think it is extremely important. As teachers of children with special needs, we are constantly tempted to use models such as presented in Table 4 as
checklists of deficiency—to "diagnose" the problem and build
our teaching strategies around remediation. Too often this procedure results in a constant struggle with incompetence in the
classroom. With the focus on deficiency, teachers, parents, and
especially the child can be blind to areas of functional strength,
which can become real learning tools. Even the most seriously
handicapped child has some capacity to learn, and, more important, approaches learning with his own special combination of
strengths as well as weaknesses. The child with limited ability to
deal with abstract concepts in words may be able to grasp sur-
prisingly complex relationships between objects presented
visually or represented in space. The child with little or no ex-

pressive language skill may be able to say a great deal through movement. The child who cannot sit still may be able to attend much longer when visual stimulation is shut down and auditory reception is emphasized. Assessment as distinct from diagnosis means looking at every area of potential competence, not one or two areas of special difficulty.

In any assessment of individual learning style, the starting point is a complete physical (and sometimes neurological) examination. The teacher then listens to what the child knows about himself, systematically observes the child in a variety of situations, and utilizes data from periodic formal and informal testing and behavior rating. The process should be ongoing, sensitive to developmental change, and carefully considered with every major shift in curriculum goals. As much as possible, the analysis should be phrased in specific terms. Statements such as "has difficulty with visual-motor functioning" or "has trouble paying attention" are less than useful to the formation of teaching strategies and goals. It is in this sense that the categories and specific skills of Table 4 can be most helpful. For example, a child can be described as reading below grade level, with low motivation and a poor self-image. Or he can be assessed more specifically as weak in phonemic, auditory memory, and auditory discrimination skills; relatively adequate in vocabulary, comprehension, and fine motor skills; and strong in visual memory and visual discrimination skills. The more complete description becomes the basis for wide-ranging curriculum choices. In the classroom, elements of the Ginn 360 Reading Program (primarily a sight approach to reading) may be selected to improve skills by capitalizing on strengths; and supplementary phonics materials, along with games emphasizing auditory discrimination skills, may be introduced in small doses for remediation. Outside the classroom, parents and child care workers can promote the growth of a more positive self-image not only by emotional support but by providing concrete opportunities for the child to be competent in activities that emphasize visual interaction with the environment.

*"Demystification" of the Academic Curriculum.* The special education curriculum is often seen as a blueprint for

highly technical, rather mysterious happenings in the classroom. Within this frame of reference, the child's learning disabilities are or are not remediated by various arcane interventions arranged by the teacher, while parents and other helpers anxiously await the outcome. Happily, an emphasis on observable skills and on individual learning style removes this implicit notion of cure from the classroom. With competence as the focus, *any curriculum can be much more usefully defined as an overall plan of action designed to optimize skills already present in the individual and to facilitate the acquisition of new skills necessary to the attainment of preselected goals.* The "specialness" of special education, then, is not that the materials used or the teacher's programmed actions have magical properties but, rather, that the strategies of teaching and the selection of specific academic goals are carefully matched with the individual learning style of each child.

In programmatic terms, this definition suggests that the academic curriculum should possess three basic attributes. First of all, it should be *comprehensible to the child.* The child should be able to understand where he is headed with a particular lesson, what skills he is using or struggling to master in a given task, and how he can use the skills he does have to program his own problem solving. In the arithmetic lesson, the child with limited ability to deal with abstract number concepts may learn to count much faster if the teacher provides concrete objects to manipulate. He or she can learn something equally useful if the teacher also explains why the blocks are part of the lesson and how similar aids could be used to help solve similar problems. Second, the academic curriculum should be directed at *concrete academic goals.* The bane of many special education classrooms is that they are saddled with nonspecific or esoteric objectives. It is very hard to tell whether "learning to learn" or "reading readiness" has taken place until such global aims have been translated into specific, observable goals which staff, children, and parents clearly understand. Also, since the classroom is usually the only place in the program where basic academic skills in reading, language arts, and arithmetic are directly addressed, progress toward the acquisition of these skills needs to remain the central focus of classroom activity whatever the general philosophy of the school. Finally, the academic curriculum should be *continuous* with the various kinds of learning taking place in other areas of the child's life. Specific academic goals can be quite distinct from goals established elsewhere in the therapeutic environment or in the home, but they do not require a totally discontinuous set of learning skills. Ideally, the individual child should experience learning to read as connected to a process of growing up and changing, which also includes learning how to make a friend, play baseball, or deal with angry feelings.

*Selection of Curriculum Materials.* The books, games, puzzles, papers, and other objects which the teacher brings into the classroom as aids to learning are part of the concrete manifestation of curriculum design. They also are important factors in defining the physical impact of the classroom as a learning environment. One of the benefits of demystifying the academic curriculum is that it clarifies the problem of choosing materials. It does not simplify the problem—individualized planning for even a small group of children remains a tremendously detailed business—but it does redefine the nature of the task. Basically, despite the fact that special education materials are often marketed as the "cure" for specific disabilities, the teacher need not assemble materials in the same way a hospital keeps particular medications on hand to treat particular symptoms. Rather, the teacher's job is to provide learning aids useful in various ways and at various stages of a dynamic process—to put together a range of materials that can be adapted to the individual learning style of each child. Two things are implied by this approach.

In the first place, the curriculum tools should be *multimodal.* In teaching skills related to reading, for instance, the teacher should have the option to use materials meant primarily to be looked at (such as books, pictures, or flash cards), listened to (such as records or tape cassettes), written on (such as workbooks and journals), manipulated (such as games and puzzles), responded to (such as programmed learning exercises), or acted out (such as oral exercises or structured language experiences), depending on the preferred learning modalities of each child.

Second, curriculum materials should be *maximally flexible,* in the same sense that a component stereo system is more flexible than a cabinet model. We have not come across any one curriculum package that provides a surefire way to teach reading, develop arithmetic skills, or promote perceptual-motor competence. The best criterion for choosing such complex materials for use with more than one child is their capability for effective use in component parts, out of sequence, and in combination with materials already in use in the classroom. This is especially important for those children whose age-appropriate interest level is not matched by age-appropriate skill in some areas of academic learning.

*The Shape of Space in the Classroom.* The shape of classroom space can be used as a physical tool for implementing curriculum objectives. Specifically, the teacher needs to make certain that the physical environment is flexible enough to be *responsive* to individual learning style and to the varying demands of the curriculum. For example, there should be at least one neutral area, where extraneous stimulation is screened out; individual desks enclosed on three sides are easy to construct and can be useful for this purpose, or small soundproofed areas adjacent to the main classroom may be even better. In the remainder of classroom space, the teacher and the children themselves should be able to adjust the environment to accommodate particular needs—opening up the space and adding stimulation for play and unstructured activity, bringing chairs and tables close together to focus on the teacher in group instruction. To assure this flexibility, the furniture in the classroom should be easily movable, and the amount of light and sound in the space should be fully adjustable.

In striving for a responsive environment, the teacher should not overlook the importance of programming the space as *instructive*—communicating the message that the classroom is a unique place, with its own rules and requirements for behavior. Specifically, the teacher should tell the children what they are expected to do at the reading table or in the science corner and should make certain that there are no hidden environmental contingencies. As we noted above, many children with special needs lack perceptual skills necessary to remain oriented in a given space or fail to make use of spatial cues in modifying their behavior. The teacher can help these children by keeping the classroom space as simple and direct as possible; that is, by carefully limiting the numbers and kinds of objects in the room, accompanying every transition to a new spatial configuration with explicit directions, and generally overdefining the connection of specific spaces to specific behaviors.

*The Climate of Surface Behavior.* Five important environmental characteristics contribute to effective and responsible behavior management in the classroom. The most obvious of these is a climate of *respect for individual differences.* Since few behavior management strategies are both effective and also valid for every child in the class, the teacher should be willing to adjust specific rules and regulations accordingly. A second general characteristic is *clarity of expectation* in all areas. There should be no mysteries in the classroom. Each step of the academic curriculum—including the teacher's expectations for behavior and the action potential of the physical materials in use—should be as clear and unambiguous as possible. Many behavior problems associated with intrapsychic conflicts in the children begin with much simpler problems of communication in the environment. A third factor that needs to be present throughout the program is an *attitude of support* for the school. A potential source of behavior difficulty in any classroom is the fact that schoolwork is sometimes restrictive, frustrating, and hard. In the face of this, all adults involved with the child must deliver the unequivocal message that success in school is worth the effort. A fourth environmental feature that promotes effective management is the presence of sufficient, instantly *available backup* to the classroom. The teacher should not have to engage extremely disruptive behavior *in class*; moreover, removal from the classroom should result in as little attention as possible—to avoid either active or covert positive reinforcement—until the child and the teacher can agree to resume the important business of going to school. Such an approach requires considerable staff teamwork and an acceptance of backup as part of the curriculum rather than as a sign of the teacher's weakness or an emergency response to the child's "bad" behavior. The last general characteristic is careful *attention to group composition* in the classroom. Extreme behavior variability can be minimized by careful grouping that takes into account behavioral, social, and affective competence skills, as well as grade levels of academic achievement.

*Administrative Structures and Linkages.* In our administrative as well as clinical experience, we have found it useful to consider all staff who work directly with children as teachers in the broadest sense. The classroom teacher orients his or her curriculum planning to one set of goals, the child care worker to another, the caseworker to a third, and so on. In working with the individual child or group of children, each staff person benefits from knowing which teaching strategies work best for the other. Therefore, an efficient staffing schedule might be devised in such a way that the child care worker can spend a part of his or her workday directly in the classroom, or the teacher can regularly participate in activities after school or in the residence. Such overlap promotes more complete understanding and respect for the importance of coordinating the environment as a whole. At the least, it seems to us, the administrative structure of any therapeutic setting should include mechanisms by which school staff and all other staff can directly share their day-to-day experiences as teachers without excessive time pressure caused by rigid scheduling and delineations of "turf."

### The Therapeutic Environment and Public School

Thus far, we have been talking about special education as a completely integrated part of the therapeutic environment. In doing so, we have stressed the notion that the whole program should be understood as a learning environment for the child and that the academic curriculum is most effectively designed as continuous with the teaching of competence skills in all areas. Such integration is not always a simple practical matter—especially in settings for troubled children where academic education is provided by various arrangements with the public schools.* Yet we believe strongly that the goal of maintaining maximum possible continuity between education in the classroom and education in the treatment program needs to be pursued, no matter what the structural organization of the setting.

*Guidelines for Assessment of the Public School.* There is wide variability in the response of public schools to children with special needs. This is true not only from community to community but also among different schools in the same system and different classrooms in the same school. The responsible child advocate is thus faced with the necessity to do some careful shopping in order to achieve the best possible match between available services and the individual learning style of each child. Ideally, of course, the treatment program should have well-established ties to the public schools, so that flexibility on the part of school staff is assured. But even if this is not the case, most states have ample legal precedents for insisting on the school's full cooperation in meeting the special educational needs of every child in a nondiscriminatory way. Public Law 94-142 spells out in detail the federal government's position on the rights of children with special needs. Both parents and interested professionals would do well to become familiar with the provisions of this landmark legislation.

In seeking to match public school resources to the special needs of each child and to the overall goals for learning established in the therapeutic program, one must begin with a clear, detailed assessment of individual learning style. The range of options in the school system can then be considered for the best possible fit. At Walker School we have found it useful to look at a number of factors in making this judgment. We begin by looking at *stated goals and objectives*—how the teachers or special education team view their work. What do they *say* they are

---

*When we talk about working with the public school, we do not mean only (or even primarily) working with separate special education classrooms. The child with special needs may be best placed in a regular classroom. See Siegel (1969) and Gearheart and Weishahn (1976) for some interesting reflections on special education in the regular public school classroom.

doing in the classroom? Especially in the special education classes, are the stated goals narrowly academic or narrowly "psychotherapeutic"? Do the stated goals sound reasonable for the particular child? How specific and measurable are they? How do they compare with goals of the therapeutic program outside the classroom? Most important, are the basic goals of classroom activity clear to the children? We also try to determine *unstated* goals—for instance, the pressure on the teacher to gear the curriculum toward performance on standardized tests, or an unspoken agreement with the principal to keep the special education children away from the rest of the school. Some *degree of segregation* from the mainstream of school activity is often a feature of special education in the public schools. In some systems the special classes are concentrated in one building or are clearly designed as self-contained and separate from all other classes. In other systems, the segregation can be quite subtle—characterized by the routine use of labels which set the child with special needs apart from "normal" children in the regular classroom. Although deliberate segregation might occasionally be desirable, a significant degree of segregation usually makes for academic and social isolation, which can be quite damaging. This factor should be carefully considered in placement.

We also assess *class size and teacher/pupil ratio.* There are no magic numbers here, but we usually consider a teacher/pupil ratio of one to four necessary for dealing with children with serious learning difficulties. In general, the larger the class, the more the children must be able to work on their own and postpone gratification. This is highly appropriate for some children but not for others. The *location of the school* also should be considered, since the school ordinarily should be close to the program. Also, the immediate neighborhood of the school building may be more or less desirable for children who are sensitive to social or physical stimulation.

We also need to assess in advance *how much self-control a child will need* in a particular setting. Specifically, how much stimulation is there in the environment (including noise, light, color, motoric activity, and subject matter of the curriculum)?

How many transitions from one activity to another or one place to another is the child required to make? How much structure and control are successfully provided by the adults? There is no "best" combination of these three which provides effective learning, yet clearly some children will be more prepared to handle unstructured and stimulating environments than others. A good match here can head off behavioral crises which can wreck a school placement.

It is also important to estimate the *resources available to the classroom*. What happens when a crisis occurs in the classroom? Who comes to help, and what do they do? Aside from crisis intervention, how many teaching specialists, tutors, aides, and guidance counselors are regularly available to the classroom? How often are they available? In many cases, the extra attention of a supportive staff member can make all the difference in school adjustment. Of course, some teachers are more open to supportive help and team work than others, and this needs to be carefully looked at.

Another important area for assessment is *classroom flexibility*. What strategies for teaching and what kinds of curriculum materials are used in the classroom? And are the school staff willing to make adjustments in established routine? Absence of flexibility is not always a disaster, but it does require that the child and the program staff have the resources to do most of the adjusting. Some of the questions to ask here include: What is the approach to the teaching of reading? How willing is the teacher to adapt this approach? Is one-to-one instruction available in areas of special difficulty? How much experience will the child have programming his own learning? Will the treatment program staff be permitted to come to school, and will the teacher be able to participate in the program? Depending on the child, answers to these questions can be vital to any sort of integration of therapeutic planning.

In striving for a good fit, we must also consider the potential *peer group*—not only from the point of view of homogeneity of academic skill levels but also on the basis of such things as the age and physical size of the children, modal behaviors within the group, degree of street sophistication, and socioeconomic background. Extreme differences between the individual and the group in any one of these areas can have a variety of detrimental influences. The child may feel demeaned in a class where the children are much younger and smaller than he is, even though academic skills are similar. Or an exceptionally street-wise youngster may cause tension in a classroom of average fifth-graders. We are not suggesting that every child needs to be exactly like every other child in the class. However, if the classroom is to be a safe place to take the risks necessary in learning, the child must recognize a basic commonality with his peers.

Finally, the *relationship of the public school to the family* should be taken into account. Does the teacher have frequent, direct contact with families? Where do the school staff members stand on the popular idea that parents are the primary cause of childhood difficulty? Are the staff able to describe what goes on in school in practical terms, free of jargon? There may be many situations where these questions are unimportant, but they are vital when parents are active in the helping process. In regard to the individual learning style of each child, parents should be able to learn a great deal from teachers, and teachers from parents.

*The Child Care Worker as Facilitator.* Making the best possible arrangement for each child is only the first step in establishing therapeutic coherence between public school and the treatment program. For continued integration, which is more than the exchange of periodic progress reports or disciplinary backup, frequent communication and a great deal of effort are required. In our view, the child care worker is the program staff member in the best position to coordinate this effort. First, the child care worker has information about the child's individual learning style that may be highly relevant in the classroom. Second, the child care worker is closest to the reality of everyday life in the program. He is in tune with the transitions to and from school, aware of changes in the child's emotional weather, knowledgeable about how much time is really available for doing homework, and the like. Finally, the child care worker is often able to use his relationship with the child and the parents in managing a variety of difficult situations. In our experience, liaison with the school should include at least weekly contact between the child care worker and the classroom teacher, in order to fully exploit all these advantages. Much vital firsthand information can get lost if contact with the public school is primarily between administrators or between caseworkers and guidance counselors, who are often one step removed from the child's daily experience.

The child care worker can perform a number of functions as facilitator of the interaction of the child, the family, and the treatment program with the public school. In the first place, he or she will need to be a careful *observer* and *recorder,* in order to keep track of the child's behavior in and out of the classroom and to make sure that all parties get the information necessary for planning. Some sort of daily log for recording contacts with the teacher and direct observations of the child's school-related behavior is usually a good idea in this regard. The child care worker also will sometimes act as an *interpreter*—making certain that the teacher and the program staff understand each other's view of what the child needs.

Part of the difficulty of having the school separate from the treatment program is purely logistical. In dealing with this problem, the child care worker will need to function at least part of the time as an *organizer* and *coordinator of resources*— seeing that the appropriate staff get together at appropriate times, helping families stay involved with the school even if they are from another community, and making it possible for the child to participate in after-school activities. This is the kind of unglamorous work (juggling schedules, organizing transportation, scrounging for money and equipment) that often gets a low priority; yet it is essential for complete coherence.

As an effective facilitator, the child care worker will also need to be a *salesperson* and public relations expert. He or she will need to convey a positive attitude about school and school-work to the child, using the collaborative relationship to support and motivate. This task is important especially if the quality of the education program is less than perfect. With school staff, the child care worker may need to be especially persuasive

—defusing head-to-head confrontations between child and teacher, advocating for the child without setting up an adversary relationship, educating the school staff as to the philosophy of the program without being patronizing, and selling the teacher on the importance of sharing as much as possible with parents and program staff. The essence of this salesmanship is to help all parties maintain respect for each other in the face of difficulty and disappointment.

Another important job of the child care worker as facilitator is to act as a *backup resource* if a behavioral crisis or any other special problem occurs. Both the school staff and the child should be able to use the child care worker as a sponge for hostility and discouragement, and to see him or her as an ally in the event of trouble. This is no easy task. It requires that the child care worker be able to relate not only to the child but to the teacher as a professional colleague handling a difficult situation. Of course, it also requires ongoing lines of communication and physical availability to the classroom.

Finally, the child care worker *as teacher* is in an excellent position to integrate work on academic skills with program goals outside the classroom. He can, for instance, help children manage their time and energy so that homework gets completed, or he can look for ways to combine academic and life-space goals in more subtle ways. During the evening routine, learning something about transitions can be combined with the promotion of reading and language acquisition skills if a regular story time or quiet reading period is built in. More generally, the child care worker can be constantly alert to helping the child acquire and process new information. Having the daily newspaper prominently available, making creative use of wall space and bulletin boards, and constantly "seeding" the environment with new words, new ideas, and new objects to experience can pay tremendous dividends in any classroom. In all of this, the classroom teacher is a potential resource regarding the selection of materials and particular strategies with individual children.

## Conclusions

An overall commitment to promoting competence skills rather than curing emotional illness is the most meaningful goal of services. However, teaching competence is a goal which is best shared by the teacher and the child care worker when the whole child is understood in terms of *individual learning style*. This understanding can be the basis of a common language for teaching.

The individual child experiences the impact of the therapeutic environment as a continuous process. He or she does not present one set of learning skills in the life space and an entirely different set in the classroom. Therefore, the curriculum for teaching competence skills should also be continuous. The whole program can be structured as a *learning environment,* in which goals in the classroom and goals in the life space are closely coordinated.

Specific techniques for working with children with special needs in the classroom should be designed first to exploit existing strengths in the child and only secondarily to remediate specific weaknesses. This is an important methodological distinction which influences program design in a number of ways.

Even when the school program is physically separate from the helping environment, coherent program implementation depends on an explicit and continuing partnership between teachers and child care workers. This partnership is a necessity for fully effective teaching both in and out of the classroom, since teacher and child care worker together are the primary change agents in the helping environment.

# 8

## Evaluating Residential Child Care Programs

In what some have described as "the age of accountability," child caring agencies have become increasingly
concerned with the question of effectiveness: Does residential
care work? For what kinds of troubled children? At what costs?
In lieu of what alternatives? Has a particular program demonstrated clinical effectiveness (that is, were positive results
achieved with this or that individual child)? What of the total
program's effectiveness (is the total agency output sufficient to
meet program objectives in a cost-effective manner)? Such questions—raised by public and voluntary funding bodies, as well as
by many within the child helping professions—have caused
group care practitioners to devote more time and attention to
the whole area of program evaluation. Another stimulus for
evaluation derives from the fact that we lack a definitive and
prescriptive model for residential care and thus need to develop
the knowledge that will allow us to do a better job of serving

troubled children and youth. Therefore, program evaluation seeks to meet the short-range objective of accountability and the longer-range objective of knowledge development.

### Problems of Program Evaluation in Residential Care

*Absence of Controls.* For ethical and practical reasons, many studies omit the use of control groups required in the classic experimental design. Although this omission leaves the interpretation of results open to question—particularly with respect to "success"—one cannot, for the sake of establishing a control group, deprive troubled children of needed care and treatment. Hence, many outcome studies have tended toward a comparison group design—testing differential approaches to residential and nonresidential treatment on a similar population of referrals.

*Poorly Defined Service Units.* In such an all-encompassing service strategy as milieu treatment, it is often difficult to specify exactly what a service unit consists of and also to identify which interventions are most potent in changing behavior. While such questions are not of paramount interest to the clinician concerned primarily with positive movement in an individual case, they are of concern to executives and planners charged with the responsibility for program expansion. An often-heard refrain in the field is "We know we are doing some things right—but we are not sure which ones."

*Improper Selection of Outcome Criteria.* All too often, residential programs have allowed themselves to be evaluated on a narrow range of criteria—grades in school, recidivism, absence of police contact—which either are not directly related to services offered or which occur in community environments where the residential program has little involvement, much less control. Such outcome studies typically show discouraging results and lead to the nihilistic conclusion that "nothing works" with these kids. The opposite problem is reflected in some outcome studies where extremely diffuse and poorly defined measures of community and personal adjustment have been used. These ratings often are based on the clinical judgment of the therapists who provided the services and are open to questions of reliability and validity.

*Sample Selection.* Troubled children and youth are seldom randomly assigned to different residential programs; instead, placement depends on such factors as severity of problem, prognosis for positive change, and available bed space. These factors may definitely bias sample selection in a number of ways. For example, some programs may engage in a "creaming-off" operation—accepting only the best-risk children—in order to positively dispose toward program successes. This problem of nonrandom assignment, particularly when coupled with the absence of a control group, can confound the interpretation of results from a program—particularly a demonstration project seeking funds for expansion on the basis of a high degree of success in the pilot phase.

*Lack of Utility.* Because many of the studies of residential child care are outcome studies—often conducted by outside researchers—many child care practitioners doubt the value of the research enterprise and feel that its findings are of little use in shaping day-to-day practice. Almost by definition, outcome research cannot be directly useful, since it does not focus on the treatment process as it is occurring but on a "payoff" that occurs, if at all, long after children have left care. Moreover, its results are cast in terms of group data—30 percent adjusted "well," 30 percent adjusted "poorly"—and offer little to the practitioner who is looking for help and direction with an individual case.

## Program Evaluation in Residential Treatment: A Selective Review

With these general problems in mind, let me briefly review some representative studies from the field of group child care. Gershenson (1956); Dinnage, Pringle, and Kellmer (1967); Shyne (1973); Kadushin (1974); and Prosser (1976) provide reviews of research in residential child care; although they do not focus on the problems of program evaluation exclusively, they provide a useful starting point for the interested practitioner.

More recently, Durkin and Durkin (1975) compiled a review on program evaluation in residential treatment for disturbed children. This lengthy review provides a thoughtful appraisal of existing studies, as well as an analysis of the strengths and weaknesses of various approaches to program evaluation. The authors identify four different types of evaluation in the existing literature: descriptive studies, outcome and follow-up studies, process evaluations, and systems analyses. Only a few representative examples from each category will be listed here. Of the four types, descriptive works are most numerous. These include case examples as well as more encompassing descriptions of a total milieu program (see Bettelheim, 1950; Redl and Wineman, 1957; Goldfarb, Mintz, and Stroock, 1969). While never intended to assess process or outcome, such descriptive studies often provide a useful conceptual framework for understanding a therapeutic milieu.

Notable among outcome studies is the pioneering study at the Ryther Child Center (Johnson and Reid, 1947) and the follow-up study at Bellefaire in Cleveland (Allerhand, Weber, and Haug, 1966). Other representative examples include Davids, Ryan, and Salvatore (1968); Goldenberg (1971); Cavior, Schmidt, and Karacki (1972); Garber (1972); and Taylor and Alpert (1973). Nearly all these outcome studies suffer from some of the methodological and organizational problems mentioned earlier. Such problems have led at least one reviewer to question traditional definitions of success and failure in residential treatment (Lerman, 1968, 1975). Outcome criteria are often not well defined, and baseline measures are typically lacking. Thus, the degree of change experienced and its relationship to the treatment effort—as opposed to, say, maturation effects —are difficult to ascertain. Further, most group studies assume a commonality of presenting problems and do not provide a differential analysis of treatment effects across different types of troubled children. Whatever their shortcomings, however, such studies have provided a wealth of information on gaps in present services. For example, both the Allerhand, Weber, and Haug study (1966) and the Taylor and Alpert study (1973) indicate that, for most children, the posttreatment environment is the determining factor in ultimate community adjustment. Such conclusions are also suggested by the research of Cavior, Schmidt, and Karacki (1972) at the Robert F. Kennedy Youth Center—a federal institution for older delinquent adolescents. These studies point clearly to the need for an extension of the treatment process into the postinstitutional environment. As noted earlier, adjustment in the institution is not necessarily a good predictor of community adjustment.

A third group of studies, process evaluations, attempt to assess changes during the course of treatment. For example, Millman and Pancost (1977) modified several behavioral rating scales to measure changes over time in cottage behavior in a large children's institution. Nelson, Singer, and Johnson (1973) suggest a sequence of evaluations including pretreatment, discharge, and posttreatment in a variety of situational contexts. Another example of a process study in residential care is provided by Monkman (1972).

As at least a partial answer to the problems inherent in the previously discussed types of studies, Durkin and Durkin (1975, p. 323) suggest a systems approach to evaluation in residential care, which would capture the following goals: treatment (an assessment of changes in mental health, interpersonal relations, attitudes, or recidivism), socialization or enculturation (an assessment of children's development of job, academic, and interpersonal skills and their own personality), custodial care (how well children are cared for in terms of their health, food, shelter, and living conditions), in-service training (the development of models for similar programs), and *isolation of* disruptive individuals (to protect society until they are ready to return to it). The authors suggest an evaluation strategy involving the total inputs and outputs of the residential program, including client behavioral ratings (before and after treatment), program participation, severity of problem, and other key client and staff variables.

## Implications for Practice

What does all this suggest for the residential program interested in evaluation? Perhaps several things. Evaluation must be seen in the context of developing a total agency information system which serves multiple purposes and which requires multiple formats for obtaining information. For example, while studies that focus on the question of staff accountability to children may be useful to residential supervisors, this kind of research is not helpful in a hearing before a funding panel. Similarly, the kind of design needed to measure the outcome of residential treatment will offer little in the way of practical and immediate help in measuring the progress of individual children while they are still in care. Thus, while the literature suggests many formats for obtaining information, the critical and prior question for the agency is: *For what purpose will this information be used?*

A second and related factor has to do with the problem of limited resources. For example, is the social systems approach proposed by Durkin and Durkin (1975) really feasible for the majority of residential child care programs, which have limited resources in collecting, analyzing, and making use of data? My own feeling is that, despite the many benefits of such an approach, most programs would find it difficult to operationalize and cumbersome to implement. They will therefore have to choose which questions and which audiences are most important to address, and they will have to decide how the questions and audiences selected can be addressed in the most cost-efficient manner. The basic tasks really involve *information retrieval* and *communication*.

Political factors also enter into the process of evaluation. In an earlier chapter, I argued for a wide range of "hard" and "soft" outcome measures rather than a single criterion such as recidivism or school grades. These indicators are important but not sufficient to capture the full impact of the services rendered. Equally important, for example, is the whole area of *consumer validation*: How do the children, their families, teachers, and referring agencies view the service and judge its usefulness? While such reactions are subjective and may not correlate with "hard" indicators of success (Berleman, Seaberg, and Steinburn, 1972), they are nonetheless *socially* important and may constitute important data in funding requests. Far too little attention has been given to this most important area of consumer validation, though some of the newer community-based programs have incorporated consumer feedback into the very core of their treatment model with good results (Wolf, Phillips, and Fixsen, 1974). A pioneering project by the National Children's Bureau in England, called "Who Cares," regularly solicits feedback from a large sample of children in and out of home care (Page and Clark, 1977).

In my judgment, we are not even close to developing a definitive model of residential treatment, and we should not design our research as if each study were going to answer the question once and for all. We do need outcome studies to build on the results already in, and these should focus on the ecological variability of the environments to which the children and youth will return. For the individual agency, research should seek to provide some immediate indicators of progress toward treatment goals, with particular emphasis on how children change while they are in the program. A review of the literature suggests to me that we have not given ourselves sufficient credit for change that occurred while the children were still in care. Given the primitive state of our treatment technology and our relative lack of control over the posttreatment environment, positive change during the course of residential care reflects no small accomplishment and should be presented as nothing less than a major achievement.

## Three Innovative Approaches

Three presently available technologies seem to me potentially useful to the group child caring agency wishing to develop some information on its effects with individual children and their families.

*Single-Subject Design.* The traditional group research designs have offered little in the way of practical help to the child care worker or therapist. As mentioned earlier, such designs do not typically differentiate between children but rather assume commonality. Furthermore, they are not designed to provide feedback during the course of treatment but yield their "results" only when the child has left the program. Finally, when the results do come in, they are couched in terms of percentages of successes and failures of the total group under study—and add little to our knowledge of why we succeeded or failed with any particular child. Thus, we need a technology that provides a valid and reliable measure of individual progress and immediate feedback on which treatment techniques and teaching formats are most effective with a given problem behavior. As a potentially useful tool for child care practitioners, the single-subject design comes closest to meeting these criteria.

The single-subject design is really a number of different research paradigms with one important common element. Rather than looking at changes *between* individuals or groups, the single-subject design (SSD) measures change *within* an individual case. For example, in residential care the child's progress toward treatment goals is measured against a pretreatment baseline of behavior. In effect, each subject provides his or her own "control group" as change is monitored precisely and differentially across different children and different behaviors. To the line child care practitioner, the "payoff" to such a research strategy comes in knowing whether or not criterion was reached for a particular goal and what specific interventions were responsible for achieving it. Though a relatively recent phenomenon in clinical practice, single-subject designs have long been used in behavioral research to identify which conditions in a given situation have the greatest impact on an individual's behavior. One early study, for example, demonstrated the powerful—though unintended—effect of social reinforcement from teachers on crying behavior in preschool children (Hart and others, 1964).

While no exhaustive review of the literature on SSD is possible here, ample materials are available for the interested child care practitioner. Browning and Stover (1971) describe the multiple uses of the SSD in a residential treatment center for severely disturbed children; Birnbrauer, Peterson, and Solnick (1974) describe the design and interpretation of single case studies; the recent volume by Hersen and Barlow (1976) provides an extensive review of the literature as well as numerous examples of applications in a variety of settings; Thoresen and Anton (1973) describe the interaction of various SSD designs and counseling procedures in a school setting; and Howe (1974) discusses the use of the SSD in casework practice; finally, Jayaratne and Levy (in press) point out the multiple uses of the SSD in a number of different community treatment settings.

One type of SSD is the *simple time series design* (AB), where a behavior is recorded for some time prior to treatment (A) and continues to be recorded throughout treatment (B). The best possible data obtainable from such an elementary design would consist of a stable baseline followed by a change in trend after the initiation of treatment. A hypothetical example might be the amount of time spent on a focused learning task before and after the initiation of praise from staff (see Figure 4). It is clear even from cursory scanning of the data that a

**Figure 4. Example of a Simple Time Series Design**

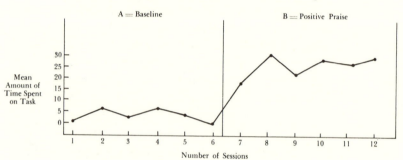

change in the desired direction occurred. Criterion will be set by the staff member and will usually be related inversely to the stability of the baseline, the less stable baseline requiring a higher criterion than the relatively stable one to demonstrate effectiveness. While such a design cannot confirm that the behavior changed because of the intervention, the mere fact that positive change occurred is sufficient for the child care practitioner, who is interested primarily in clinical progress. Even at this elementary level, the SSD provides a way of organizing a treatment intervention by recording a baseline, specifying target behavior, specifying intervention, and recording change.

In some research, the problem of alternative explanations is at least partially solved by a return to baseline conditions and then a return of treatment to see whether criterion is again met

(ABAB). This so-called *repeated time series design* (and there are numerous variations) probably has little relevance for child care work practice, since it involves the dubious ethics of attempting to reverse treatment gains. More relevant is the *multiple treatment baseline design,* which evaluates different treatment strategems under the same conditions and thus permits comparisons between them. For example, one study with obvious implications for residential programs occurred in a classroom where the goal was to increase task-oriented behavior in children through the use of a behavioral paradigm which included token reinforcement for appropriate behavior, social reinforcement with the administration of tokens, and time out for disruptive behavior. In this design (Walker, Mattson and Buckley, 1971) a baseline was taken with all three treatments in effect. Each of the three treatments was then removed serially with a return to baseline in between as follows:

1. A (Baseline) . . . All three treatment components in effect
2. $B_1$        . . . Removal of the token reinforcement (rate of task-oriented behavior remains the same)
3. A          . . . Return to baseline
4. $B_2$        . . . Removal of positive social reinforcement (rate of task-oriented behavior declines markedly)
5. A          . . . Return to baseline
6. $B_3$        . . . Removal of time out (rate of task-oriented behavior again declines)

What we have, in effect, is a valid comparison of each of the treatment conditions with a baseline. The results suggested that the social reinforcement and the time out were functional aspects of the program and that the token reinforcement alone was ineffective in altering behavior. Furthermore, of the two functional components, social reinforcement appeared to be the more potent. This seems to me precisely the kind of paradigm we need to determine which "mix" of components makes most sense in designing a treatment intervention for a group of youngsters. While the order of the treatments may well have influenced results, we still have some reasonably valid data on which to base program decisions. Another version of this design might vary a single treatment along some parameter. For example, what length of time out is most effective in extinguishing low-level disruptive behavior?

Other variations of the single-subject design include the *multiresponse baseline design,* where two or more behaviors are recorded during baseline and then treated sequentially in a number of different phases. This design allows valid conclusions that change occurred and that the treatment was responsible, because dependent measures are continuous and because there is within-subject replication (Birnbrauer, Peterson, and Solnick, 1974, p. 198). Another variant, the *multiple baseline design,* takes several forms. That is, the same treatment may be applied sequentially (1) to separate target behaviors in a single subject, (2) across matched subjects presumably exposed to "identical" environmental conditions, or (3) to a single subject or group of subjects across independent situations (Hersen and Barlow, 1976, pp. 228-229). This multiple baseline design seems particularly useful in the group care program, where the same behavior is often a problem in different settings: the cottage, the classroom, and the child's home. Such a design allows for systematic monitoring of the same behavior across various settings as well as careful introduction of targeted treatment procedures.

While we have only barely scratched the surface of single-subject research, there do appear to be some potentially positive benefits to the use of this technology in residential child care:

1. The SSD provides precise feedback on the effects of our treatment interventions.
2. The SSD yields useful information on the individual child's progress and provides at least a partial data base for ongoing evaluation.
3. The SSD allows us to "change horses in midstream" by providing rapid feedback as to which interventions are working with a particular child and which are not.

4. The SSD moves us one notch up from clinical "hunches" in generalizing from past experiences to new children in care.
5. The SSD yields data that are readily communicable to line staff, parents, teachers, and other care givers—as well as to the child himself.

There are, as well, some limitations with single-subject research:

1. Many of the behaviors we seek to change are complex and do not readily yield specific targets or specific interventions.
2. A host of important variables (feelings, attitudes, self-concept, and the like) are not captured in the SSD.
3. Measurement itself—particularly continuous recording—presents logistical problems as well as problems of reliability—especially when child care staff who are already overburdened with direct care responsibilities are expected to do the major portion of the behavioral recording.
4. Even though the SSD need not be restricted to behavioral treatment, the choice of the research paradigm forces the staff to become more behaviorally specific with respect to target behaviors and procedures. As Browning and Stover (1971) noted, some staff may find the use of such behavioral technology "restrictive" and "unnatural."
5. The validity of the SSD has not yet been determined.

In sum, the SSD is not a panacea for the child care program interested in evaluation and, in fact, constitutes only one segment of a total agency information system. It is not without limitations in both implementation and interpretation. Despite these problems, it appears to be a potentially useful technology for measuring progress of individual children and providing feedback on the efficacy of treatment procedures.

*Goal Attainment Procedures.* While the single-subject design is useful for providing information about specific behaviors and therapeutic interventions, it does not provide a comprehensive framework for organizing information about the child's total progress. How is such material, related to major presenting problems and change goals, to be collected and utilized? My experience is that a great many group care programs collect reams of information about the child's progress—much of it written in narrative form—which is not useful in individual clinical evaluation, much less program evaluation. To be sure, the judgments of child care workers and therapists are useful, but only insofar as they attempt to specify exactly what the child's gains were and how they were attained. Clinical speculation provides a rich source of hypotheses, but it needs to be clearly separated from statements of fact in the record lest the two become confused. Many record-keeping systems are also plagued by an absence of baselines and/or pretreatment goals, so that the degree of change in an individual child is difficult to assess objectively. Clinical evaluation demands some systematic way of recording problems and progress toward proximate and long-term goals. Such a system can also provide at least a partial base for program evaluation designed to measure the effectiveness of the total agency in meeting its mission. Some residential programs have found both goal-oriented and problem-oriented recording systems useful in this regard.

The most widely used goal-oriented system is the Goal Attainment Scale (GAS) developed by Kiresuk and Sherman (1968). The GAS—first developed in community mental health and much modified—has been widely disseminated and employed in a variety of social and health agencies (for core bibliography see Garwick, McCree and Brintnall, 1976). Johnson and associates (Johnson, 1974; Johnson and others, 1976) describe a major adaptation of the GAS concept at a residential treatment center for adolescent girls. The process involves developing with each individual girl a range of short- and long-term goals, the means through which they are to be achieved and a range of expected outcomes: "most desirable . . . . . . least desirable." Goal statements are behaviorally specific and typically reflect a wide range of developmental areas—social, academic, and vocational. All staff who will be working directly with the girls are involved in the goal setting process. Goal statements may be altered and updated and progress is reviewed on a regular basis. The authors provide a useful discussion of some of the practical problems involved in implementing GAS in a large, complex treatment institution. Benedict (1976) and Benedict and Bruce (1975) describe a similar adaptation of GAS in four residential treatment programs for disturbed adolescents. Although such adaptations show promise, some recent critics argue that GAS has been too widely distributed without proper attention being paid to its limitations. Typically, these include problems with deciding just what a goal is, how it should be described, and what respective roles clients and therapists should play in the actual rating of goal attainment (Seaberg and Gillespie, 1977; Willer and Miller, 1976).

Despite these potential limitations, GAS does seem to offer much that is useful to the smaller residential child care program. What struck me most forcefully in the two examples previously cited was the extent to which children were actively involved in developing a set of reasonable goals for themselves and figuring out how they would best be achieved. The involvement of all key staff—child care workers, teachers, and social workers—along with parents helps to ensure that expectations are clear from the outset. The process of goal setting itself gives a direction to the inevitable assessment phase when a child first enters the residence and helps to take the mystery out of treatment by pinpointing some clearly defined objectives for the short and long term. Just as the single subject design provides a useful framework for assessing the effectiveness of a particular treatment intervention, the GAS offers a helpful framework for assessing a total case plan at regular intervals. It is, in short, a useful tool for organizing the endless bits of information collected on individual children in care and relating them to a set of basic treatment goals.

Finally, the GAS and other scales for rating child behavior (see Wahler, House, and Stambaugh, 1976; Patterson and associates, 1975; Spivack and Swift, 1967; Schaefer and Millman, 1973; and Millman and Pancost, 1977) provide at least the potential as a basic data source for a more comprehensive evaluation of program. The need for such information is crucial when one surveys the status of evaluation in the field as a whole. A comprehensive survey of Alberta's residential treatments centers yields a conclusion that is probably generally accurate: "The majority of centers don't have criteria for success and

failure written down. ... Most directors have never calculated
their percentage of successes at discharge or follow up. Comparison between the effects of different treatments, between different interventions and between the effects of treatment and
maturation have all been informal in nature" (Johnson and
others, 1976, p. 281).

*Consumer Evaluation.* Wolf (1976, p. 24) suggests that if
services are to be ultimately effective, they must at some point
reflect what the various consumer groups feel is "socially important": "Earlier in our history, Watson and Skinner argued forcefully against subjective measurement because they were concerned about the inappropriate causal roles that hypothetical,
internal variables, subjectively separated, were playing in social
science. As a result, many of us concluded that all subjective
measurement was inappropriate. A new consensus seems to be
developing. It seems that if we aspire to social importance then we
must develop systems that allow our consumers to provide us
feedback about how our applications relate to their values, to
their reinforcers. This is not a rejection of our heritage. Our use of
subjective measures does not relate to internal causal variables.
Instead, it is an attempt to assess the dimensions of complex
reinforcers in socially acceptable and practical ways."

Wolf's brief for social validity does not rest on purely philosophical grounds. As one of the principal investigators in the
Achievement Place Project, frequently cited in this volume, he
describes how the project failed in its first attempt to replicate the
group home model in a new community—in large measure because
there were no mechanisms to elicit feedback from the community
until it was too late. In fact, this particular project has developed
what is very nearly a model for obtaining consumer feedback
from relevant groups—including youth, parents, teachers, em-
ployers, and community agencies—and then incorporating that
feedback into the program (Wolf, Phillips, and Fixsen, 1974; Willner and associates, 1977).*

Needless to say, subjective appraisals of service do not

*For further information on the consumer evaluation procedures
developed in this model, contact Elery L. Phillips, Deputy Director for
Youth Care, Father Flanagan's Boys Home, Boys Town, Nebraska, 68010.

always coincide with more objective indicators. For example, in the delinquency prevention experiment reported by Berleman, Seaberg, and Steinburn (1972), parents' and children's evaluations of services were overwhelmingly positive, even though the evaluation of effectiveness during the treatment period and during the eight months following treatment indicated no positive impact on disruptive behavior in school, police contacts, or the rate of institutionalization. How are such apparently conflicting sets of data to be reconciled? In this particular study, I suspect, the services offered were not sufficient to accomplish the aims of the project and thus constituted an unfair measure of effectiveness. This problem occurs again and again in the delinquency field and leads to the general conclusion that we should be extremely circumspect and cautious in defining objectives for limited service strategies. The second point is frankly speculative, but suggests to me that perhaps the parents and children were reporting a change in behavior or condition that the "objective" data-gathering instruments of the study were not sensitive to. In any event, the mere fact that the consumer of the service responded overwhelmingly positively toward it is to me an extremely significant and *socially relevant* indicator that should be central to any overall evaluation of effectiveness. Our goal in group child care programs should be to regularly report such subjective appraisal and demonstrate how it alters and improves services offered. One model for obtaining this information is the previously cited "Who Cares" Project of the National Children's Bureau in England (Page and Clark, 1977). This project regularly brings together children and youth in substitute care settings to elicit their views on a wide range of questions, for example which staff are most helpful to them and how connected do they feel to the community in which they reside. It seems to me that such a format could easily be extended to other consumers—parents, teachers, and referring agencies, for example—and thus provide a continuing source of data on residential child care throughout the community.

## Suggestions on Implementation

Because many of the strategies of program evaluation were developed by researchers and organizational analysts, some child care practitioners are hesitant to challenge their appropriateness for a particular group care setting. It is well to remind ourselves, however, that program evaluation is, by definition, a value-oriented process and not simply a scientific endeavor. Program evaluation is concerned at its most essential level with questions of "bestness" and "rightness," which are, fundamentally and properly, questions of value. What do we consider a "successfully" treated delinquent? What constitutes the "least restrictive alternative" in services? What determines "accountability" in children's services? What factors distinguish "quality care" from "adequate care"? Such questions cannot be answered in a purely rational, totally objective process divorced from the conflicting value assumptions from which they arise. Thus, while a commitment to thorough and ongoing program evaluation does move us more toward a scientific, objective approach to practice, it also takes us deeper into the political area, where we as practitioners need to fight tenaciously for what we believe is "right" and "best" and not allow ourselves to be the docile subjects for somebody else's "objective" research.

I have argued consistently throughout this chapter that practitioners need to get involved in the process of evaluation—specifically, in problem formulation, instrument development, data collection, and analysis. Many programs, however, lack the staff resources in both time and expertise to adequately address the question of evaluation. Some options include purchasing the time of a research consultant, designating a portion of staff time to evaluation, and/or forming an agency-wide committee to deal with evaluation. This kind of in-house capability is particularly critical when an external agency—usually a funding source—is actively involved in setting both the criteria for evaluation and the means by which they will be measured. External evaluation is desirable, but it should articulate with and be sensitive to the agency's own attempts to assess effectiveness. This is particularly important when the purpose for evaluation may differ considerably according to the source. The question for the group child care program faced with an external evaluation is this: Does sufficient expertise reside within the staff and/or consultants to critically analyze and modify an externally generated program evaluation? If the answer is "no,' {the program may find itself in the position of going to trial without a properly trained defense attorney.

Another problem attendant to implementation has to do with the mutual perceptions (or misperceptions) of clinicians and researchers. There are clearly differences in training, socialization, and orientation—though the stereotypes probably greatly exaggerate the differences. Clearly, all researchers are not "cold," "numbers oriented," "uncaring," and "narrow"; and clinicians are not necessarily "soft," "fuzzy headed," and "unscientific." The researcher or program evaluation consultant needs to understand the process of treatment if he or she is to evaluate it effectively. Similarly, the clinician and child care worker need to understand the requirements of the research enterprise in order to tell the story of what the program has accomplished. The best way to reach this understanding is to engage in a process of mutual education around the development of an evaluation package that makes sense for the particular group care setting, rather than simply "farming out" evaluation to the external consultant. The ideal exists in those group care programs where the research endeavor and the clinical process are intertwined and mutually reinforcing.

In my experience, many attempts at program evaluation have failed because they are too cumbersome, unwieldy, or ambitious. Data collection and analysis do take time, effort, and energy and often fall most heavily on those who also have primary responsibility for service delivery—the child care workers. This takes us back to the basic question of what it is we wish to know and for what purpose it shall be used. Economy of effort suggests not attempting to do everything at once, but rather phasing in components of a total evaluation package over time.

Another problem concerns the fact that evaluation stimulates anxiety on the part of those being evaluated. Properly used, this anxiety can be helpful in improving the quality of the program. For example, the child care staff member who receives corrective feedback on his or her behavior management skills can learn to become more effective in managing noisy and troublesome behavior in the cottage. The key element here is that the evaluation be seen as a tool used in the service of making the program better, not as an end in itself. Also critical is the commitment to evaluation across the total agency. For example, child care staff should have an opportunity to evaluate the effectiveness of their supervisors and administrators. The system needs to be perceived as essentially open to change at all levels if formative evaluation is to work at maximum effectiveness.

Finally, each child caring program should regularly evaluate the "evaluation package" (including consultants) to see if it is doing the job intended. Just as treatment needs change with organizational maturity and/or changes in client population, so do the needs for evaluation. Evaluation programs can grow to the point where the time required to fill out forms or code data seriously impinges on staff's ability to be with the children. In such instances, the research design itself has negatively affected the efficacy of treatment and should be modified. Procedures should be regularly reviewed to see if they are redundant and if the information they generate is serving a useful purpose.

# 9 Jerome Beker

# Training and Professional Development in Child Care

The concept of ecological child treatment developed in this book recognizes the differential needs of some troubled children for temporary out-of-home care, as well as the needs of all youngsters to move toward normal developmental objectives in the context of family and community life. Integrating these factors is an intricate, sophisticated process requiring skilled personnel, viewed here as generic child care professionals, who are sensitive to the requirements of effective functioning in the life space and to ways in which they can help the developmental process to move in this direction.

### Historical Perspective

The institutionalization of deviant youngsters in the United States essentially began in the early nineteenth century (Rothman, 1971). Before that, children we would now label as

205

dependent, neglected, disturbed, or delinquent remained at home or were "placed out" with relatives or others in the community. As cities grew, such youngsters were often sent to live with farm families, where they were cared for and provided a source of additional labor. Others made their own way on the city streets. There were a variety of economic and other reasons for this situation, but the key point is that the community served as the locus of intervention, and social roles were provided in the community for youngsters even if they had special problems. After 1800, for a variety of reasons, many of these youngsters were placed in institutions, largely in isolation from the outside world. The complexities of urbanization and industrial development reduced opportunities for deviant youngsters in the community, and it seemed easier to send them away. The institution was also viewed as a place where appropriate "moral training," including work, could be provided away from the "corrupting" influences of the city streets. Presumably, the youngsters could then return home "reformed," to take their places as good citizens (Whittaker, 1973b). These early institutions providing care were not solely punitive, although "discipline" was regarded as an essential element of the program. Institutional staff members worked with large groups, but the literature of the period reflects their genuine concern for the healthy development of the individual child in the context of nineteenth-century thinking (Marks, 1973; Rothman, 1971). These were the first child care workers, untrained and nonprofessional, certainly custodial by the standards of today, but apparently committed to enhancing the development and welfare of the youngsters in their care.

Around the time of the Civil War, it was recognized that this system was not having its desired effects. The observation of Brace (1872) that "the longer he [a child] is in the Asylum, the less likely he is to do well in outside life" will hardly come as a surprise to those familiar with the work of Polsky (1962) and others a century later. It remains an apt characterization of the impact of many institutions even today. There was a wave of reform in the late nineteenth century, however, in which foster home and cottage-type institutions were created and in which child care responsibilities were increasingly handled by houseparents. Greater attention was given to humanitarian care by these parent surrogates, although the emphasis was still on conformity, work, and retraining for society. During the period that followed, as described in Chapter Three, ideas of mental hygiene and child treatment emerged and led to the child guidance movement and the psychiatric team of psychiatrist, clinical psychologist, and social worker. Between 1910 and 1930, these concepts and the associated clinical model were grafted onto the programs of many children's institutions. What had been the relative autonomy of houseparents (at least as long as they were able to keep the youngsters under control) changed to a situation where they found themselves subservient to clinical professionals, whose values, goals, and methods were often vastly different both from their own and from those of the children in care. As a result, conflicts developed between the newcomers, who worked with the children primarily through relatively brief, one-to-one office contacts, and the child care personnel, who were still viewed as nonprofessionals but carried responsibility for living with groups of troubled youngsters around the clock (Weber, 1961, 1973; Piliavin, 1970). As noted earlier, social workers, who occupied most of the clinical positions closest to the child care workers and frequently supervised them, were engaged in a status struggle of their own, which contributed to the distance that developed between the two groups. Thus, child care workers continued to be viewed as nonprofessional, primarily custodial personnel, necessary for institutional functioning but largely irrelevant to the treatment enterprise—a view that persists in practice if not in theory in many settings today.

When the idea of milieu therapy began to be clearly articulated (Bettelheim and Sylvester, 1948; Jones, 1956; Redl, 1959), it became increasingly evident that the unique rehabilitation potential of the institution lay in the opportunity it provided for consistent, round-the-clock impact on those in care and that it was ill used as a mere holding pen for children awaiting weekly or even daily sessions with the "therapist" in an isolated office. As Trieschman, Whittaker, and Brendtro (1969) described, "the other 23 hours" are crucial to effective treatment; and other researchers have demonstrated that child care personnel are the most influential group of institutional staff (Beker, 1965; Portnoy, Biller, and Davids, 1972; Portnoy, 1973; Portnoy and Biller, 1973). From this perspective, child care workers are at least as important as representatives of the other, established clinical groups.

Throughout this period of the evolution of residential treatment, the established clinical professions have also taken leadership roles in and controlled most child guidance clinics and other outpatient settings. New techniques such as play therapy and activity group therapy have been introduced as extensions of traditional methods to be applied by professionals. Only in the last two decades have significant inroads been made in this guild system, with paraprofessional and other human service personnel trained to work (usually as assistants) in treatment roles. Until very recently, there have been no roles for child care specialists in these settings. We have relatively little in the way of success to show for the past century of development and change in children's services. Brace's comment finds its echo in the earlier reported work of Polsky (1962), which was conducted in a highly professionalized, clinically sophisticated, treatment-oriented institution. It is reflected dramatically in testimony within the past decade that has characterized our juvenile correctional institutions as "crime hatcheries where children are tutored in crime if they are not assaulted by other inmates or the guards first," or as facilities that "take an 11-year-old and in twelve years turn out a finely honed weapon against society" (Joint Commission on Mental Health of Children, 1969, p. 5). Follow-up studies of residential and outpatient programs suggest that they are often ineffective and institutions in particular seem to have failed and are in wide disrepute. However, Wolins (1974) and others offer convincing evidence that failure is not intrinsic to group care, and many sophisticated child care professionals are working to establish group care program models that can succeed. Furthermore, as the institution is increasingly recognized as but one element in a network of services, new roles for child care workers outside institutions are emerging.

In addition, studies of residential programs argue persuasively that the nature and effectiveness of the reentry process into the community, more than what happens to the youngster during residential placement, determines postinstitutional adjustment (Allerhand, Weber, and Haug, 1966; Taylor and Alpert, 1973). The current emphasis on a network of services, in which community-based programs are fundamental, is based on a careful assessment of experience to date. Implicit in such a model are new roles for child care professionals in working more closely with families, schools, and other community agencies.

Group homes comprise a major step in this direction. Although they are still primarily residential, the youngsters they serve are almost of necessity more closely related to the surrounding community than are most residents of institutions. Group homes also require a broader range of skills on the part of the child care worker, who cannot depend on immediate backup in any of numerous specialty areas as needed.

Child care personnel in some settings are moving even more directly into the community. Frequently, they are modeling effective child management techniques for parents and are teaching parents directly. Increasingly, they are working in traditional social agencies, in schools, in probation situations, in drop-in centers, on the street—in the youngster's life space, wherever that may be at a given time. Traditional child care workers are not, of course, prepared by training, experience, or role expectations for tasks of this magnitude, nor can they expect support and encouragement from most professionals in traditional clinical disciplines, who perceive this "turf" as belonging to them. However, child care workers have been moving on their own and in collaboration with concerned colleagues from other fields to enhance their qualifications and to professionalize their own roles in accordance with growing general recognition of the importance of their potential contribution. As always, the growing edge is uneven in this field, with some workers striving beyond their competence and others unable to find positions commensurate with what they can do. The movement toward community-based services has also left many behind, still trying to integrate their roles as institutional personnel. Nonetheless, the need for well-trained personnel at all points on the continuum will continue to increase. This is the state of the field today, as we turn to look more closely at current efforts to pull it together organizationally and conceptually.

## The Place of Child Care in the Human Service Field

As child care workers have become more aware of the importance of their work, the technical sophistication and broad expertise required to do it effectively, and the interests they share with their colleagues in child care, efforts to join together to improve their lot and the services they provide have emerged. These have followed three major lines of development: unionization, merger with an established professional group, and creation of a new professional or quasi-professional structure. Additionally, the paraprofessional and/or the associated human services professional movement may come to have an increasingly significant impact on the development of the field.

*Unionization.* The development and consequences of unionization among direct care personnel have been described by Cleland and Brandt (1970). Although their analysis is focused on attendants in institutions for the retarded, much of it applies to the child care field as a whole. In the child care field, however, unionization has frequently not provided the benefits —such as enhanced status for child care personnel, relative improvement in remuneration and working conditions commensurate with the importance of the task, and the development of meaningful reference groups—that its proponents had hoped for and that theoretical considerations might lead one to expect. The problem is that unions in human service agencies have typically organized the entire nonsupervisory staff—maintenance and clerical, child care, education, social work—rather than focusing on child care workers as a distinct group. Essentially, they tend to be vertical or "industrial" unions rather than horizontal or "craft" unions; that is, the local unit or chapter consists of a given agency rather than the child care workers in a given area. As a result, where this model of unionization pertains, child care personnel face the same difficulties with their agency colleagues as they formerly did in dealing with administration. Neither the nonprofessionals nor the established professionals are prepared to support changes that would enhance the position of child care workers relative to their own. Consequently, negotiations with management tend to be conducted for changes "across the board" rather than with reference to the differential needs of child care personnel or the needs of children, which might suggest new divisions of labor or other changes. For these reasons and others, including the traditional passivity of child care workers as a group, unions have by and large not proven to be effective agents for upgrading the quality and stature of the child care field per se, although they may have helped to improve personnel practices in children's service programs in general.

*Merger with an Established Profession.* Many sensitive observers and child care practitioners have urged that the field look toward an alliance or merger with one of the established helping professions. Maier (1963), for example, has viewed child care work as a fourth method of social work, to be added to the more traditional casework, group work, and community organization. Others have emphasized its roots in education, psychology, and pediatric or psychiatric nursing. Typical staff roles, practice settings, and the knowledge base within each of these established disciplines overlap in many areas. However, they are identifiably different to the extent that it has proven intellectually and practically viable to conceptualize them in separate helping professions. Each has its own training programs, credentialing procedures, professional associations, and the like, although traditional lines between them are increasingly being bridged as growing recognition of their commonalities and sociopolitical pressures combine to stimulate multidisciplinary efforts. However, there remains some risk that crystallization of child care within one of the allied fields could tend to exclude from full recognition some practitioners who have come to their work through other disciplines.

Nor has child care benefited significantly to date from the blurring of traditional professional differentiations, probably at least in part because relatively few child care practitioners are full members of any of the recognized helping professions. It is no longer unusual to hear of a psychologist heading a traditional social work agency or a social worker leading the mental health team in a school system. At the same time, child care workers are typically viewed in the context of the particular orientation of the agency where they happen to be working, and most avenues for advancement beyond the first step or two are closed to them unless they affiliate with another, more established discipline and meet its requirements.* As a result, the most competent personnel are forced to leave the field for new professional identities and loyalties if they seek advancement, while the less motivated and probably less effective workers tend to remain or drift away, to be replaced by inexperienced newcomers who repeat the cycle.

Thus, although the idea of merging child care into an established profession seems attractive as a means of helping to avoid undue proliferation among human service professions, the field has not been able to move significantly in that direction. Established helping professions—particularly social work, since most child care personnel work in settings where they relate most closely to social workers—have not opened themselves to child care as an equal partner, despite their protestations to the contrary. As Whittaker (1971-72, p. 75) has pointed out, " 'We are all equal partners in the treatment team' is the cry. 'But some of us are more equal than others' is the refrain." Largely as a result, merger has not worked from a practical point of view.

The desirability of merging child care with an established helping profession can also be questioned on conceptual grounds. Although the body of knowledge on which child care practice rests has not yet been fully articulated, it clearly draws

---

*A few instances have been reported where meaningful career ladders have been established for child care workers *qua* child care workers in practice settings (see Stevens and Mueller, 1976; Goocher, 1978). The highest levels usually remain closed to them unless they have advanced degrees in allied fields, however, perhaps because graduate programs in child care are rarely offered.

significantly from many disciplines, adds its own components, and integrates these elements in a new way. Whether rooted in education, nursing, psychiatry, psychology, social work, or another field, even distinctly different models of child care have much in common, usually more than that which differentiates them. This follows from the similar structural or built-in requirements with which all must deal—getting groups of youngsters up, washed, dressed, fed, and able to negotiate other necessary tasks and requirements of the life space successfully—as well as shared ideological or value orientations and goals for the youngsters (Beker, 1976a, 1976b). All models of child rearing acceptable in our culture require humane treatment and emphasize developmental objectives. Thus, although the body of knowledge that undergirds child care is in some ways allied to those of the established helping professions, it transcends those of any other single professional discipline.

*Creation of a New Profession.* In recent years, a movement has developed among some child care workers and others interested in the field to develop it as a new autonomous profession analogous to social work, education, and others. In part, these efforts have developed as a means of alleviating problems such as low pay, inadequate recognition, long and inconvenient working hours, high turnover, and limited opportunity for advancement. The thrust toward professionalization has remained largely distinct from unionization efforts, however, partly because of the problems in unionization for child care workers noted above. In addition, those favoring professionalization (a relatively small but increasingly powerful number of child care workers) have had somewhat broader and more ambitious objectives.

First, they have attempted to show that the key tasks and requirements of effective child care work require a professional level of training, sophistication, and skill. Advocates believe that neither unions, as they are presently structured in the human service field, nor the existing professions provide a compatible environment for the development of child care on this level. They believe that child care work must evolve as a viable, recognized career option rather than a stepping stone to advancement in an allied field—a perspective that has militated against greater willingness to "join" an existing profession.

*Paraprofessionals and Generic Human Service Professionals.* Although still tentative and widely variable, the interrelated paraprofessional and generic human service professional movements may have important implications for the development of the child care field. Already, the federal government has sponsored the Child Development Associate Program, an approach to providing a competency-based credential for direct practitioners on what is essentially a paraprofessional level in day care (Klein, 1973).

The paraprofessional concept in the human services, although not totally new (there have been practical nurses and nurse's aides for a long time), was forcefully advanced in the 1960s in an effort to accomplish several objectives. Some advocates believed that "indigenous paraprofessionals" might be the most appropriate providers of direct services to the community; such personnel, they believed, would be better able to understand, identify with, and help poor, minority-group clients than traditional, more highly trained professionals would be. The paraprofessional movement was also seen as providing meaningful employment for traditionally underemployed and undervalued groups and as a way of providing meaningful social roles for former clients. The lines between client and helper were blurred, often intentionally, in an effort to view the alleviation of social and human relationship difficulties as a problem we all bear and a task we all share. Further, given the scarcity of personnel trained in the helping professions in relation to the need, paraprofessionals provided the only readily available resource that might help to fill the gap (Pearl and Riessman, 1965; Sobey, 1970; Gartner, 1971).

Thoughtful observers have noted both strengths and shortcomings in the paraprofessional model and its influence. Much of what would be called professional "mystique" has increasingly been seen as an unnecessary and sometimes harmful accouterment to the work of helping people, serving primarily to maintain professional distance between clients and traditional helping professions. However, the need for a relevant body of knowledge and its skilled, sensitive application is apparent. Perhaps a systematic mix of professional and paraprofessional personnel would be most effective in the human services. For example, the field of nursing has long recognized the utility of such a hierarchy of training and skills, represented by aides, practical nurses, and registered nurses, as well as the need for specialization in the care of different kinds of ailments, different age groups, and the like. Teachers' aides and bachelor's degree social workers, paramedics, and paralegal personnel represent more recent efforts in this direction in other fields. At least partly as a result of experience with paraprofessionals, a significant movement toward the development of a comprehensive, generic human service profession has also emerged. While allowing for appropriate subspecialties and levels of training and service, it would provide under a single professional umbrella many of the social services that are now so badly fragmented that clients often can neither understand them nor use them effectively. The direction, pace, and ultimate impact of these developments are not yet clear, but they have influenced the evolution of the child care field and seem likely to continue to do so in the future (Cohen and Mesrop, in press).

The emergence of the paraprofessional movement in the 1960s, around the time when child care was beginning to assert its own autonomy more directly, may have indirectly retarded the professionalization process in child care. It provided a convenient label and category which administrators and others could use to provide enhanced status for child care workers without threatening the established professionals. If they were not really equal members of the treatment team, they were at least no longer custodial staff on the same level as maintenance and clerical personnel. The new designation seemed to fit their general level of preparation—they had some training but usually not much, and it was often not directly relevant, so that much of their learning occurred on the job. Finally, there was no child care profession anyway, and "paraprofessional" seemed to many observers to be an appropriate designation for the field.

Just as in other fields, however, it has since become increasingly clear that effective service requires more of a body of knowledge and techniques for its effective application than paraprofessionals can be expected to provide alone. Developmental emphases in child treatment require specialists who are able to foster and monitor developmental progress, not simply to participate in occasional therapy sessions. The basic task in child care is preparation for effective, productive living, and most of this can be accomplished only in the kind of living environment where it will be practiced. With the development of the generic human services professional, however, a more viable model for child care may have been created. Essentially, the child care worker is a human service professional with a generic approach to children's services. Depending on the particular circumstances, he or she may be counseling an individual youngster, organizing a group activity, modeling effective parental behavior in a parent training program, or consulting with any of a variety of other professional specialists about a client. As community-based services and the number of small-group settings expand, the need for this kind of generic child care worker to function in tandem with paraprofessional assistants and colleagues with other specialties seems likely to increase. Thus, the developing generic human service profession may come to encompass child care as one of its specialties.

### The Professional Development of Child Care

It is difficult to put a precise date on the emergence of the professional movement in the child care field. Burmeister (1960) titled her book *The Professional Houseparent* and explained that, "Whatever the term whereby child care workers are known, the word 'professional' represents an aspiration and a goal toward which they are discernibly and universally moving" (p. vi). Still, her use of the designation *professional* seems intended to reflect the idea that houseparents are "valuable" and need a certain body of knowledge and skill to do their jobs well, rather than a conception of the emergence of a profession in the technical sense of the term (see, for example, Greenwood, 1957; Moore, 1970).

Hromadka (1966) reports a study of the tasks and working conditions of child care personnel that, while still based on a limited concept of professionalization, documents the emergence of the child care worker as a formally recognized treatment agent in most of the participating institutions. More recently, in reviewing the literature in this area, Toigo (1975) concludes that "Child care as an occupational specialty appears to have certain, but not all, of the characteristics of a profession" (p. 15). He continues:

> Change appears to be occurring, however. Perhaps the greatest current indicator is the exploratory literature now being produced regarding training methods, standards, and curriculum development. It would be unwise to dismiss these current expressions of the "state of the art" as the posturing of those within a marginal occupational specialty seeking to upgrade their own status through the use of an occupational model borrowed from the established professions. The current literature would suggest, rather, an internal process of self-development, as those within child care explore the dimensions of their own personal and occupational experience. As it has become clear that "common sense" is not enough to make an adequate child care worker, both those who teach and practice in the field have begun to articulate a set of common goals and understandings, an important first step in the development of a professional specialty within the human services sector. Even though this is an ongoing process, it is fair to suggest that it is already well under way.

This "internal process of self-development" is reflected in a variety of indications that the field has, for the first time, begun to demonstrate its staying power as an organized entity. For example, there are at this writing about twenty regional, state, and local child care workers' associations, most of which are expanding in membership, activities, and influence; and others are in the process of being established. These associations hold regular meetings primarily for members, sponsor conferences and workshops for a broader range of child care workers and others in the field, publish newsletters, and are affiliated with a variety of groups devoted to improving child care services and programs. Increasingly, such associations are also becoming involved in standard setting and establishing certification procedures for child care personnel, working with colleges and universities to establish training programs at the associate, bachelor's and master's degree levels. Their membership often encompasses supervisory and administrative personnel in addition to line child care workers, reflecting growing recognition of the need for broad-based involvement at all levels of the emerging professional career ladder (Beker, 1977).

At least one state association provides group professional liability insurance at low cost for its members. This would probably not even have been seriously considered a decade earlier, but it seems particularly appropriate now in view of the broadening applicability of child abuse laws to child care workers, frequently with mandatory reporting provisions, and it attests to the growing professionalism of the field.

Association representatives also joined together in 1975 as the National Task Force on Child Care Associations, a group that in 1977 established the National Organization of Child Care Worker Associations, which is designed to unite the field as an identifiable national movement while maintaining the autonomy of the state associations. This group issues a quarterly newsletter, *Child Care Work in Focus,* and sponsors extensive meetings in conjunction with the Annual Conference of the American Orthopsychiatric Association as well as sessions at conventions of the Child Welfare League of America and other relevant groups. At this writing, it seems poised to move into an even more active role on the national scene when the necessary initial focus of its work, establishing a viable internal structure, has moved further ahead. Meanwhile, several of the founding associations in the eastern part of the country have conducted the first three annual Inter-Association Child Care Conferences, attended by hundreds of child care workers and their colleagues primarily from that region but with a liberal sprinkling of participants from throughout the country and from Canada. A similar regional conference was held for the first time in 1977 in the Midwest. It seems clear that, after numerous false starts around the country, the field has developed enough internal professional organizational momentum to sustain and enhance its growth for the foreseeable future.

Despite the occasional protestations of social work and, less frequently, other fields that child care work should be within their scope, these allied disciplines have not moved formally to bring child care personnel into their established professional associations, credentialing processes, and the like. There is one transdisciplinary group, the American Association of Workers for Children (AAWC), through which leaders in a variety of allied fields are attempting to clarify and upgrade the role and status of child care as a professional discipline in the United States, but the long-range program and probable impact of AAWC remain unclear. Constituted as the chartered American branch of the major international body of this field, the Association Internationale des Éducateurs de Jeunes Inadaptés (International Association of Workers for Maladjusted Children), AAWC seeks to cull experience in this field in other countries, some of which is reviewed below, for possible relevance here. The only other formal efforts based in the traditional helping professions to admit child care to their ranks appear to have been developed in the context of particular child care models, also to be discussed later in this chapter.

The preceding discussion pertains primarily to child care workers in residential care and treatment settings, but other groups of workers with children may increasingly identify and unite with this group—to the benefit of both groups as well as the children they serve (Beker, 1976a). In particular, day care personnel and juvenile probation workers have also begun to move toward more professional status and bring a great deal of experience with and sophistication in community-based service to the child care enterprise. Many workers in newly emerging kinds of youth programs—such as youth service bureaus, respite centers, shelters, homes for runaways, and storefronts—are also still in need of a clear, consistent professional identity as well. Although training programs for and associations of foster parents are appearing on the scene, the position of foster parents in the field is still unclear. The accelerating development of preparation-for-parenthood programs in many secondary schools and other agencies, often including fieldwork in child care settings, represents another broadening of the field in the community not reflected above. Education and social work have made some attempts to encompass some of these kinds of groups that care for children, but independent development in the context of a comprehensive child care profession remains a viable possibility.

The child care field has also begun to develop a significant literature, an important requisite for professionalization. *Child Care Quarterly* appeared in 1971 as the first independent journal wholly devoted to the field. It had been preceded by a few agency-based, "house organ" periodicals, often published sporadically, and occasional relevant "special issues" of journals in related fields. Articles directed to or about the child care field have appeared from time to time in other journals as well, particularly *Child Welfare* and the *American Journal of Orthopsychiatry*. Other periodicals in the field include the newsletters mentioned above and publications directed to particular subgroups, such as the *Journal of the Association for the Care of Children in Hospitals*. The number and quality of books, pamphlets, and informally published material about or closely related to child care work have also increased markedly in the 1970s. In addition, the Child Care Information Center in Hampton, Virginia, distributes a large number of audiotapes in the field, and a variety of audiovisual aids for training are available. Together, these resources comprise a respectable, rapidly growing literature and represent tangibly the still somewhat amorphous body of knowledge underlying the new professional discipline.

## Training and Practice Models in Child Care

As is reflected in the historical overview, child care practice was seen as primarily custodial in nature. With growing recognition of the importance of the work, however, training opportunities have increased. Training ranges from informal in-service programs to formal undergraduate and graduate degree curricula; a small number of doctoral programs encompass child care with allied fields in a joint degree. Most of the few conceptually clear training models that exist are associated with university-based training programs. In-service training tends, naturally enough, to reflect the needs and philosophy of the agency involved, rather than a comprehensive model of professional child care. Extension or continuing education courses, credit and noncredit, are offered by community and four-year colleges and universities, sometimes on the college campus but often in agency settings and occasionally as correspondence courses. In some instances, funding that has recently become available through Title XX of the Social Security Act has permitted the establishment of new and expanded child care training programs under college and university auspices; for example, the State University of New York has centers at Albany and Stony Brook. Child care associations and independent groups also offer courses in the field from time to time. Usually consisting of one or two courses, these Title XX programs focus more on skill building than on professional development in the context of a coherent practice model.

There are exceptions, however. The two-year program offered by the Michigan Association of Children's Agencies (MACA), for example, provides what is probably the most comprehensive training in the field available outside a formal college program (Rozentals, Piper, and Whipple, 1974). The courses, workshops, and certificate offered by the Group Child Care Consultant Services, at the University of North Carolina School of Social Work, have also achieved prominence as nondegree training resources, and this group has recently developed a sophisticated introductory training package in residential child care work with the financial support of the federal Office of Child Development. In recent years, many community colleges have begun to offer one-year certificate programs and/or two-year associate degree programs in child care or in broader areas such as human services with a specialization in child care (VanderVen, 1976). Some—such as those at Bristol Community College in Fall River, Massachusetts; the Human Services Institute of the City Colleges of Chicago; and the Pedology Program at the Community College of Allegheny County in Pittsburgh (a spinoff from the University of Pittsburgh program to be discussed below)—have earned national recognition. Community college child care programs still tend, however, to train personnel to work in the context of currently predominant child care roles and models. They appear to produce more knowledgeable and more highly skilled personnel but are usually not directly concerned with the development and implementation of new, more professional modes and contexts of practice.

It is at the bachelor's degree level that one begins to see reciprocal efforts between the academy and the practice arena to influence and improve basic concepts affecting the delivery of child care services. The comparatively few bachelor's degree and graduate programs that have been established are usually relatively clear in purpose and approach and actively committed to professional development. The first university concentration in this field was established at the University of Pittsburgh in 1952 under the leadership of Benjamin Spock. At first, it offered only a master's program in child development and child care through the Department of Psychiatry. In 1969 this program evolved into the Department of Child Development and Child Care in the then newly established School of Health Related Professions. A preprofessional certificate program had been added earlier and was transferred to Allegheny Community College in 1968. In 1970 the bachelor's degree program was initiated, and it has grown with the support of funding from the National Institute of Mental Health into the mid 1970s (VanderVen and Mattingly, 1975). The University of Pittsburgh programs, characterized as the developmental child care model, prepare students for service in a wide variety of child care settings and remain the most widely known bachelor's and master's degree programs in the field.

With the encouragement and collaboration of child care associations, groups of agencies, and units of government in some cases, a number of other bachelor's degree programs in child care have been developed. St. Thomas Aquinas College in

Sparkill, New York, for example, offers a child care specialization through its psychology department, a program developed jointly by the college and that state's Association of Child Care Workers. Adelphi University and the Institute for Child Mental Health in New York City offer a joint curriculum leading to a bachelor's degree in child care as well. Working closely with the Texas Association of Child Care Workers and the State Department of Mental Health and Mental Retardation, the Center for Child Care Training and Research in Texas has initiated child care programs at both the bachelor's and the master's degree levels through Incarnate Word College in San Antonio. The Child Welfare Project at the University of Washington School of Social Work also provides child care training at the bachelor's degree and graduate levels. Goddard College, based in Vermont, offers bachelor's and master's degrees in child care through supervised independent study in various locations. These and a variety of other such programs in the United States and Canada tend to be eclectic, and they are oriented toward preparing child care professionals who can better meet the needs of the existing and emerging system of children's services rather than providing comprehensive alternative theoretical or practice models as the basis for the child care role.

Other training programs are specifically targeted toward preparing child care workers who differ from their predecessors not only in levels of knowledge, skill, and professional identity but also in their overall approach to the job. Perhaps the most clear-cut example of such a training regimen is that provided in several centers around the country in connection with the Teaching-Family Model developed in the Achievement Place Project and currently being implemented at Boys Town in Nebraska (Maloney and others, in press). The essential program components of this model were presented in Chapter Three. Prospective teaching-parents are expected to complete successfully a clearly specified one-year training sequence, most of which is comprised of closely monitored on-the-job experience. Academic requirements for entry into the program are somewhat flexible, and the certification that marks its successful completion is generally recognized as a credential only for settings using the Teaching-Family Model. This model is most closely related to the field of psychology, with considerable but not exclusive emphasis on behavior modification approaches. (This program also emphasizes the training and employment of married couples as a team—an echo in modern form of the older "houseparents" approach, which has tended to be discarded in the last few decades, and possibly a harbinger of a broader movement back in that direction as we place additional stress on good child care and child rearing in contrast to treatment per se.)

Some leaders in children's services, aware of the failures of most traditional programs in the United States, have explored approaches used in other countries in an effort to determine how our programs might best be improved. Most attention has been given to the *éducateur,* a generic child care and treatment specialist in France, Switzerland, and, with some modifications, in French Canada (Linton, 1973). The term is sometimes extended to encompass children's service personnel in other countries as well, such as the Dutch *orthopedagogue.* Proponents in the United States believe that this approach represents "good" child care practice in contrast to current patterns (Linton, 1971).

Briefly, the task of the *éducateur* is "to encourage the development of the character of maladjusted youths, while helping them to mature socially, through activities or situations that he shares with them, either within an institution or service or in their natural environment, by means of his influence over both the youth and his environment" (Ginger, 1971, p. 19). At first glance, this does not appear to be radically different from widely held conceptions of an effective child care worker in the United States. However, the notions that treatment occurs primarily in the living environment rather than in the therapeutic hour and that the child care worker—the *éducateur*—is responsible for coordinating the work of the other clinical professionals do not reflect typical procedures in youth service programs in this country. Numerous attempts have been made to import *éducateur* ideology and practice, appropriately adapted, to the United States. Barnes and Kelman (1974) have reported on one such program in Pennsylvania. In addition, Southern

Connecticut State College has recently initiated a training program designed to produce *éducateurs* through its Department of Special Education. Although a comprehensive, innovative *psychoéducateur* program has been in existence for about thirty years in the French-speaking community in the province of Quebec, Canada, encompassing a separate unit of the University of Montreal for training and a variety of service settings (Guindon, in press), English-speaking Canada has not moved quickly to adapt such a model. Recently, however, a bachelor's degree program based in large part on the *éducateur* concept has been initiated at the University of Victoria, British Columbia, and there are at least two English-language *éducateur* training programs in the province of Quebec.

Other program models in the United States have drawn explicitly on *éducateur* concepts and perhaps have been inspired by them but encompass enough other perspectives to be viewed as essentially different models. One prominent example, cited in an earlier chapter, is the group of programs encompassed by Project Re-Ed. The line child care worker in the Re-Ed model, called a teacher-counselor, is typically a teacher with an additional year of specialized preparation leading to a master's degree in special education with emphasis in the area of emotional disturbance. Professionally, teacher-counselors usually identify themselves with the field of special education and can achieve both lateral mobility to and from classroom settings and vertical mobility in Re-Ed schools or other special education settings (Lewis, in press).

Another model based partly on the *éducateur* is that developed in the Child Mental Health Specialist Training Program in California, which encompasses training at the associate, bachelor's, and master's degree levels (Rieger and Devries, 1974). It is rooted in child psychiatry and focuses on the training and preparation of effective personnel for a variety of educational and mental health settings rather than for work within a particular practice model such as Re-Ed. The training regimen includes, in addition to relevant academic and practice courses, participation in a planned series of clinical rotations, following the model used in medical education. Thus, while the Teaching-Family Model and Re-Ed training are explicitly linked to clearly articulated program or practice models and have developed their approaches to training accordingly, the Child Mental Health Specialist Training Program represents a model of training for individuals as generic professionals in child mental health who are exposed to a variety of settings and are presumably competent to provide service effectively wherever they may be needed. They may specialize in classroom work with normal youngsters or in special education (for instance, in residential treatment). Any statement as to which approach is more effective would be largely conjectural at this point and would depend on an evaluation of the prescribed program models as well as the training in the case of Teaching-Family and Re-Ed. (All three of these models—Re-Ed, the Teaching-Family Model, and the Child Mental Health Specialist—as well as the baccalaureate program at the University of Pittsburgh were assisted in their development and implementation by substantial federal funding through the National Institute of Mental Health. The federal government has thereby made a significant investment in the development of more effective children's services based on the establishment of more effective child care program and training models.)

These are the major avenues to training in child care work. Most current care practitioners, however, even those in positions of professional leadership, have come to the field through other routes, frequently before many, if any, of these programs were in existence. Many were originally trained as educators, nurses, psychologists, or social workers; a few, as psychiatrists or in other disciplines. Some began their work in child care without formal training in any of the helping professions and have been able to advance with or without acquiring professional credentials along the way. Thus, those in the field at present represent a wide variety of backgrounds, reflecting the state of flux in which the entire field of child treatment now finds itself.

## Reintegration: A Look to the Future

Our failure to provide effective treatment services for children, only recently acknowledged, has led to our current reappraisal of existing agencies. Many institutions and techniques, like the juvenile court and the traditional treatment hour, have been challenged as ineffective, counterproductive, or at best uneconomical. Such concepts as "community-based treatment" and the "rights of children," both often ill defined, have been advanced as requisites for providing a better foundation for healthy child development as well as the more caring society perceived as necessary for fostering optimal social conditions and human growth in the long run. Growing concern with evaluation and cost effectiveness also reflects, at least in part, a sense that children's treatment programs—along with the human services in general—have failed to deliver on their promises. With established human service professions being called to task for what they have done or failed to do in the past, the time may be auspicious for the new child care professionals now arriving on the scene.

To succeed, this enterprise must avoid the excesses of the established helping professions while incorporating much of their expertise into its own base of knowledge and practice. It must be prepared, much more than were the traditional helping professions at the comparable state in their own development, to subject its practice to continuing, systematic, sophisticated outside scrutiny, including that of professional groups that may be most concerned with protecting their own prerogatives from encroachment by the new discipline. This is an opportunity as well as a threat, since, if the child care field accepts its responsibility to be accountable and to develop its practice flexibly, it can be revised as may be indicated when it is assessed. Finally, in the service of its own integrity as well as the needs of those it serves, the new profession will need to adopt a strong advocacy role in cooperation with appropriate citizens' groups, sometimes sacrificing at least its apparent short-term vested interests, in a society that has to date shown itself all too willing to short-change the needs of its children.

All this will require unity of purpose and a great deal of cooperative effort among those with varying specialties, who may continue to advocate different practice models but share similar objectives for the field and for our youth. A unified child care profession encompassing day care workers, child treatment personnel in the kinds of settings described in this book, hospital child care workers, and others in the field seems needed as an umbrella for this kind of joint effort. It is important not only for the strength that lies in numbers but also to facilitate the refinement of the knowledge and practice base that undergirds the field (Beker, 1976a, 1976b). Teaching-parents and child mental health specialists, for example, are working with many of the same types of youngsters in structurally similar types of settings. They need to be able to compare notes as colleagues, and it is important to the field that they be able to do so as a continuing source of enrichment and improvement of the knowledge base and of practice.

A unified profession will also enhance opportunities for both lateral and vertical mobility in the field. Degrees, certification, and other credentials will be more easily transferable, as are those of other professionals. Service systems built around child care professionals will provide the career ladder opportunities that have taken so long to develop, making it more likely that competent people will enter the field with realistic expectations of making a career commitment to it. The structure of the field should provide the most effective direct care practitioners with the option of advancing in career status and income by continuing direct work with clients, perhaps the most difficult cases, rather than linking advancement solely to the acceptance of supervisory and administrative responsibilities. The former is the pattern in law and medicine, for example, while the latter usually applies in education, nursing, social work, and other fields (Beker, 1975). The "master teacher" role in some educational systems represents an analogous attempt to reward excellence within the context of direct practice, and the most talented university professors have traditionally continued to teach, usually focusing on the most talented and highly specialized students.

Realistically, child care is unlikely to join the highest-status professions such as medicine and law, where private practice is the norm, since organizations and agencies continue to be involved in the delivery of children's treatment services. Thus, for the foreseeable future, child care professionals are likely to occupy positions somewhat like those of teachers, social workers, and nurses: working within and achieving upward mobility through bureaucratic structures. The professional status of child care will be that of "bureaucratic profession" or "semiprofession" (Etzioni, 1969).*

As explained by Toren (1969, p. 153), "Semiprofessionalism denotes that the profession does not rest on a firm theoretical knowledge base; the period of training involved is relatively short; members cannot claim monopoly of exclusive skills; and the special area of their competence is less well defined" than that of such professions as law and medicine. Toren also discusses the concept of "heteronomy" in the semiprofessions, referring to the extent to which "members of the profession are guided and controlled not only from within—that is, by internalized professional norms, expert knowledge, and the professional community—but also by administrative rules and by superiors in the organizational hierarchy" (1969, p. 153). However, she continues, *"direct* supervision in the semiprofessions is always carried out by senior or ex-professionals who have risen from the ranks—the school principal, the head nurse, the social work supervisor, and the like" (p. 154). It seems clear that child care is moving toward, but has not yet achieved, the status of a semiprofession.

Joffe (1975) has used the term *weak profession* to refer to groups that are "actively engaged in *negotiating* an occupational identity," in contrast to the semiprofessions, "about which there are a fairly stabilized set of understandings." In this sense, child care currently appears to occupy the position of a "weak profession," with its concomitant marginality among professional groups and relatively greater dependence on the

---

*Such designations as these and *weak profession,* to follow, are used in their technical, sociological sense to describe the situation that exists, and not pejoratively. Nevertheless, the persistent status differences between, for example, medicine and law, on the one hand, and education, nursing and social work, on the other, cannot be ignored. That the categories represent parts of a continuum rather than discrete entities is illustrated by the position of psychology, which appears to be between the two groupings just cited.

support of its clientele for its legitimacy. Since the occupational identity of this field is unclear and its function is not currently ceded to it by sanction or tradition, no monopoly exists and prospective clients (youngsters and their families, juvenile courts, or other agencies able to purchase services) are free to select among a variety of service providers, including special schools, social work agencies, and others in addition to professional child care agencies. As a result, child care is in the position of having to negotiate with its proposed clientele to establish its role, a difficult situation for any group aspiring to professional prerogatives but one providing an unusual opportunity for a field that seeks to remain truly client-oriented. In addition, many of the professional decision makers with whom child care must negotiate represent professional groups (especially social work) that tend to view it competitively. In this connection, the field will need to do more to make common cause with its ultimate clientele, youngsters and their families. The outcome of this effort will go far toward determining the eventual position of the child care field in delivery of services to young people and their families, and perhaps the nature and quality of those services as well.

In this light, the development of a broader, unified generic human services discipline, which could attain clear professional recognition and autonomy, may be the most effective long-range solution. It would require established, vested interests to give way to genuine professional concern for client needs and welfare—something that runs counter to apparent trends, even in such high-status professions as medicine and the law. In spite of these trends, the vast and fundamental changes under way in the human service delivery systems have given the professions involved a rare opportunity to unify so as to organize themselves more effectively for service delivery as well. In any case, those committed to enhancing child care services must accelerate their own professionalization processes, so that they can join and influence a unified effort as full partners, or proceed effectively on their own if necessary, to provide the best possible services for children and youth.

# References

Adler, J. *The Child Care Worker: Concepts, Tasks, and Relationships.* New York: Brunner/Mazel, 1976.

Aichorn, A. *Wayward Youth.* New York: Viking Press, 1935.

Allen, K. E., and Harris, F. R. "Elimination of a Child's Excessive Scratching by Training the Mother in Reinforcement Procedures." *Behavior Research and Therapy,* 1966, *4,* 79-84.

Allen, K. E., and others. "Effects of Social Reinforcement on Isolate Behavior of a Nursery School Child." *Child Development,* 1964, *35,* 511-518.

Allerhand, M. E., Weber, R., and Haug, M. *Adaptation and Adaptability: The Bellefaire Follow-Up Study.* New York: Child Welfare League of America, 1966.

Allport, G. W. *ABC's of Scapegoating.* New York: Anti-Defamation League of B'nai Brith, 1966.

American Association of Children's Residential Centers (Ed.). *From Chaos to Order: A Collective View of the Residential*

*Treatment of Children.* New York: Child Welfare League of America, 1972.

Apter, S. J. "Family Advocacy in the BRIDGE Program." Paper presented at the 85th annual convention of the American Psychological Association, San Francisco, August 1977.

Apter, S. J. "Applications of Ecological Theory: Toward a Community Special Education Model for Troubled Children." *Exceptional Children,* in press.

Ayllon, T., and Azrin, M. *The Token Economy.* New York: Appleton-Century-Crofts, 1968.

Ayllon, T., and Michael, J. "The Psychiatric Nurse as a Behavioral Engineer." *Journal of the Experimental Analysis of Behavior,* 1959, *2,* 323-334.

Bakal, Y. (Ed.). *Closing Correctional Institutions.* Lexington, Mass.: Heath, 1973.

Balthazar, E. E., and Stevens, H. A. *The Emotionally Disturbed Mentally Retarded: A Historical and Contemporary Perspective.* Englewood Cliffs, N.J.: Prentice-Hall, 1975.

Bangs, T. *Language and Learning Disorders of the Pre-Academic Child.* New York: Appleton-Century-Crofts, 1968.

Bardill, R. R. "Group Therapy Techniques with Preadolescent Boys in a Residential Treatment Center." *Child Welfare,* 1973, *52* (8), 533-541.

Barker, R. *Ecological Psychology.* Stanford, Calif.: Stanford University Press, 1968.

Barnes, F. H., and Kelman, S. M. "From Slogans to Concepts: A Basis for Change in Child Care Work." *Child Care Quarterly,* 1974, *3* (1), 7-24.

Becker, W. *Parents Are Teachers.* Champaign, Ill.: Research Press, 1971.

Beker, J. "Male Adolescent Inmates' Perceptions of 'Helping Persons.' " *Social Work,* 1965, *10* (2), 18-26.

Beker, J. *Critical Incidents in Child Care: A Casebook.* New York: Behavioral Publications, 1972.

Beker, J. "Development of a Professional Identity for the Child Care Worker." *Child Welfare,* 1975, *54,* 421-431.

Beker, J. "Editorial: On Defining the Child Care Profession— II." *Child Care Quarterly,* 1976a, *5,* 245-247.

Beker, J. "Toward the Unification of the Child Care Field as a Profession." *Journal of the Association for the Care of Children in Hospitals,* 1976b, *1,* 14-19.

Beker, J. "Editorial: On Defining the Child Care Profession— V." *Child Care Quarterly,* 1977, *6,* 165-166.

Benedict, W. R. "A Programme Evaluation Approach to Consensus Community-Oriented Goal Setting in Residential Treatment." In G. Garwick and J. Brintnall (Eds.), *Proceedings of the Second Goal Attainment Scaling Conference.* Minneapolis: Program Evaluation Resource Center, 1976.

Benedict, W. R., and Bruce, D. A. *Treatment Expectations and Outcome Results for Adolescents in Residential Treatment.* Stoughton, Wis.: Martin Luther Centers, Lutheran Social Services of Wisconsin and Upper Michigan, 1975.

Berkowitz, B. P., and Graziano, A. M. "Training Parents as Behavior Therapists: A Review." In A. M. Graziano (Ed.), *Behavior Therapy with Children.* Vol. 2. Chicago: Aldine, 1975.

Berleman, W. C., Seaberg, J. R., and Steinburn, T. W. "The Delinquency Prevention Experiment of the Seattle Atlantic Street Center: A Final Evaluation." *Social Service Review,* 1972, *46* (3), 323-347.

Bernstein, B., Snider, D., and Meezan, W. *A Preliminary Report: Foster Care Needs and Alternatives to Placement.* New York: Board of Social Welfare, 1975.

Bertcher, H., and Maple, F. "Elements and Issues in Group Composition." In P. Glasser, R. C. Sarri, and R. D. Vinter (Eds.), *Individual Change Through Small Groups.* New York: Free Press, 1974.

Bettelheim, B. *Love Is Not Enough.* New York: Free Press, 1950.

Bettelheim, B. *Truants from Life.* New York: Free Press, 1955.

Bettelheim, B. "Feral Children and Autistic Children." *American Journal of Sociology,* 1959, *64* (5), 455-467.

Bettelheim, B. *The Empty Fortress.* New York: Free Press, 1967.

Bettelheim, B. *A Home for the Heart.* New York: Knopf, 1974.

Bettelheim, B., and Sylvester, E. "A Therapeutic Milieu." *Amer-*

*ican Journal of Orthopsychiatry,* 1948, *18* (2), 191-206. Also in H. W. Polsky, D. S. Claster, and C. Goldberg (Eds.), *Social System Perspectives in Residential Institutions.* East Lansing: Michigan State University Press, 1970.

Bijou, S. *The Exceptional Child: Conditional Learning and Teaching Ideas.* New York: M.S.S. Information Corp., 1971.

Birnbrauer, J. S., Peterson, C. R., and Solnick, J. V. "Design and Interpretation of Studies of Single Subjects." *American Journal of Mental Deficiency,* 1974, *79* (2), 191-203.

Bower, E. M., and others. *Project Re-Ed.* Nashville, Tenn.: George Peabody College, 1969.

Brace, C. L. *The Dangerous Classes of New York, and Twenty Years' Work Among Them.* New York: Wynkoop and Hallenbeck, 1872.

Bradfield, R. *Behavior Modification of Learning Disabilities.* San Rafael, Calif.: Academic Therapy Press, 1971.

Braud, L. W., Lupin, M. N., and Braud, W. G. "The Use of Electromyographic Biofeedback in the Control of Hyperactivity." *Journal of Learning Disabilities,* 1975, *8* (7), 21-26.

Braukman, C. J., and others. "Behavioral Approaches to Treatment in the Crime and Delinquency Field." *Criminology,* 1975, *13,* 199-331.

Brendtro, L. K. "Establishing Relationship Beachheads." In A. E. Trieschman, J. K. Whittaker, and L. K. Brendtro, *The Other 23 Hours: Child Care Work in a Therapeutic Milieu.* Chicago: Aldine, 1969.

Brintnall, J., and Garwick, G. *Applications of Goal Attainment Scaling.* Minneapolis: Program Evaluation Research Center, 1976.

Brodie, R. D. "Some Aspects of Psychotherapy in a Residential Treatment Center." In J. K. Whittaker and A. E. Trieschman (Eds.), *Children Away from Home: A Sourcebook of Residential Treatment.* Chicago: Aldine, 1972.

Bronfenbrenner, U. "Toward an Experimental Ecology of Human Development." *American Psychologist,* 1977, *32* (7), 513-532.

Browning, R. M., and Stover, D. O. *Behavior Modification in Child Treatment.* Chicago: Aldine, 1971.

Buckley, W. (Ed.). *Modern Systems Research for the Behavioral Scientist.* Chicago: Aldine, 1968.

Burmeister, E. *The Professional Houseparent.* New York: Columbia University Press, 1960.

Carpenter, P., and Carom, R. "Green Stamp Therapy: Modification of Delinquent Behavior Through Food Trading Stamps." *Proceedings, 76th Annual Convention, American Psychological Association,* 1968, *3,* 531-532.

Cavior, E. C., Schmidt, A., and Karacki, L. *An Evaluation of the Kennedy Youth Center Differential Treatment Program.* Washington, D.C.: U.S. Bureau of Prisons, 1972.

Chomsky, N. *Reflections on Language.* New York: Random House, 1975.

Churchill, S. "Prestructuring Group Content." *Social Work,* 1959, *4* (3), 52-55.

Cleland, C. C., and Brandt, F. S. "Unionization of Institutions: A Therapeutic Event." *Community Mental Health Journal,* 1970, *6,* 51-62.

Coates, R. B., and Miller, A. D. "Neutralization of Community Resistance to Group Homes." In Y. Bakal (Ed.), *Closing Correctional Institutions.* Lexington, Mass.: Heath, 1973.

Cohen, A. C., and Mesrop, A. "Child Care and the Profession of Human Services." In J. Beker (Ed.), *The Child Care Worker in the United States: A Comparative Analysis of Evolving Role Models.* New York: Human Sciences Press, in press.

Cohen, H. L., and Filipczak, J. *A New Learning Environment: A Case for Learning.* San Francisco: Jossey-Bass, 1971.

Coleman, J. V. "Institutional Child Care—Some Principles." *Social Work Today,* 1940, *7.*

Collins, A. H., and Pancoast, D. L. *Natural Helping Networks.* Washington, D.C.: National Association of Social Workers, 1976.

Condon, W. S. "Multiple Response to Sound in Dysfunctional Children." *Journal of Autism and Childhood Schizophrenia,* 1975, *5* (1), 37-56.

Costurn, C. *The Day Treatment Program.* Everett, Wash.: Luther Child Center, 1978.

Coughlin, B. J. "Deinstitutionalization: A Matter of Social Order and Deviance." *Child Welfare,* 1977, *56* (5), 293-301.

Creak, M. "Schizophrenic Syndrome in Children: Further Progress Report of Working Party." *Developmental Medicine and Child Neurology,* 1964, *4,* 530.

Cruickshank, W. M. *Learning Disabilities in Home, School, and Community.* Syracuse, N.Y.: Syracuse University Press, 1971.

Cruickshank, W. M., and Johnson, G. *Education of Exceptional Children and Youth.* Englewood Cliffs, N.J.: Prentice-Hall, 1975.

Cummings, J., and Cummings, E. *Ego and Milieu.* New York: Atherton Press, 1963.

Davids, A., Ryan, R., and Salvatore, P. "Effectiveness of Residential Treatment." *American Journal of Orthopsychiatry,* 1968, *38,* 469-475.

Davidson, W. S., and Seidman, E. "Studies of Behavior Modification and Juvenile Delinquency." *Psychological Bulletin,* 1974, *81,* 998-1011.

Davis, J. S. "The Education Component of Residential Treatment Centers." In American Association of Children's Residential Centers (Ed.), *From Chaos to Order: A Collective View of the Residential Treatment of Children.* New York: Child Welfare League of America, 1972.

Dentler, R. A., and Mackler, B. "The Socialization of Retarded Children in an Institution." *Journal of Health and Human Behavior,* 1961, *2,* 243-252.

Dimock, E. T. "Youth Crisis Services: Short-Term Community-Based Residential Treatment." *Child Welfare,* 1977, *56* (3), 187-196.

Dinkmeyer, D., and McKay, G. *Raising the Responsible Child.* New York: Simon & Schuster, 1973.

Dinnage, R., Pringle, M., and Kellmer, M. L. *Residential Care— Facts and Fallacies.* New York: Humanities Press, 1967.

Dittman, A. T., and Kitchener, H. L. "Life Space Interviewing and Individual Play Therapy: A Comparison of Techniques." *American Journal of Orthopsychiatry,* 1959, *29* (1), 19-27.

Dokecki, P. R., and Hutton, R. "The Liaison Specialist." Paper presented at the 85th annual convention of the American Psychological Association, San Francisco, 1977.

Dreikurs, R. *Children: The Challenge.* New York: Hawthorn, 1964.

Dreikurs, R., and Grey, C. *Logical Consequences: A Handbook to Discipline.* New York: Hawthorn, 1968.

Durkin, R. P., and Durkin, A. B. "Evaluating Residential Treatment Programs for Disturbed Children." In M. Guttentag and E. L. Struening (Eds.), *Handbook of Evaluation Research.* Vol. 2. Beverly Hills, Calif.: Sage, 1975.

Empey, L. T., and Lubeck, S. G. *The Silverlake Experiment.* Chicago: Aldine, 1972.

English, O. S., and Finch, S. M. *Introduction to Psychiatry.* New York: Norton, 1954.

English, O. S., and Pearson, G. H. *Emotional Problems of Living.* New York: Norton, 1957.

Erikson, E. H. *Childhood and Society.* (2nd ed.) New York: Norton, 1963.

Erikson, E. H. "Toys and Reasons." In M. R. Haworth (Ed.), *Child Psychotherapy.* New York: Basic Books, 1964.

Etzioni, A. (Ed.). *The Semi-Professions and Their Organization.* New York: Free Press, 1969.

Fagen, S. A., Long, N. J., and Stevens, D. J. *Teaching Children Self-Control.* Columbus, Ohio: Merrill, 1975.

Fanshel, D. "Status Changes of Children in Foster Care." *Child Welfare,* 1976, *55* (3), 143-172.

Fanshel, D., and Shinn, E. B. *Children in Foster Care.* New York: Columbia University Press, 1977.

Feldman, R. A., and Wodarski, J. S. *Contemporary Approaches to Group Treatment: Traditional, Behavior-Modification, and Group-Centered Methods.* San Francisco: Jossey-Bass, 1975.

Feldman, R. A., and others. "Treating Delinquents in Traditional Agencies." *Social Work,* 1972, *17,* 72-77.

Finch, A. J., and others. "Modification of an Impulsive Cognitive Tempo in Emotionally Disturbed Boys." *Journal of Abnormal Child Psychology,* 1975, *3* (1), 49-52.

Fineman, K. R. "An Operant Conditioning Program in a Juvenile Detention Facility." *Psychological Reports,* 1968, *22,* 1119-1120.

Finkelstein, N. E. "Family Participation in Residential Treatment." *Child Welfare,* 1974, *53* (9), 570-576.

Flackett, J. M., and Flackett, G. "Criswell House: An Alternative to Institutional Treatment for Juvenile Offenders." *Federal Probation,* 1970, *34,* 30-37.

Folks, H. "Effective and Adequate Child Caring Work" [1904]. In S. Zimand (Ed.), *Public Health and Welfare: The Collected Papers of Homer Folks.* New York: Macmillan, 1958.

Foster, G. W., and others. *Child Care Work with Emotionally Disturbed Children.* Pittsburgh: University of Pittsburgh Press, 1972.

Frostig, M. *Education for Dignity.* New York: Grune & Stratton, 1976.

Frostig, M., and Maslow, P. *Learning Problems in the Classroom.* New York: Grune & Stratton, 1973.

Furman, E. *A Child's Parent Dies: Studies in Childhood Bereavement.* New Haven, Conn.: Yale University Press, 1974.

Garbarino, J. "A Preliminary Study of Some Ecological Correlates of Child Abuse: The Impact of Socioeconomic Stress on Mothers." *Child Development,* 1976, *47,* 178-185.

Garbarino, J. "Child Abuse and Juvenile Delinquency: The Developmental Impact of Social Isolation." Unpublished paper. Boys Town, Neb.: Boys Town Center for the Study of Youth Development, 1977a.

Garbarino, J. "Studying the Human Ecology of Child Maltreatment: The Role of Isolation from Potent Support Systems." Unpublished paper. Boys Town, Neb.: Boys Town Center for the Study of Youth Development, 1977b.

Garber, B. *Follow-Up Study of Hospitalized Adolescents.* New York: Brunner/Mazel, 1972.

Gardner, R. *Boys and Girls Book About Divorce.* New York: Aronson, 1971.

Garland, J. A., Jones, H., and Kolodny, R. L. "A Model for Stages of Development in Social Work Groups." In S. Bernstein (Ed.), *Explorations in Group Work.* Boston: School of Social Work, Boston University, 1965.

Garland, J. A., and Kolodny, R. L. *Characteristics and Resolution of Scapegoating.* In J. K. Whittaker and A. E. Trieschman (Eds.), *Children Away from Home: A Sourcebook of Residential Treatment.* Chicago: Aldine, 1972.

Gartner, A. *Paraprofessionals and Their Performance: A Survey of Education, Health, and Social Service Programs.* New York: Praeger, 1971.

Garwick, G., McCree, S., and Brintnall, J. *Bibliography on Goal Attainment Scaling and Associated Methodologies.* Minneapolis: Program Evaluation Research Center, 1976.

Gatti, F., and Colman, C. "Community Network Therapy: An Approach to Aiding Families with Troubled Children." *American Journal of Orthopsychiatry,* 1976, *46* (4), 608-618.

Gearheart, B., and Weishahn, M. *The Handicapped Child in the Regular Classroom.* St. Louis: Mosby, 1976.

Gershenson, C. P. "Residential Treatment of Children: Research Problems and Possibilities." *Social Service Review,* 1956, *30* (3), 268-275.

Gillespie, D. F., and Seaberg, J. R. "Individual Problem Rating: A Proposed Scale." *Administration in Mental Health,* in press.

Ginger, S. "The Problem-*Éducateur.*" *International Child Welfare Review,* 1971, *9,* 16-23.

Ginott, H. G. *Between Parent and Child.* New York: Macmillan, 1965.

Glasser, P., Sarri, R. C., and Vinter, R. D. (Eds.). *Individual Change Through Small Groups.* New York: Free Press, 1974.

Goffman, E. *Asylums.* Chicago: Aldine, 1962.

Goldenberg, I. *Build Me a Mountain.* Cambridge, Mass.: M.I.T. Press, 1971.

Goldfarb, W. "Parental Perplexity and Childhood Confusion." In A. H. Esmand (Ed.), *New Frontiers in Child Guidance.* New York: International Universities Press, 1958.

Goldfarb, W., Mintz, I., and Stroock, K. W. *A Time To Heal.* New York: International Universities Press, 1969.

Goocher, B. "Behavioral Applications of an Educateur Model in Child Care." *Child Care Quarterly,* 1975, *4* (2), 84-92.

Goocher, B. "Ages and Stages in Professional Child Care Training." *Child Care Quarterly,* 1978, *7,* in press.

Gordon, T. *Parent Effectiveness Training.* New York: Wyden, 1971.

Graziano, A. M. (Ed.). *Behavior Therapy with Children.* Vol. 1. Chicago: Aldine, 1971.

Graziano, A. M. (Ed.). *Behavior Therapy with Children.* Vol. 2. Chicago: Aldine, 1975.

Greenfeld, J. *A Child Called Noah.* New York: Holt, Rinehart and Winston, 1972.

Greenwood, E. "Attributes of a Profession." *Social Work,* 1957, *2,* 45-55.

Gross, M. B., and Wilson, W. C. *Minimal Brain Dysfunction.* New York: Brunner/Mazel, 1974.

Grossbard, H. "Ego Deficiency in Delinquents." *Social Casework,* 1962, *43,* 171-178.

Gruber, C. "A Case History of Multiple Learning Disorders." Unpublished paper, Walker School, Needham, Mass., 1975.

Guindon, J. *Les Étapes de la Rééducation* [*Stages in Reeducation*]. Paris: Éditions Fleurus, 1970.

Guindon, J. "The *Psychoéducateur* Model." In J. Beker (Ed.), *The Child Care Worker in the United States: A Comparative Analysis of Evolving Role Models.* New York: Human Sciences Press, in press.

Gump, P., and Sutton-Smith, B. "Activity Setting and Social Interaction: A Field Study." *American Journal of Orthopsychiatry,* 1955, *25* (3), 755-760.

Harris, F. R., and others. "Effects of Positive Social Reinforcement on Regressed Crawling of a Nursery School Child." *Journal of Educational Psychology,* 1964, *55,* 35-41.

Harstad, C. "Guided Group Interaction: Positive Peer Culture." *Child Care Quarterly,* 1976, *5* (2), 109-120.

Hart, B. M., and others. "Effects of Social Reinforcement on Operant Crying." *Journal of Experimental Child Psychology,* 1964, *1,* 145-153.

Henry, J. "The Culture of Interpersonal Relations in a Therapeutic Institution for Emotionally Disturbed Children." *American Journal of Orthopsychiatry,* 1957, *27* (4), 725-735.

Herron, R., and Sutton-Smith, B. *Child's Play.* New York: Wiley, 1971.

Hersen, M., and Barlow, D. H. *Single Case Experiment Designs.* Elmsford, New York: Pergamon Press, 1976.

Herstein, N. "Reflections on the Primacy of the One-to-One Model in Residential Treatment." *Child Welfare,* 1977, *56* (5), 311-321.

Hewett, F. *The Emotionally Disturbed Child in the Classroom.* Boston: Allyn & Bacon, 1969.

Hobbs, N. "The Process of Reeducation." Unpublished paper. Nashville, Tenn.: George Peabody College, 1964.

Hobbs, N. "Helping Disturbed Children: Psychological and Ecological Strategies." *American Psychologist,* 1966, *21* (12), 1105-1151.

Hobbs, N. "The Reeducation of Emotionally Disturbed Children." In E. M. Bower and W. G. Hollister (Eds.), *Behavioral Science Frontiers in Education.* New York: Wiley, 1967.

Hobbs, N. *The Futures of Children: Categories, Labels, and Their Consequences.* San Francisco: Jossey-Bass, 1975a.

Hobbs, N. (Ed.). *Issues in the Classification of Children: A Sourcebook on Categories, Labels, and Their Consequences.* (2 vols.) San Francisco: Jossey-Bass, 1975b.

Homme, L. *How to Use Contingency Contracting in the Classroom.* Champaign, Ill.: Research Press, 1969.

Howe, M. "Casework Self-Evaluation: A Single Subject Approach." *Social Service Review,* 1974, *48* (1), 1-24.

Hromadka, V. G. *Child Care Worker on the Road to Professionalization.* New York: Hawthorne Center for the Study of Adolescent Behavior, 1966.

Huessy, H. R. "Study of the Prevalence and Therapy of the Choreiform Syndrome of Hyperkinesis in Rural Vermont." *Acta Paedopsychiatrica,* 1967, *34,* 130-135.

Itard, J. M. *The Wild Boy of Aveyron.* (G. Humphrey and M. Humphrey, Trans.) New York: Appleton-Century-Crofts, 1962.

Jayaratne, S., and Levy, R. *The Clinical-Research Model of Intervention.* New York: Columbia University Press, in press.

Jesness, C. F. "Comparative Effectiveness of Behavior Modification and Transactional Analysis Programs for Delinquents." *Journal of Consulting and Clinical Psychology,* 1975, *42,* 758-779.

Joffe, C. "Client Control and the Weak Profession." Paper presented at the 70th annual meeting of the American Sociological Association, San Francisco, 1975.

Johnson, A. M. "Sanctions for Superego Lacunae of Adolescents." In K. R. Eissler (Ed.), *Searchlights on Delinquency.* New York: International Universities Press, 1950.

Johnson, A. M., and Szurek, S. "The Genesis of Antisocial Acting-Out in Children and Adults." In I. N. Berlin and S. Szurek (Eds.), *Learning and Its Disorders.* Vol. 2. Palo Alto, Calif.: Science and Behavior Books, 1965.

Johnson, C. A., and Katz, R. C. "Using Parents as Change Agents for Their Children: A Review." *Journal of Child Psychology and Child Psychiatry,* 1973, *14,* 181-200.

Johnson, H. L. *Demonstration of Goal Planning and Evaluative Research in a Residential Treatment Center.* Unpublished report. Edmonton, Alberta, Canada: Mapleridge Residential Treatment Center, 1974.

Johnson, H. L., and others. "Program Evaluation in Residential Treatment." *Child Welfare,* 1976, *55* (4), 279-291.

Johnson, L., and Reid, J. *An Evaluation of Ten Years' Work with Emotionally Disturbed Children.* Seattle: Ryther Child Center, 1947.

Joint Commission on Mental Health of Children. *The Digest of Crisis in Child Mental Health: Challenge for the 70s.* Washington, D.C.: Joint Commission on Mental Health of Children, 1969.

Joint Commission on Mental Health of Children. *Crisis in Child Mental Health: Challenge for the 1970s.* New York: Harper & Row, 1970.

Jones, M. "The Concept of a Therapeutic Community." *American Journal of Psychiatry,* 1956, *112,* 647-650. Also in H. W. Polsky, D. S. Claster, and C. Goldberg (Eds.), *Social System Perspectives in Residential Institutions.* East Lansing: Michigan State University Press, 1970.

Kadushin, A. *Child Welfare Services.* (2nd ed.) New York: Macmillan, 1974.

Kanner, L. "Autistic Disturbances of Affective Content." *Nervous Child,* 1943, *2,* 217-250.

Karacki, L., and Levinson, R. B. "A Token Economy in a Correctional Institution for Youthful Offenders." *Howard Journal of Penology and Crime Prevention*, 1970, *13*, 20-30.

Kazdin, A. E. *The Token Economy*. New York: Plenum, 1977.

Kelly, J. G. "Toward an Ecological Conception of Preventive Interventions." In J. W. Carter (Ed.), *Research Contributions from Psychology to Community Mental Health*. New York: Behavioral Publications, 1969.

Kiresuk, T. J., and Sherman, R. "Goal Attainment Scaling: A General Method for Evaluating Community Mental Health Programs." *Community Mental Health Journal*, 1968, *4* (6), 443-453.

Kirk, S. A. *The Diagnosis and Remediation of Psycholinguistic Abilities*. Urbana: University of Illinois Press, 1966.

Klein, J. "Toward Competency in Child Care." *Educational Leadership*, 1973.

Konopka, G. *Therapeutic Group Work with Children*. Minneapolis: University of Minnesota Press, 1946.

Konopka, G. *Group Work in the Institution*. New York: Association Press, 1954.

Koret, S. "Family Therapy as a Therapeutic Technique in Residential Treatment." *Child Welfare*, 1973, *52* (4), 235-248.

Koshel, J. *Deinstitutionalization—Dependent and Neglected Children*. Washington, D.C.: Urban Institute, 1973.

Kozloff, M. A. *Reaching the Autistic Child in a Parent Training Program*. Champaign, Ill.: Research Press, 1975.

Langer, J. *Theories of Development*. New York: Holt, Rinehart and Winston, 1969.

Lerman, P. "Evaluating Studies in Institutions for Delinquents." *Social Work*, 1968, *13*, 55-64.

Lerman, P. *Community Treatment and Social Control: A Critical Analysis of Juvenile Correctional Policy*. Chicago: University of Chicago Press, 1975.

Levine, T. "Community Based Treatment for Adolescents: Myths and Realities." *Social Work*, 1977, *22* (22), 144-147.

Levitt, E. "Research on Psychotherapy with Children." In A. E. Bergin and S. L. Garfield (Eds.), *Handbook of Psychotherapy and Behavior Change*. New York: Wiley, 1971.

Lewis, W. W. "The Re-Ed Teacher Counselor." In J. Beker

(Ed.), *The Child Care Worker in the United States: A Comparative Analysis of Evolving Role Models.* New York: Human Sciences Press, in press.

Lievens, P. "The Organic Psychosyndrome of Early Childhood and Its Effects on Learning." *Journal of Learning Disabilities,* 1974, *7,* 626-631.

Linton, T. E. "The Éducateur Model: A Theoretical Monograph." *Journal of Special Education,* 1971, *5,* 155-190.

Linton, T. E. "The *Éducateur*: A European Model for the Care of 'Problem' Children." *International Journal of Mental Health,* 1973, *2* (1), 1-88.

Litwak, E., and Meyer, H. J. *School, Family, and Neighborhood: The Theory and Practice of School-Community Relations.* New York: Columbia University Press, 1974.

London, P. "The End of Ideology in Behavior Modification." *American Psychologist,* 1972, *27,* 913-919.

Long, N. J., Morse, W. C., and Newman, R. G. *Conflict in the Classroom.* (2nd ed.) Belmont, Calif.: Wadsworth, 1971.

Lovaas, O. I. "A Behavior Therapy Approach to the Treatment of Childhood Schizophrenia." In J. P. Hill (Ed.), *Minnesota Symposium on Child Psychology.* Minneapolis: University of Minnesota Press, 1967.

McCorkle, L. W., Elias, A., and Bixby, F. L. *The Highfields Story.* New York: Holt, Rinehart and Winston, 1958.

MacGregor, R., and others. *Multiple Impact Family Therapy with Families.* New York: McGraw-Hill, 1964.

McInnis, E. T., and Marholin, D. "Individualizing Behavior Therapy for Children in Group Settings." *Child Welfare,* 1977, *56* (7), 445-465.

McNeil, E. "The European *Éducateur* Program for Disturbed Children: A Response." *Forum for Residential Therapy,* 1969, *2* (1), 15-20.

Magnus, R. A. "Teaching Parent to Parent: Parent Involvement in Residential Treatment Programs." *Children Today,* 1974, *3,* 26.

Mahler, M., Furer, M., and Settlage, C. F. "Severe Emotional Disturbances in Childhood: Psychosis." In S. Arieti (Ed.), *American Handbook of Psychiatry.* Toronto: University of Toronto Press, 1959.

Mahoney, M. J. *Cognition and Behavior Modification.* Philadelphia: Ballinger, 1974.

Maier, H. W. "Child Care as a Method of Social Work." In H. W. Maier (Ed.), *Training for Child Care Staff.* New York: Child Welfare League of America, 1963.

Maier, H. W. *Group Work as Part of Residential Treatment.* Washington, D.C.: National Association of Social Workers, 1965.

Maier, H. W. "Child Care Workers." In R. Morris (Ed.), *Encyclopedia of Social Work.* Washington, D.C.: National Association of Social Workers, 1971.

Makarenko, A. S. *The Road to Life: An Epic of Education.* Moscow: Foreign Languages Publishing House, 1955.

Maloney, K. B., and others. "Behavior Technology in Child Care: The Teaching-Parent and the Teaching-Family Model." In J. Beker (Ed.), *The Child Care Worker in the United States: A Comparative Analysis of Evolving Role Models.* New York: Human Sciences Press, in press.

Maluccio, A. N., and Marlow, W. D. "Residential Treatment of Emotionally Disturbed Children: A Review of the Literature." *Social Service Review,* 1972, *46* (2), 230-251.

Mann, L., and Sabatino, D. *The Second Review of Special Education.* New York: Grune & Stratton, 1974.

Marcus, L. "Patterns of Coping in Families of Psychotic Children." *American Journal of Orthopsychiatry,* 1977, *47* (3), 388-400.

Marks, R. B. "Institutions for Dependent and Delinquent Children: Histories, Nineteenth-Century Statistics, and Recurrent Goals." In D. M. Pappenfort, D. M. Kilpatrick, and R. W. Roberts (Eds.), *Child Caring: Social Policy and the Institution.* Chicago: Aldine, 1973.

Matsushima, J. "Some Aspects of Defining 'Success' in Residential Treatment." *Child Welfare,* 1965, *44,* 272-277.

Mayer, M. F. "The Parental Figures in Residential Treatment." *Social Service Review,* 1960, *34* (3), 273-285.

Mayer, M. F., and Blum, A. (Eds.). *Healing Through Living: A Symposium on Residential Treatment.* Springfield, Ill.: Thomas, 1971.

Mayer, M. F., Richman, L. H., and Balcerzak, E. A. *Group Care of Children: Crossroads and Transitions.* New York: Child Welfare League of America, 1977.

Meichenbaum, D. *Cognitive-Behavior Modification.* New York: Plenum, 1977.

Meisels, L. "The Student's Social Contract: Learning Social Competence in the Classroom." *Teaching Exceptional Children,* 1974, 7 (1), 34-36.

Meyer, H., Borgatta, E., and Jones, W. *Girls at Vocational High.* New York: Russell Sage Foundation, 1965.

Meyer, M., Odom, E. E., and Wax, B. J. "Birth and Life of an Incentive System in a Residential Institution for Adolescents." *Child Welfare,* 1973, *52* (8), 503-509.

Middleman, R. *The Nonverbal Method in Working with Groups.* New York: Association Press, 1968.

Miller, J., and Ohlin, L. E. "The New Corrections: The Case of Massachusetts." In M. K. Rosenheim (Ed.), *Pursuing Justice for the Child.* Chicago: University of Chicago Press, 1976.

Millman, H. L., and Pancost, R. O. "Program Evaluation in a Residential Treatment Center." *Behavioral Disorders,* 1977, *2,* 66-75.

Monkman, M. *A Milieu Therapy Program for Behaviorally Disturbed Children.* Springfield, Ill.: Thomas, 1972.

Montessori, M. *The Montessori Method* [1912]. New York: Schocken Books, 1964.

Montessori, M. *From Childhood to Adolescence* [1939]. (A. M. Joosten, Trans.) New York: Schocken Books, 1973.

Moore, W. E. *The Professions: Roles and Rules.* New York: Russell Sage Foundation, 1970.

Morrison, I. A. "Deinstitutionalization: Panacea or Sophistry?" *Residential Group Care,* 1977, *2* (1), 11-16.

Morrison, J. E., and Stewart, M. A. "The Psychiatric Status of the Legal Families of Adopted Hyperactive Children." *Archives of General Psychiatry,* 1973, *28,* 888-891.

Morse, W. C., and Small, E. R. "Group Life Space Interviewing in a Therapeutic Camp." *American Journal of Orthopsychiatry,* 1959, *29* (1), 27-45.

Morse, W. C., and Wineman, D. "Group Interviewing in a Camp for Disturbed Boys." *Journal of Social Issues,* 1957, *13* (1), 23-32.

Nelson, R. H., Singer, M. J., and Johnson, L. O. "Community Considerations in the Evaluation of a Children's Residential Treatment Center." *Proceedings, 81st Annual Convention, American Psychological Association,* 1973, *8,* 951-952.

Noshpitz, J. D. "Notes on the Theory of Residential Treatment." *Journal of American Academy of Child Psychiatry,* 1962, *1* (2), 284-296.

Noshpitz, J. D. "The Psychotherapist in Residential Treatment." In M. F. Mayer and A. Blum (Eds.), *Healing Through Living: A Symposium on Residential Treatment.* Springfield, Ill.: Thomas, 1971.

Ohlin, L. E., Coates, R. B., and Miller, A. D. "Radical Correctional Reform: A Case Study of the Massachusetts Youth Correctional System." In H. Rodham (Ed.), *The Rights of Children.* Cambridge, Mass.: Harvard Educational Review, 1974.

Page, R., and Clark, G. A. (Eds.). *Who Cares?* London: National Children's Bureau, 1977.

Pappenfort, D. M., Kilpatrick, D. M., and Roberts, R. W. (Eds.). *Child Caring: Social Policy and the Institution.* Chicago: Aldine, 1973.

Paradise, R. "The Factor of Timing in the Addition of New Members to Established Groups." *Child Welfare,* 1968, *47* (9), 529-542.

Paradise, R., and Daniels, R. "Group Composition as a Treatment Tool with Children." In S. Bernstein (Ed.), *Further Explorations in Group Work.* Boston: Boston University Bookstore, 1970.

Patterson, G. R. "A Learning Theory Approach to the Treatment of the School Phobic Child." In L. P. Ullmann and L. Krasner (Eds.), *Case Studies in Behavior Modification.* New York: Holt, Rinehart and Winston, 1965.

Patterson, G. R. *Families.* Champaign, Ill.: Research Press, 1971.

Patterson, G. R., and Gullion, M. *Living with Children.* Champaign, Ill.: Research Press, 1968.

Patterson, G. R., and others. *A Social Learning Approach to Family Intervention.* Eugene, Ore.: Castalia, 1975.

Pearl, A. L., and Riessman, F. *New Careers for the Poor.* New York: Free Press, 1965.

Peters, J. E., and others. *Physician's Handbook Screening for MBD.* New York: CIBA, 1973.

Phillips, E. L., and others. "Achievement Place: Behavior Shaping Works for Delinquents." *Psychology Today,* 1973a, *7* (1), 74-80.

Phillips, E. L., and others. "Achievement Place: Development of an Elected Manager System." *Journal of Applied Behavior Analysis,* 1973b, *6* (4), 541-563.

Piaget, J. *The Language and Thought of the Child.* New York: Basic Books, 1963.

Piaget, J. *Science of Education and the Psychology of the Child.* New York: Grossman, Orion Press, 1970.

Piaget, J., and Inhelder, B. *The Psychology of the Child.* New York: Basic Books, 1969.

Piliavin, I. "Conflict Between Cottage Parents and Caseworkers." *Social Service Review,* 1963, *37,* 17-25. Also in H. W. Polsky, D. S. Claster, and C. Goldberg (Eds.), *Social System Perspectives in Residential Institutions.* East Lansing: Michigan State University Press, 1970.

Pilnick, S. "Guided Group Interaction." In R. Morris (Ed.), *Encyclopedia of Social Work.* Vol. 1. Washington, D.C.: National Association of Social Workers, 1971.

Polsky, H. W. *Cottage Six—The Social System of Delinquent Boys in Residential Treatment.* New York: Russell Sage Foundation, 1962.

Polsky, H. W. "Residential Treatment Homes." In R. Morris (Ed.), *Encyclopedia of Social Work.* Vol. 1. Washington, D.C.: National Association of Social Workers, 1971.

Polsky, H. W., and Claster, D. S. *The Dynamics of Residential Treatment: A Social System Analysis.* Chapel Hill: University of North Carolina Press, 1968.

Portnoy, S. M. "Power of Child Care Worker and Therapist Figures and Their Effectiveness as Models for Emotionally Disturbed Children in Residential Treatment." *Journal of Consulting and Clinical Psychology,* 1973, *40,* 15-19.

Portnoy, S. M., and Biller, H. B. "Comparison of Children's Perceptions of Child Care Workers and Therapists." *Journal of Clinical Psychology,* 1973, *29,* 96.

Portnoy, S. M., Biller, H. B., and Davids, A. "The Influence of the Child Care Worker in Residential Treatment." *American Journal of Orthopsychiatry,* 1972, *42,* 719-722.

Prechtl, J. J. R., and Stemmer, C. J. "The Choreiform Syndrome in Children." *Developmental Medicine and Child Neurology,* 1962, *4,* 119-127.

Premack, D. "Toward Empirical Behavior Laws. I: Positive Reinforcement." *Psychological Review,* 1959, *66* (4), 219-233.

*Profiles of Children—1970 White House Conference on Children.* Washington, D.C.: U.S. Government Printing Office, 1972.

Prosser, H. *Perspectives on Residential Child Care.* Windsor, England: National Federation for Educational Research [National Children's Bureau Reports], 1976.

Quay, H. C., and Werry, J. S. (Eds.). *Psychopathological Disorders of Childhood.* New York: Wiley, 1972.

Raush, H. L., Dittman, A. T., and Taylor, J. J. "The Interpersonal Behavior of Children in Residential Treatment." *Journal of Abnormal and Social Psychology,* 1959, *58,* 9-26.

Redl, F. "The Concept of a 'Therapeutic Milieu.'" *American Journal of Orthopsychiatry,* 1959, *29,* 721-736. Also in G. H. Weber and B. J. Haberlein (Eds.), *Residential Treatment of Emotionally Disturbed Children.* New York: Behavioral Publications, 1972.

Redl, F. *When We Deal with Children.* New York: Free Press, 1966.

Redl, F., and Wattenberg, M. W. *Mental Hygiene in Teaching.* New York: Harcourt Brace Jovanovich, 1959.

Redl, F., and Wineman, D. *The Aggressive Child.* New York: Free Press, 1957.

Reid, J. H. "From the Executive Director." *Child Welfare League Newsletter,* 1974, *4* (2), 1.

Reid, W. J., and Epstein, L. *Task-Centered Casework.* New York: Columbia University Press, 1972.

Reid, W. J., and Epstein, L. *Task-Centered Practice.* New York: Columbia University Press, 1977.

Repucci, N. D., and Saunders, J. T. "Social Psychology of Behavior Modification: Problems of Implementation in Natural Settings." *American Psychologist,* 1974, *29,* 649-660.

Resnik, D. "The Social Worker as Coordinator in Residential Treatment." *Social Casework,* 1967, *48,* 293-298.

Rhodes, W. C. "A Community Participation Analysis of Emotional Disturbance in Children." *Exceptional Children,* 1970, *34* (5), 309-314.

Rhodes, W. C. "Problems in the Development of Incentive Programs." *Child Welfare,* 1977, *56* (3), 173-180.

Rhodes, W. C., and Tracy, M. L. *A Study of Child Variance.* Ann Arbor: University of Michigan Press, 1972.

Rice, R. D. "Educo-Therapy: A New Approach to Delinquent Behavior." *Journal of Learning Disabilities,* 1970, *3,* 16-23.

Rieger, N. I., and Devries, A. G. "The Need and Some Specific Suggestions for a Standardized Training Program for a New Professional: The Child Care Mental Health Specialist." *Child Care Quarterly,* 1974, *3,* 177-187.

Robinson, N. M., and Robinson, H. B. *The Mentally Retarded Child.* (2nd ed.) New York: McGraw-Hill, 1976.

Rogers-Warren, A., and Warren, S. F. (Eds.). *Ecological Perspectives in Behavior Analysis.* Baltimore: University Park Press, 1977.

Rose, S. D. *Treating Children in Groups: A Behavioral Approach.* San Francisco: Jossey-Bass, 1972.

Rosenheim, M. Presentation to the National Conference on Group Care, Child Welfare League of America, New Orleans, January 1976.

Rothman, D. J. *The Discovery of the Asylum: Social Order and Disorder in the New Republic.* Boston: Little, Brown, 1971.

Rourke, B. P. "Brain Behavior Relationships in Children with Learning Disabilities." *American Psychologist,* 1975, *30,* 911-921.

Rozentals, V., Piper, A. C., and Whipple, H. "Professionalizing the Child Care Worker." *Child Welfare,* 1974, *53,* 565-569.

Ruesch, J., and Bateson, G. *Communication: The Social Matrix of Psychiatry.* New York: Norton, 1951.

Rutter, M. "Concepts of Autism: A Review of Research." In S. Chess and A. Thomas (Eds.), *Child Psychiatry and Child Development.* New York: Brunner/Mazel, 1969.

Sapir, S. G., and Nitzburg, A. C. *Children with Learning Problems.* New York: Brunner/Mazel, 1973.

Sarason, I. G., and Ganzer, V. J. *Modeling: An Approach to the Rehabilitation of Juvenile Offenders.* Washington, D.C.: Social and Rehabilitation Service, Department of Health, Education and Welfare, 1971.

Sarason, I. G., and Sarason, B. R. *Modeling and Role-Playing in the Schools.* Los Angeles: Human Interaction Research Institute, 1973.

Sarri, R. C., and Selo, E. "Evaluation Process and Outcome in Juvenile Corrections: A Grim Tale." In P. O. Davidson, F. W. Clark, and L. A. Hamerlynck (Eds.), *Evaluation of Community Programs.* Champaign, Ill.: Research Press, 1974.

Scallon, R. J., Vitale, J., and Eschenauer, R. "Behavior Modification in a Residence and School for Adolescent Boys: A Team Approach." *Child Welfare,* 1976, *55* (8), 561-573.

Schaefer, C. E., and Millman, H. L. "The Use of Behavior Ratings in Assessing the Effect of Residential Treatment with Latency Age Boys." *Child Psychiatry and Human Development,* 1973, *3,* 157-164.

Schopler, E. "Parents of Psychotic Children as Scapegoats." *Journal of Contemporary Psychology,* 1971, *4* (1), 17-22.

Schopler, E., and Loftin, J. "Thinking Disorders in Parents of Young Psychotic Children." *Journal of Abnormal Psychology,* 1969a, *74* (3), 281-287.

Schopler, E., and Loftin, J. "Thought Disorders in Parents of Psychotic Children: A Function of Test Anxiety." *Archives of General Psychology,* 1969b, *20,* 174-181.

Schopler, E., and Reichler, R. J. "Parents as Cotherapists in the Treatment of Psychotic Children." *Journal of Autism and Childhood Schizophrenia,* 1971a, *1* (1), 87-102.

Schopler, E., and Reichler, R. J. "Psychobiological Referents for the Treatment of Autism." In D. W. Churchill, G. D. Alpern, and M. K. Demyer (Eds.), *Infantile Autism: Proceedings of the Indiana Symposium.* Springfield, Ill.: Thomas, 1971b.

Schopler, E., and Reichler, R. J. *Psychopathology and Child Development: Research and Treatment.* New York: Plenum, 1976.

Schulze, S. (Ed.). *Creative Group Living in a Children's Institution.* New York: Association Press, 1951.

Schwebel, M., and Ralph, J. *Piaget in the Classroom.* New York: Basic Books, 1973.

Seaberg, J. R., and Gillespie, D. F. "Goal Attainment Scaling: A Critique." *Social Work Research and Abstracts,* 1977, *13* (2), 4-10.

Seymour, F. W., and Stokes, T. F. "Self-Rewarding in Training Girls to Increase Work and Evoke Staff Praise in an Institution for Offenders." *Journal of Applied Behavior Analysis,* 1976, *9,* 41-54.

Shalinsky, W. "Group Composition as an Element in Social Group Work Practice." *Social Service Review,* 1969, *43* (1), 42-50.

Shyne, A. W. "Research on Child Caring Institutions." In D. M. Pappenfort, D. M. Kilpatrick, and R. W. Roberts (Eds.), *Child Caring: Social Policy and the Institution.* Chicago: Aldine, 1973.

Siegel, E. *Special Education in the Regular Classroom.* New York: Day, 1969.

Silberman, C. *The Open Classroom Reader.* New York: Random House, 1973.

Singer, J. L. *The Child's World of Make-Believe.* New York: Academic Press, 1973.

Skillman, A. G. "Verbal Communication Between Mothers and Sons in Learning Problem Families." *Smith College Studies in Social Work,* 1964, *34* (2), 141-160.

Slavson, S. R., and Schiffer, M. *Group Psychotherapies with Children.* New York: International Universities Press, 1975.

Small, R. W. "A Summary of the Walker School Program." *Child Care Quarterly,* 1976, *5* (2), 136-143.

Small, R. W., and Whittaker, J. K. "Residential Group Care and Home-Based Care: Toward a Continuity of Family Service." In T. Walz (Ed.), *Home-Based Services for Children and Their Families.* Springfield, Ill.: Thomas, in Press.

Sobey, F. *The Nonprofessional Revolution in Mental Health.* New York: Columbia University Press, 1970.

*Social Work in the New Age of Accountability.* Seattle: University of Washington School of Social Work, 1973.

Spivack, G., and Swift, M. S. *Devereux Elementary School Be-*

*havior Rating Scale Manual.* Devon, Penn.: Devereux Foundation, 1967.

Spock, B. *Baby and Child Care: New Revised Edition.* New York: Hawthorn, 1968.

Stedman, J. M., Patton, W. F., and Walton, K. F. *Clinical Studies in Behavior Therapy with Children, Adolescents, and Their Families.* Springfield, Ill.: Thomas, 1973.

Stein, T. J., and Gambrill, E. D. "Behavioral Techniques in Foster Care." *Social Work,* 1976, *21* (1), 34-40.

Stephenson, R. M., and Scarpitti, F. R. *Group Interaction as Therapy: The Use of the Small Group in Corrections.* Westport, Conn.: Greenwood, 1974.

Stevens, G. T., and Mueller, C. "A Child Care Ladder." *Child Welfare,* 1976, *55,* 319-328.

Stumphauzer, J. J. *Behavior Therapy with Delinquents.* Springfield, Ill.: Thomas, 1973.

Swift, M., and Spivack, G. "Therapeutic Teaching: A Review of Teaching Methods for Behaviorally Troubled Children." *Journal of Special Education,* 1974, *8* (3), 259-289.

Taft, J. "Relation of Personality Study to Child Placing." *Proceedings: National Conference on Social Welfare,* 1919, *46,* 595-598.

Taylor, D. A., and Alpert, S. W. *Continuity and Support Following Residential Treatment.* New York: Child Welfare League of America, 1973.

Tharp, R. G., and Wetzel, R. J. *Behavior Modification in the Natural Environment.* New York: Academic Press, 1969.

Thoresen, C. E., and Anton, J. L. "Intensive Counseling." *Focus on Guidance,* 1973, *6* (2), 1-11.

Toigo, R. "Child Care Manpower Development: A Literature Review." *Child Care Quarterly,* 1975, *4,* 6-17.

Toren, N. "Semi-Professionalism and Social Work: A Theoretical Perspective." In A. Etzioni (Ed.), *The Semi-Professions and Their Organization.* New York: Free Press, 1969.

Trieschman, A. E. "The Walker School: An Education Based Model." *Child Care Quarterly,* 1976, *5* (2), 123-135.

Trieschman, A. E., and Levine, B. "Helping Children Learn to Deal with Sadness." In J. K. Whittaker and A. E. Trieschman

(Eds.), *Children Away from Home: A Sourcebook of Residential Treatment.* Chicago: Aldine, 1972.

Trieschman, A. E., Whittaker, J. K., and Brendtro, L. K. *The Other 23 Hours: Child Care Work in a Therapeutic Milieu.* Chicago: Aldine, 1969.

VanderVen, K. D. "Activity Programming." In G. W. Foster and others (Eds.), *Child Care Work with Emotionally Disturbed Children.* Pittsburgh: University of Pittsburgh Press, 1972.

VanderVen, K. D. "A Compendium of Training Programs in the Child Care Professions." *Child Care Quarterly,* 1976, *5,* 319-329.

VanderVen, K. D., and Mattingly, M. A. *The Developmental Child Care Model of Education: The Baccalaureate Program in Child Development and Child Care.* Pittsburgh: Department of Child Development and Child Care, School of Health Related Professions, University of Pittsburgh, 1975.

Vinter, R. "Program Activities: An Analysis of Their Effects on Participant Behavior." In P. Glasser, R. C. Sarri, and R. D. Vinter (Eds.), *Individual Change Through Small Groups.* New York: Free Press, 1974.

Vorrath, H. H., and Brendtro, L. K. *Positive Peer Culture.* Chicago: Aldine, 1974.

Wahler, R. G. "Some Structural Aspects of Deviant Child Behavior." *Journal of Applied Behavior Analysis,* 1975, *8* (1), 27-43.

Wahler, R. G., House, A. E., and Stambaugh, E. E. *Ecological Assessment of Child Problem Behavior.* Elmsford, New York: Pergamon Press, 1976.

Walker, H. M., Mattson, R. H., and Buckley, N. K. "The Functional Analysis of Behavior Within an Experimental Setting." In W. C. Becker (Ed.), *An Empirical Basis for Change in Education.* Chicago: Science Research Associates, 1971.

Walzer, S., and Wolff, P. (Eds.). *Minimal Cerebral Dysfunction in Children.* New York: Grune & Stratton, 1973.

Waxler, N. E., and Mishler, E. G. "Parental Interaction with Schizophrenic Children and Well Siblings: An Experimental Test of Some Etiological Theories." In S. Chess and A. Thomas (Eds.), *Annual Progress in Child Psychiatry and Child Development.* New York: Brunner/Mazel, 1972.

Weber, G. H. "Emotional and Defensive Reactions of Cottage Parents." In D. R. Cressey (Ed.), *The Prisons: Studies in Institutional Organization and Change.* New York: Holt, Rinehart and Winston, 1961.

Weber, G. H. "Conflicts Between Professional and Nonprofessional Personnel in Institutional Treatment." In G. H. Weber and B. J. Haberlein (Eds.), *Residential Treatment of Emotionally Disturbed Children.* New York: Behavioral Publications, 1973.

Weber, G. H., and Haberlein, B. J. (Eds.). *Residential Treatment of Emotionally Disturbed Children.* New York: Behavioral Publications, 1972.

Weeks, H. A. *Youthful Offenders at Highfields.* Ann Arbor: University of Michigan Press, 1963.

Weinstein, L. *Evaluation of a Program for Re-educating Disturbed Children: A Follow-Up Comparison with Untreated Children.* Washington, D.C.: U.S. Office of Education, Department of Health, Education, and Welfare, 1974.

Weintrob, A. "Changing Population in Adolescent Residential Treatment: New Problems for Program and Staff." *American Journal of Orthopsychiatry,* 1974, *44* (4), 604-611.

Werder, P., Stenson, S., and Carlson, L. *A Survival Skills Program for Adolescents in a Delinquency Institution.* Snoqualmie, Wash.: Echo Glen Children's Center, 1976.

Werry, J. S., Weiss, G., and Douglas, V. "Studies of the Hyperactive Child: Some Preliminary Findings." *Canadian Psychiatric Association Journal,* 1964, *9,* 120-130.

White, R. W. "Motivation Reconsidered: The Concept of Competence." *Psychological Review,* 1959, *66,* 297-333.

White, R. W. "Competence and the Psychosexual Stages of Development." In M. R. Jones (Ed.), *Nebraska Symposium on Motivation.* Lincoln: University of Nebraska Press, 1960.

White, R. W. *Ego and Reality in Psychoanalytic Theory.* New York: International Universities Press, 1963.

Whittaker, J. K. "Developing a Unified Theory of Residential Treatment." *Mental Hygiene,* 1970a, *54* (1), 166-169.

Whittaker, J. K. "Training Child Care Staff: Pitfalls and Promises." *Mental Hygiene,* 1970b, *54* (4), 516-519.

Whittaker, J. K. "Planning for Child Caring Institutions." Unpublished doctoral dissertation, University of Minnesota, 1970c.

Whittaker, J. K. "Models of Group Development: Implications for Social Group Work Practice." *Social Service Review,* 1970d, *44* (3), 308-322.

Whittaker, J. K. "Colonial Child Care Institutions: Our Heritage of Care." *Child Welfare,* 1971a, *50* (7), 396-400.

Whittaker, J. K. "Mental Hygiene Influences in Children's Institutions: Organization and Technology for Treatment." *Mental Hygiene,* 1971b, *55* (4), 444-450.

Whittaker, J. K. "I've Been Down So Long—It Looks Like Up to Me." *Child Care Quarterly,* 1971-72, *1,* 75-84.

Whittaker, J. K. "Group Care for Children: Guidelines for Planning." *Social Work,* 1972, *17* (1), 51-61.

Whittaker, J. K. "The Child Care Continuum: New Directions for Children's Residential Centers." *Child Care Quarterly,* 1973a, *2* (2), 124-135.

Whittaker, J. K. "Nineteenth Century Innovations in Delinquency Institutions." *Child Care Quarterly,* 1973b, *2,* 14-24.

Whittaker, J. K. "Program Activities: Their Selection and Use in a Therapeutic Milieu." In P. Glasser, R. C. Sarri, and R. D. Vinter (Eds.), *Individual Change Through Small Groups.* New York: Free Press, 1974.

Whittaker, J. K. "The Ecology of Child Treatment: A Developmental-Educational Approach to the Therapeutic Milieu." *Journal of Autism and Childhood Schizophrenia,* 1975, *5* (3), 223-237.

Whittaker, J. K. "Causes of Childhood Disorders: New Findings." *Social Work,* 1976a, *21* (2), 91-96.

Whittaker, J. K. "Differential Use of Program Activities in Child Treatment Groups." *Child Welfare,* 1976b, *55* (7), 459-467.

Whittaker, J. K., and Small, R. W. "Differential Approaches to Group Treatment of Children and Adolescents." *Child and Youth Services,* 1977, *1* (1), 1-13.

Whittaker, J. K., and Trieschman, A. E. (Eds.). *Children Away from Home: A Sourcebook in Residential Treatment.* Chicago: Aldine, 1972.

Willer, B., and Miller, G. "On the Validity of Goal Attainment

Scaling as an Outcome Measure in Mental Health." *American Journal of Public Health,* 1976, *66* (12), 1197-1198.

Willner, A. G., and others. "The Training and Validation of Youth-Preferred Social Behaviors." *Journal of Applied Behavior Analysis,* 1977, *10* (2), 219-231.

Wolf, M. M. "Social Validity: The Case for Subjective Measurement." Paper presented to the Division of the Experimental Analysis of Behavior, American Psychological Association, Washington, D.C., 1976.

Wolf, M. M., Mees, H., and Risley, T. "Application of Operant Conditioning Procedures to the Behavior Problems of an Autistic Child." *Behavior Research and Therapy,* 1964, *1,* 305-312.

Wolf, M. M., Phillips, E. L., and Fixsen, D. L. *Achievement Place: Phase II.* Bethesda, Md.: National Institute of Mental Health, 1974.

Wolfensberger, W. *Normalization.* New York: National Institute on Mental Retardation, 1972.

Wolins, M. (Ed.). *Successful Group Care: Explorations in the Powerful Environment.* Chicago: Aldine, 1974.

Wolins, M., and Gottesman, M. *Group Care: An Israeli Approach.* New York: Gordon & Breach, 1971.

Wright, L. S. "Conduct Problem or Learning Disability?" *Journal of Special Education,* 1974, *8* (4), 331-336.

Wynne, L., and Singer, M. "Thought Disorder and Family Relations of Schizophrenics." *Archives of General Psychiatry,* 1963, *9,* 199-206.

# Name Index

Lovaas, O. J., 57, 64, 244
Lubeck, S. G., 67, 69, 237
Lupin, M. N., 25, 234

McCallum, C., 72
McCorkle, L. W., 69, 244
McCree, S., 198, 239
MacGregor, R., 148, 244
McInnis, E. T., 95, 244
McKay, G., 143, 236
Mackler, B., 66, 236
McNeil, E., 77, 244
Magnus, R. A., 137, 244
Mahler, M., 244
Mahoney, M. J., 123, 245
Maier, H. W., 99, 114, 211, 245
Makarenko, A. S., 72, 74n, 245
Maloney, K. B., 223, 245
Maluccio, A. N., 11, 20, 245
Mann, L., 155, 245
Maple, F., 114, 233
Marcus, L., 146, 245
Marholin, D., 95, 244
Marks, R. B., 206, 245
Marlow, W. D., 11, 20, 245
Maslow, P., 156, 238
Matsushima, J., 245
Mattingly, M. A., 222, 254
Mattson, R. H., 195, 254
Mayer, M. F., 11, 44, 114, 125, 137, 157, 245-246
Mees, H., 57, 257
Meezan, W., 138, 233
Meichenbaum, D., 123, 246
Meisels, L., 156, 246
Mesrop, A., 215, 235
Meyer, H., 246
Meyer, H. J., 133, 244
Meyer, M., 88, 89, 246
Michael, J., 96, 232
Middleman, R., 246
Miller, A. D., 5, 127-128, 235, 247
Miller, G., 199, 256-257
Miller, J., 246
Millman, H. L., 190, 199, 246, 251
Mintz, I., 45, 189, 239
Mishler, E. G., 254
Monkman, M., 190, 246
Montessori, M., 156, 246
Moore, W. E., 216, 246

Morrison, I. A., 5, 246
Morrison, J. E., 33, 246
Morse, W. C., 24, 39, 50, 103, 114, 244, 246
Mueller, C., 212n, 253

Nelson, R. H., 190, 247
Newman, R. G., 24, 39, 50, 103, 244
Nitzburg, A. C., 32, 33, 250
Noshpitz, J. D., 45, 56, 247

Odom, E. E., 88, 89, 246
Ohlin, L. E., 5, 246, 247

Page, R., 192, 201, 247
Pancoast, D. L., 2, 125, 132, 235
Pancost, R. O., 190, 199, 246
Pappenfort, D. M., 19, 52, 247
Paradise, R., 114, 247
Patterson, G. R., 7, 11, 25, 51, 58, 64, 103, 122, 143, 148, 199, 247
Patton, W. F., 88, 253
Pearl, A. L., 214, 247
Pearson, G. H., 32-33, 237
Peters, J. E., 23, 248
Peterson, C. R., 193, 196, 234
Phillips, E. L., 11, 12, 58, 59, 60, 61, 81, 88-89, 91n, 118, 123, 192, 200, 248, 257
Piaget, J., 156, 165, 248
Piliavin, I., 66, 207, 248
Pilnick, S., 67, 112, 248
Piper, A. C., 221, 250
Polsky, H. W., 12, 27, 55-56, 66-67, 114, 138, 206, 208, 248
Portnoy, S. M., 208, 248-249
Prechtl, J. J. R., 34, 249
Premack, D., 103, 249
Pringle, M., 188, 236
Prosser, H., 188, 249

Quay, H. C., 34, 62, 249

Ralph, J., 156, 252
Raush, H. L., 66, 249
Redl, F., 21, 22, 24, 39, 44-45, 48-52, 55, 80, 83, 99, 114, 122, 157, 189, 207, 249
Reichler, R. J., 7, 47, 64, 146, 251
Reid, J., 189, 242

# Subject Index